Chasing
Quetzalcoatl
to the
American Dream

Garret Godwin

Author's Tranquility Press
MARIETTA, GEORGIA

Garret Godwin/Author's Tranquility Press
2706 Station Club Drive SW
Marietta, GA 30060
www.authorstranquilitypress.com

Publisher's Note: This is a work of fiction. Names, characters, places, and incidents are a product of the author's imagination. Locales and public names are sometimes used for atmospheric purposes. Any resemblance to actual people, living or dead, or to businesses, companies, events, institutions, or locales is completely coincidental.

Ordering Information:
Quantity sales. Special discounts are available on quantity purchases by corporations, associations, and others. For details, contact the "Special Sales Department" at the address above.

Chasing Quetzalcoatl to the American Dream/Garret Godwin
Hardback: 978-1-959197-30-0
Paperback: 978-1-959197-31-7
eBook: 978-1-959197-32-4

CONTENTS

CHAPTER 1

A BOY NAMED TRICK

What do you get when you cross the Lone Ranger and Tonto? One tough hombre. And believe it or not, such a man actually exists. Born on the San Dea Navajo Indian Reservation in 1953, he was raised by his Navajo mother while his father worked as a cowboy on a cattle ranch. They named him Trick. In 1957, the family moved from the reservation to a small host town named Galileo. Galileo was an old mining town back in the nineteen hundreds. The truth about Galileo was that the old miner's ghosts still roamed the abandoned streets and caused mysterious happenings in the town. Jackson Hartland was a visionary, and he wanted to rebuild Galileo and make it a tourist attraction. He would hire cowboys to reenact Western gunfights and build a brand new saloon that would be a showcase. Running Deer, Trick's mother, loved the new town. Their adobe hut on the outskirts of town became a Mecca for cowboys and Navajo Indians from across the region. When he played, Trick couldn't decide whether he liked being a cowboy or an Indian better. He had both costumes, but he tended to like being a cowboy better. He would point his six-shooter at the cactus outside his house and pretend that they were Indians. Trick appeared more white than red, so he tended to identify more with the cowboys than the Indians.

There weren't any other children to play with in Galileo, so Trick invented an invisible friend. His name was Carlos. Carlos and Trick formed a blood brotherhood. One day, Trick cut his wrist and let the blood drip onto a rock. He formed the concept in his mind that Carlos was the rock, and he had learned the incantation of the Navajo from his mother. It worked; after that, Carlos never left him.

By the end of 1958, the saloon had been built and the plans for a new hotel were being drawn up. There were also plans for a corral, where the gunfights would be reenacted, a stable for the horses, and a wishing well. Everybody loves wishing wells.

Trick and Carlos would romp through the streets of Galileo, killing Indians, killing outlaws, and staging battles with the likes of Jesse James and Billy the Kid.

Trick and Carlos never lost, of course. They were an unbeatable team. Carlos was the perfect scout and information gatherer. He would give Trick the information he needed to be victorious. One of the things that never failed Trick was his "trick" finger. He had the uncanny ability to pull the trigger on his gun faster than his brain signals reached his finger. He wondered if that's why his parents named him Trick. He really did have a magic finger that worked faster than his brain.

Carlos knew this, and always gave him the correct location of his enemies. All Trick needed to know was the location of his enemy, and he would always be victorious in a gunfight.

Sometimes Carlos would play tricks on Trick. He would give him misinformation and see if Trick could figure out the untruth. Trick got to the point where he could always tell if Carlos was telling the truth or not. After all, Carlos was only a figment of Trick's imagination. In time, Trick became sharper and sharper at discerning the truth. By the time he was six, he knew instantaneously when Carlos was telling the truth and when he wasn't.

Running Deer was aware of Trick's friend. She delighted in the fact Trick had a friend to play with, even if he was only imaginary. Running Deer would set a place for Carlos at the table to make Trick happy. Running Deer told Jackson about Trick's new friend. He smiled at her and asked if he was white or an Indian.

"He's Navajo, of course," Running Deer said.

Jackson was a little disappointed with this, but he let it go. He was still thinking about that contract to build the horse stable.

Trick's sixth birthday occurred on November 21, 1959. Running Deer set a place for Carlos and put a piece of cake at Carlos' place.

"Thanks, Mom," Trick said.

Trick's first girlfriend was named Little Dove. She was a Navajo girl from the San Dea Reservation and her mother was a friend of Running Deer. She wore her hair in two braided ponytails and her skin was the color of molasses.

One day Trick told Little Dove that he had a secret.

"I have a secret friend," he said. "His name is Carlos and he helps me win my battles."

"Where is he?" Little Dove asked.

"I think that only I can see him, but I know he's there," Trick said.

"O.K.," Little Dove said.

"Let's go to the wishing well," Trick said.

So Carlos, Little Dove, and Trick made their way to the wishing well. When they got there, Trick threw a penny into the wishing well and made a wish to be the best warrior in the world. And he knew that with Carlos' help, he could do it.

"How does Carlos help you?" Little Dove asked.

"He tells me where my enemies are, and that's all I need to know," Trick replied.

"Why is that?" she asked.

"Because I have a trick finger that never loses in a gunfight," Trick said.

"Even faster than Crazy Horses' arrows?" Little Dove asked.

"Yep, and then some," Trick replied.

2
CHAPTER

SNOW DANCE

Trick was now seven. It was the winter of 1960, and Trick was thrilled that it was snowing. A fine powder snow was covering the hills and valleys of Galileo, and Trick wanted to go outside and play in it. His parents had bought him a toboggan last Christmas, and he wanted to try it and see how well it worked. There was already an inch of snow on the ground, and it looked like it was going to come down for at least a few more hours. Trick called Little Dove on the phone.

"Can you come over and go tobogganing with me?"

Little Dove said she would be over in half an hour.

Trick brought his toboggan up out of the basement and took it outside and propped it up against the wall. What a beautiful snowfall it was. The flakes were tiny and powdery, but the big snowflakes you get with a wet snow. This kind of snow was perfect for sledding – there was very little friction between the runners and the snow. Trick saw Little Dove walking up the driveway.

"Let's go," he said as he grabbed the toboggan, took the tether, and started up the hill.

From the top of a pretty big hill, Trick let Little Dove climb in first, and then he gave the toboggan a push over the edge of the hill before climbing in himself.

They started out slow because the grade wasn't that steep, then they started going faster and faster as the gradient became steeper. Down they went, missing a sequoia cactus, veering to the left to avoid a rock. Little Dove was starting to get a little afraid due to the speed, but Trick reassured her that she was going to be O.K.

Riding over one bump after another, it seemed like this downhill trek would never come to an end. Carlos was telling Trick which way to turn to avoid running into something. Trick kept Carlos' directions to himself – he wanted Little Dove to think that he was the one who was doing the driving. Finally, they reached the bottom of the canyon. There was a small creek running through the canyon and they stopped just short of it.

Little Dove got out of the toboggan and said, "That was fun!"

Trick saw the gleam in her eyes. He knew that she had a crush on him, and he wanted her to take notice of his good steering.

"Let's go again," he said. Trick grabbed the rope and started pulling the toboggan behind him. Up over one crest to the next one, slowly they climbed back up to the crest.

"Let's do a snow dance," Little Dove said.

"What's a snow dance?" Trick asked.

"It's just a rain dance, except that with the snow on the ground, we keep dancing until we make a circle where there's no snow," Little Dove explained.

"O.K.," Trick said excitedly. "Let's do it."

And so Little Dove and Trick started dancing in a circle in the snow, and each time they went around, the circle became more and more distinct and easy to follow. By the time they had gone around a half a dozen times, there was a perfectly defined circle in the snow.

"Now let's make snow angels in the circle," Little Dove said.

Trick and Little Dove laid down in the circle about three feet apart and started waving their arms up and down. Their circle had been about twenty feet in diameter, and Trick and Little Dove were small, so their snow angels were small inside the circle.

****

"How about that Sam," Jackson Hartland said triumphantly. He had hired Sam to play Wyatt Earp in his gunslinger show, and boy did he play the role well. He was only eighteen years old, but his mustache made him look much older.

Sam's job was to outdraw and shoot down the Clanton gang. Of course, he had Doc Holliday on his side, which didn't hurt. Sam looked spectacular with his silver spurs on his black boots, his black hat, and black vest with his silver five-pointed star sheriff's badge pinned on it.

Sam stood around six feet tall, but with his black cowboy hat, he looked much taller. He had to look impressive; after all, he was the star of the show – Doc Holliday was only a sidekick.

Slowly word spread across central New Mexico that the gun show in Galileo was pretty good, and soon parents from all over the region were bringing their children there to witness the event. Admission was only one dollar, and that fit almost everyone's budget.

Trick loved the show. He wanted to grow up to be Wyatt Earp. He practiced drawing his guns every day so that one day he could play Wyatt Earp at the O.K. Corral.

Soon after the gun show started, there was enough profit coming in to finish building the saloon. When it was done, Jackson sprinkled sawdust on the floor to give it that lived in Western feel. Besides drinks, the saloon also sold fast-food meals, and soon the saloon/restaurant became a bigger moneymaker than the gunslinger show.

Jackson was delighted. His vision was finally starting to become a reality. He expanded the parking lot, started charging a parking fee, on top of the admission fee to his Western ghost town. Soon more and more people from outside the region started to hear about Galileo. There were no other places like it in the state of New Mexico – there were in Arizona, but not in New Mexico.

Every day, Sam blew away the Clanton gang and the people loved it. The teenagers Jackson hired did such a good job dying on demand that after a few months he gave them a raise. They deserved it. They were throwing themselves over hitching posts, falling into water troughs, flailing themselves upon stones on the ground, and doing whatever was necessary to impress the crowd.

Trick watched the two o'clock show just about every day and lined up the Clanton gang in his gun sights just like Wyatt Earp did. One day, he knew he would play Wyatt Earp.

3
CHAPTER

NOVEMBER 22, 1963

Yesterday was Trick's tenth birthday. Three kids from the Montessori school and Little Dove had been there for his birthday party. No one saw Carlos except Trick, but he was there too. Lately, Trick noticed that Carlos had been appearing to him less and less. And the times when Carlos did appear didn't last as long. Something was happening, but Trick didn't understand it. Although there were only five kids including Trick, the birthday party was still a huge success. Nobody had a better time than Trick, who seemed intent on showing his appreciation for his gifts by demonstrating his charm and quick wit. Little Dove gave him a dreamcatcher talisman. He really loved that. He went to bed that night grateful that he had such wonderful parents and friends.

At school the next day, things started out just like every other day – Trick went to language class then he went to science class. Then everything changed at around 9:00 a.m. Someone had a radio on somewhere and heard that President Kennedy had been shot. The principal's voice came over the loudspeaker system and confirmed it – President Kennedy had been shot in the head during his motorcade ride through Dallas.

Classes were halted, and the children were asked to go to their homerooms. Television sets were turned on in almost every classroom. No one spoke – not even the teachers.

Trick knew his parents would be devastated – they loved JFK. Who could possibly do such a thing? The answer to that question would be known before the end of the day.

Meanwhile, Trick and Little Dove conferred on the matter. He had wondered what her reaction would be. She was terrified. She didn't know that such violence still existed in the world.

By midafternoon, all hope for JFK surviving was over. The President didn't make it – he was declared officially dead at 3:00 p.m. Lyndon Johnson was to be sworn in as President of the United States.

****

There are mysteries in some children that parents just can't understand. Jackson and Running Deer Hartland understood the need for Trick to create an imaginary friend because there just weren't that many kids to play with in central New Mexico. They were actually happy for him that his imagination was so keen. What they couldn't get a grasp on were certain new behaviors in Trick that didn't seem to go with his pleasant fun-loving personality.

Trick started collecting scorpions and setting them in a sandbox to fight with each other. He would watch them fight and cheer for one or the other of them. He took an interest in watching vultures eat dead bodies of jackrabbits and other road kill. He wasn't as interested in playing with Little Dove as he used to be, and he would go out for long walks by himself, and when he came home, he wouldn't be very specific about where he went. Running Deer, in particular, was getting concerned. His grades in school weren't suffering, but his personality was becoming less joyful, more somber, and serious. She watched out the back window as he pitted the scorpions against each other, and he didn't like the intensity Trick displayed as he watched the death match.

One day she finally confronted him. "Trick, why do you catch scorpions and pit them against each other in the sandbox?" she asked.

"Because I like to see what maneuvers the winning scorpion uses," he said in a flat tone.

"Aren't you sad for the loser?" his mother asked.

"Nope. That's life. The better fighter always wins," he said as he grabbed his knapsack of books and headed out the door.

4
CHAPTER

FIRST FIGHT

It was probably inevitable. With all that practice in drawing his guns and watching scorpions duel to the death, someday Trick would find himself in a real fight. That day occurred in the summer of 1964 when Trick was eleven years old.

There were various cliques at school, but the one that Trick wanted in was the Rangers. There were six or so boys who called themselves the rangers and they went camping together, took telescopes outside to look at the stars, launched rockets and hot air balloons, and generally did "scientific" things that appealed to their wide range of interests.

There was another boy named Bob who also wanted to join the rangers. One day, riding on the school bus, Bob stuck out his leg and tripped Trick as he was walking down the center aisle. Trick cushioned the impact by sticking out his hands, but he landed with a thud. Trick's green eyes looked back at Bob and made it clear that someday he would seek retribution.

That day would be the very next. Trick invited Bob over to his house on the pretext that he wanted to show Bob his collection of model airplanes. What he really wanted was to beat Bob to a pulp. Trick told his mother what had happened on the bus, and she agreed to be a referee to a fight for revenge.

As Bob entered through the patio gate, Running Deer explained to Bob that she was going to referee a fight between him and Trick. Bob looked remorseful but said O.K.

The opponents stared into each other's eyes. Finally, Trick made the first move. He grabbed Bob's arm, spun himself around, and somehow managed to completely flip Bob over his shoulder onto the ground. Trick stared down into Bob's shocked eyes and then proceeded to punch him in the stomach. Bob curled over onto his side. Trick was satisfied. He had taken enough revenge. Running deer declared the match over. Bob left through the gate holding his stomach.

5

CHAPTER

OF THINGS FORETOLD

Deep in the northwest corner of the San Dea reservation, among the high mesas and close to Bandolier, lived a Navajo shaman by the name of White Buffalo. He was named White Buffalo because as a small child it was clear how rare his powers were. By the time he was six, he was able to predict future events without fail. As he entered young manhood, his powers expanded to include healing as well as prophecy.

Running Deer knew White Buffalo because they were the same age and attended the same Indian school. He told Running Deer that one day she would have a very special child. This greatly pleased her and she always hoped that that prophesy had been fulfilled because she knew that Trick would indeed be special one day.

After Trick's defeat of Bob, Running Deer decided that she wanted Trick to meet White Buffalo. The arrangements were made and Running Deer looked forward to the meeting.

When the day came, they jumped into the station wagon and headed north. Trick was excited too – he didn't know what a shaman was, but from what he'd heard, he knew it was going to be a special day.

They pulled up to an adobe house up on top of a mesa and pulled up to the top of the driveway. They walked over the stone path that led to the door. Running Deer knocked on the door. After a few seconds, the door opened.

"Please come in," a Navajo woman said.

Inside, the stucco walls were decorated with paintings by Indian artists, and Navajo pottery adorned the shelves, and Navajo rugs covered the hardwood floors. Soon a tall Navajo man with long black hair appeared from a room off to the left of the living room.

"Let's go sit down in the dining room," he said.

White Buffalo and his wife, Pale Moon, sat down next to each other, and Running Deer and Trick sat down directly across from them. White Buffalo was staring at Trick. Then he smiled.

"Do you want me to tell you of things to come?" White Buffalo asked Running Deer. She only hesitated for a second before answering "Yes."

White Buffalo sat back in his chair, closed his eyes, and looked upward.

"There will come a time when this boy will change the world as we know it," White Buffalo said. "It will not be in a way that will be immediately apparent, and it will not occur until after he becomes a great warrior. You will witness it Running Deer, but your husband will not."

"How will he change the world?" Running Deer asked.

"All I can tell you is that it will not be in any way that you will be able to understand," White Buffalo replied.

Running Deer looked disappointed but accepted the answer. Trick was in awe of White Buffalo. When White Buffalo tilted his head back his eyes rolled into the back of their sockets and all you could see was the whites of his eyes. Trick wondered if that was how White Buffalo got his name.

"There's one more thing I must tell you," White Buffalo said. "I see a choice that Trick will have to make one day involving an aspect of his feminine side, and I hope he makes the right decision," White Buffalo said.

"He will," Running Deer said. And with that, she knew the session was over. "Thank you White Buffalo," Running Deer said. She knew she had a special son and White Buffalo had just confirmed it.

6
CHAPTER

BOY SCOUTS
IS FOR KIDS

The Methodist Church that Jackson belonged to hosted a Boy Scout troop. Some of the white children came from Las Cruces and some came from the military base at White Sands. In all, there were about twenty boys ranging in age from ten to eighteen. Sometimes only half the troop showed up, and on other occasions, the full contingent showed up.

At first, Trick loved the Boy Scouts. He loved the uniform, and the whole concept of badges enthralled him. He was sworn in as a Boy Scout second class and he wanted to earn badges slowly and build up his sash one badge at a time.

He knew how to live off the land, and he figured that would be an advantage compared to the other all-white boys. Somehow he wanted to impress the scoutmaster and get him to give him special consideration for being the only half-Navajo in the troop.

Trick loved the trips to the Boy Scout camps. On these trips, Trick had a tendency to wander off on his own Trick always felt safe wandering into the desert by himself; after all, he always had Carlos with him. He was quick as hell and there were no things in the desert landscape that scared him. If he got thirsty, he knew which cacti to cut that had water inside. He had put away his toy guns and graduated to his first real weapon – a bowie knife. That's all he needed to cut the cactus open, slice off a snake's head, or scare off the vultures.

One night he crept out of his tent, grabbed the ax lying next to his scoutmaster's tent, and walked out into the desert with it. He walked north for about a half mile until he came to a stand of pine trees. He started chopping down every dead tree he could find. After four of them, he started chopping them up into two-foot-long logs. He worked through the night, and when he was done, he carried two longs at a time, one under each arm, until he had stacked all the logs against a lean-to.

As the sun rose, the cord or so of wood was neatly stacked against the lean-to. When the scoutmaster walked out of his tent and saw it, he couldn't believe his eyes. "Who did this?" he asked.

"I did sir," Trick replied.

"How in the world did you do it?" the scoutmaster asked incredulously.

"I couldn't sleep, sir, so I chopped wood all night so that we would have enough wood for the rest of the camping trip," Trick said.

"Well, I'm going to order a merit badge for this for going above and beyond the call of duty," the scoutmaster said.

"People who don't take initiative never accomplish anything," Trick said.

****

The Rangers were made up of the smartest kids in the neighborhood. They funded their endeavors by charging admission to the movies of their rocket launches. The Rangers would line up about thirty or so folding chairs in Trick's garage and hope that word of mouth would get around the neighborhood. Admission was fifty cents. Sometimes only three or four kids would show up and sometimes the garage would be filled.

The launches took place in the foothills of Galileo. There was so much undeveloped land in the sixties around Galileo that no man-made objects could be seen for miles around. There were rumors of Indian ghosts who roamed this land, but none of the Rangers ever saw one.

Almost every kid within a ten-mile radius of Galileo had heard about the Rangers. There was a period when all the club did was make hot air balloons out of tissue paper. Some of the balloons were twelve to fifteen feet tall. They were made by buying rolls of tissue paper and gluing them together at the seams. A round wire rim at the bottom provided the hole where the hot air from a fire would expand the balloon. After the balloon was full of hot air, it would ascend upwards to between five and ten thousand feet. It took hours for them to descend, and the Rangers had to follow them on bicycle to retrieve them.

On one occasion, a balloon blew over the White sands military base. It was picked up on radar, and MPs with machine guns were scrambling around trying to find out what the UFO was. When the hot air balloon descended, they figured it must have come from that rocket club called the Rangers who lived in the Galileo area. They called the president of the club – they knew his name from the newspaper article – and told him to never let it happen again.

Trick's main enjoyment from the club wasn't the construction of rockets or balloons but in the retrieval operations. His eyesight was so acute he would see a rocket or balloon even at ten thousand feet. Not only that, but he could also ride his bike and still keep focused on the object in the air. He was usually at the front of the bicycle vanguard, leading the others on in their pursuit. The other Rangers trusted his instincts and always followed him turn after turn.

One day one of his fellow Rangers asked him how he could unfailingly see a speck in the sky.

"I have eagle vision," Trick said.

"What is eagle vision?" his friend asked him.

"I can spot a mouse from two miles away and tell you how many whiskers it has under its nose," Trick said with confidence.

7
CHAPTER

INDIGENOUS SPECIES

A round Galileo, jackrabbits would run around and play amongst the sagebrush. Jackrabbits are approximately twice the size of an eastern cottontail rabbit. They can jump five or six feet in a single stride. Jackson would take out his 22, the only rifle he owned, and shoot at them once in a while. Trick loved the creatures, and when Jackson offered him the 22 one time he refused.

There were also rattlesnakes, vultures, hawks, falcons, condors, hummingbirds, coyotes, and then there were the insects – the largest being the scorpions. When Trick went on his walks in the desert he could always sense where the rattlesnakes were. He didn't have to hear the rattle of their tail to know when he was approaching one – he just sensed it somehow. It was almost as if he could feel their vibration.

This "gift" came in very handy one day when he and Little Dove went on a hiking expedition. Little Dove was in front and veered off onto a barely visible trail on her left. Trick sensed something was there and he told her to stop. Sure enough, as Trick went ahead to explore, there was a rattler waiting in the crevice between two big rocks.

"How did you know it was there?" Little Dove asked.

"I just felt it," Trick replied.

"Well that's some gift," she said as she turned back to take the trail on the right.

****

Trick's twelfth winter was a nature study in the contrast between seasons. New Mexico is known for its dry heat, but in the winter it could get pretty cold. It snowed on Thanksgiving Day 1965 – not the typical one or two inches, but a whopper – twenty-plus inches. Sometimes Little Dove would come over and they would go sledding together. Other times, they made snowmen and dressed them up with stovepipe hats and all.

On this Thanksgiving Day, however, Trick wanted to go skating. His parents had bought him a new set of skates for his birthday and he wanted to try them out. There was a skating rink about a half-hour away and Trick asked his mother if she would drive them over there.

Running Deer consented and took them over to the ice skating rink. After they put their skates on, they met on the rink. Trick's ability was uncanny. While Little Dove kept falling on her bum every minute or so, Trick, after only a few minutes' practice, was skating backwards, then forward, then on one skate. And his speed was extraordinary. He was like a dervish on the ice, whipping past the young and the old, turning on a dime, and instantaneously gaining inertia to propel himself from one end of the rink to the other in a matter of seconds. Little Dove was in awe.

"How do you do it?" she asked.

"I don't know – it just comes naturally," Trick replied.

8
CHAPTER

CARLOS PLAYS A TRICK ON TRICK

Sometimes there are omens in this world that should never be ignored. Trick had developed an early warning system for such omens and knew that each omen had practical applications. In the summer of 1966, such an omen occurred and Trick by this time was smart enough to take it to heart.

The omen involved Carlos. Now that trick was almost a teenager, Carlos had been making fewer and fewer appearances. No longer did Carlos point out where Trick's enemies were; he pretty much-left Trick fend for himself now. Carlos started playing a new game with Trick – hide and seek. Carlos would whisper in Trick's ear "I'm here, can you find me?" and Trick would have to scout out every hiding place in sight before he could find Carlos. Sometimes Carlos would be hiding behind a rock and sometimes he would be hiding behind a cactus. Other times he would just stand up after blending in with some sagebrush.

One day in the middle of July 1966, Carlos played a trick on Trick. Carlos disguised himself as a condor. The condor was flying overhead as Trick was checking out every hiding place he could see. He noticed the condor circling overhead, but he didn't even consider that it might be Carlos disguising himself.

Trick knew that Carlos was around because he could "feel" his presence, but this was the first time that he couldn't find him. Finally, the condor landed about twenty feet ahead of Trick. There was something unusual about this condor's eyes, but Trick didn't think that he was looking at Carlos in disguise. Then the condor started to get larger and larger and the wings slowly disappeared and were replaced with arms, and the legs started to take on a human shape, and the head became human until it finally became Carlos as he had always appeared to Trick before.

"That was a pretty good disguise," Trick said. "I didn't know that you could make yourself into a bird."

"I can make myself into any creature I want to," said Carlos, "but I really like making myself into a bird because I love to fly."

"Well, I guess from now on it's going to be a lot tougher to find you," Trick said.

"Deep down inside, when you first spotted me in the sky, you knew it was me," Carlos said.

Trick thought about that for a minute, considering whether that was true or not.

9
CHAPTER

FIRST LOVE

It happened in the fall of Trick's twelfth year. For the first time in his life, he experienced loss. He and Little Dove had always been the best of friends, but they were also prepubescent boyfriend and girlfriend. They admired each other's bodies and had secretly vowed to each other that someday when they were grown, they would get married.

So it came as such a surprise when Trick saw Little Dove walking home from school with Billy Williams one day. They weren't just walking home together they were also holding hands. Billy Williams was a smart white kid who had blond hair and blue eyes, and a nice smile. He also had an effervescent, outgoing personality that Little Dove apparently liked.

Little Dove had never officially "broken up" with Trick, but he knew from what he saw that he was no longer the number one man in her life. He couldn't put into words his feelings, he just knew what it felt like. It felt like the proverbial little "pang," or twitch in his heart. Whenever he remembered that image of Billy and Little Dove together, he actually felt pain in his heart.

Finally, Trick decided that he had to confront her. He saw her in the hallway in between classes and asked her to meet him at the soccer field after school.

"I see that you really like Billy Williams," Trick said.

"Yes I do," she replied.

"What about our promise that we would get married when we're grown up?" Trick asked.

"I'm sorry Trick, but I don't think that's going to happen now," Little Dove said.

"You really Billy Williams more than me?" Trick asked.

"No, I like both of you in different ways," Little Dove said in a melancholy tone.

"I'm sorry Trick, you're the best friend a girl could ever have in this world; I just think it's time for us to start hanging out with other people," Little Dove said.

With that, Trick was satisfied. Little Dove just wanted to expand her horizons, and he had to accept it. Maybe it was time for him to expand his horizons too.

****

One morning, Trick jumped up out of his bed and dashed to the bathroom to see what was wrong with his forehead. It was sore right between his eyes. As he looked in the mirror, he couldn't believe it – there, right between his eyes – was a red mound the size of a pea full of pus. It took him five or six seconds to decide to try and pop it. The yellow pus came out with the first squeeze. Trick put his fingers under the running water to get rid of the ooze.

This was his first introduction to puberty. Lately, he had also started having wet dreams. His dream lovers were usually Navajo girls with their black hair braided and they had curvaceous hips and breasts. Once a month or so now when he woke up in the morning there would be semen in his undershorts, and then he would remember the dream that caused it. He realized that most of the girls were variations of Little Dove. God, was he jealous of Billy Williams!

Trick was an early bloomer. He knew that most kids didn't reach puberty until fifteen or sixteen, but he knew he was becoming a man earlier. As his body started manufacturing testosterone with ever-increasing intensity, Trick's voice deepened, he started growing an inch a month, and he began having sexual fantasies about all kinds of girls. Usually, the girls were Navajo, but not all of them. Sometimes they were white girls with blond hair and blue eyes or white brunettes with brown eyes. Trick knew that it was time to put away his child's toys and act more like a man – or a warrior.

10
CHAPTER
TRANSCEDENTAL WARRIOR

As pimple after pimple began to appear on Trick's face and he continued to pop them one by one, tiny pockmarks and scars were left behind. All traces of baby fat were gone from his face now, and Trick cursed his white blood because he knew that was the source of his misery. Very rarely did Navajo boys develop acne. On the other hand, almost every white teenage boy had the problem.

By the Time Trick was fifteen, he had lost interest in the Boy Scots and the Rangers, and it was clear that what fascinated him was the shaman magic of White Buffalo. He felt he had sort of outgrown the Boy Scouts, and the rangers were just a tad too nerdy for him.

Trick had started visiting White Buffalo and Pale Moon more and more frequently. He wanted to understand the powers that White Buffalo possessed. It was well-known that White Buffalo was the best shaman of the San Dea tribe of Navajo. He had healed many people, even some whites, who came to him for healing. His prophetic powers he used much more sparingly. He enjoyed Trick's visits and tried to impart some wisdom to him every time they met.

One day, Trick told White Buffalo about Carlos.

"I suspected that," White Buffalo said. "He is your ally, and I can feel that he is a very strong one too," he added.

"I don't see him near as often as I used to," Trick admitted.

"That's because you are growing stronger every day on your own and don't need him so much. He will always be a part of you though," White Buffalo said.

"He can take the shape of any living creature," Trick said.

"Yes, I felt that you have a very cunning and clever ally," White Buffalo said. Then he paused for a moment as though he were searching for exactly the right words.

"You must remember that your ally, Carlos, is always there for you. There will come a time when you will definitely need him. Remember that his powers come from the spirit world; he is not limited by this world. He is pure Navajo, and his purpose is to serve you in becoming a great warrior."

"I thought that was Carlos' goal, but I wasn't sure," Trick said. "As a child, when he would appear, we were just buddies who played together, but as I got older I realized that he was teaching me things, like how to run as though there was no gravity, and how to "feel" danger. Now I am beginning to understand that he was really teaching me the way of the warrior."

"Yes, and he is a more powerful teacher than I can ever be because he is a part of you, and he knows you better than I ever will," White Buffalo said.

****

Sometimes there are tests that come up in life, and one can only move forward if they are passed successfully. In Trick's case, his first major test occurred when he was sixteen years old. He had to pass a warrior's test.

As part of a school project, Trick's social studies teacher planned a field trip to the state penitentiary in Las Cruces. There were criminals of all types there. Some were murderers, some were rapists, some were child molesters, some were drug dealers, and some were thieves. A few were on death row.

A few of the almost rehabilitated were allowed to talk to the students. One after the next criminal stood up and gave their "scared straight" speech, not to go bad and commit a crime. The last criminal to give his testimony was different – he was scheduled to die on death row for murder. He was evil-looking, his eyes had a perpetual squint as though he was trying to see through something. He walked up to the front of the room and started to tell his woeful tale.

"I am here because I am a murderer. I killed two people while I was robbing a convenience store. I didn't want any witnesses, so I shot them both at point-blank range. One was a fifty-eight-year-old man, the owner of the store, and one was a female seventeen-year-old cashier. I shot them both without remorse because I was a cold-blooded killer without a conscience. Now I've seen the light and given my life over to Jesus."

Trick could see the evil lurking behind those sinister eyes. He saw a man who acted on animal instinct, a cold-blooded killer who wasn't raised to have a conscience.

At one point, the killer locked eyes with Trick. Something transpired. Some sort of communication was taking place on a higher plane. Trick sensed it after a few seconds. And then Trick sensed that this staring competition was some kind of test. Trick started to see that there was a warrior too, but one who was more of an animal than a human being. White Buffalo had told Trick that there were good warriors and bad warriors. The good warriors did have a conscience and never used their skills to hurt the innocent. True warriors lived by principles, the principles that brought out the best and loftiest attributes of being human. Trick realized that what he was looking at and listening to was the opposite of that, an animal who loved on the animal plane.

As these thoughts crystallized in Trick's mind, he realized that he was passing the test. He felt no compassion for this criminal; there was no redeeming social value to this outlaw. Trick wanted to be the opposite of this loser – a warrior with a good cause, a noble, caring, compassionate warrior whose cause was noble and whose mission was good.

11
CHAPTER
ADRIFT ON A HIGH MESA

Trick's body was getting bigger and stronger every day. He already stood five foot six and weighed a hundred and thirty pounds. But most importantly, his muscles were becoming harder, and more taut. Because of his hiking throughout the desert, his legs were like steel. From ascending to the top of mesas, his abdominal rib cage looked like a washer board, and from pulling himself up to higher and higher ledges, his shoulders were becoming very broad and his arms had a sinewy toughness.

At school, girls started to notice the changes in Trick's body. As they passed him in the hallways, some of them would stare at him to let him know that they were interested. He was becoming very good-looking in a rugged sort of way. He had his father's fine sandy hair but his mother's molasses skin. His father's eyes were blue, but somehow Trick's eyes were green.

Most days after school, Trick would go hiking on the many trails around Galileo. One day, he took a trail to the north, which led to some very high mesas. He picked which one he wanted to ascend and spotted a difficult but doable approach to the top. This mesa was about five hundred feet high, and the angle of ascent was steep. One of Trick's strengths as a climber was his sure-footedness. He always was careful never to let himself slip on a stone or loose earth. It took him about an hour to reach the plateau.

It was a spectacular day, seventy-five degrees and only a few wisps of clouds. The air seemed buoyant, almost negating the effect of gravity. From the top of this mesa, Trick could see twenty miles in every direction. To the south were the desert lowlands and Galileo, to the east was flat desert, to the west were the San Dea Mountains, and to the north was the Pecos National Forest, part of the Rockies. When he concentrated on the scenery of the west and north, he was glad he was born here, this beautiful Land of Enchantment, this historical place where monks and Indians and Spaniards left their mark. He started to run, and he would leap into the air, and it was as if time stood still at the apex of his jump. He felt like a gazelle, another creature that apparently had the ability to almost defy gravity. His airborne leaps left him suspended in mid-air for longer than what should have been, and he thought that he had an enormous gift that only a few people on this planet had ever known.

****

It was the summer of 1971, and Trick had been accepted to New Mexico State University in Las Cruces. He wanted to go there for two years to get his associate's degree, and then he wanted to go into the military. He was an ace at math and had no trouble getting into NMSU. His acceptance letter had come in April and all he could think about was starting college in the fall. Jackson and Running Deer were elated. Las Cruces was only an hour and a half away from Galileo, which meant that Trick would be able to come home most weekends if he wanted to.

Trick goofed off in school after receiving his acceptance letter. He did the required minimum to get through his remaining courses and worked hard on what he wanted to work on the most – his body. Trick knew that his legs didn't need any work – the muscles in his legs were like steel, but he did want to bulk up his upper body a bit more, and the only way he could do that was with weights. So every day he went to the school's gym and lifted free weights and dumbbells. He didn't want to look like Mr. Universe, but he wanted a little more definition on top than he now had.

He started with ten-pound free weights, did that for a month before graduating to twenty-pound free weights. He could bench-press a hundred and fifty pounds with great effort, and he knew he needed to get to the point where it required little effort. To really work on his biceps, he did chin-ups, ten at a time, with three repetitions.

By high school graduation, Trick was really buff, and he knew many girls were interested in getting to know him better. But he didn't want to get involved with any girls from his high school; he was already looking ahead to college – and maybe there he would take a chance at love. He knew from his experience with Little Dove that girls could be fickle, and he wanted to be more sure of himself before he put his heart out on his sleeve.

12
CHAPTER

HIGHWAY 25

I t was September 3, 1971, and Trick was driving down Highway 25 towards Las Cruces. He didn't want to wait until the first day of classes; he wanted to get there early so he could get situated in his dorm room and explore the town a little bit. He had worked hard all summer trying to get enough money together to buy a car, and he was successful in that endeavor. He bought himself a little red Fiat sports car. It was only a two-seater, but so what – he wasn't planning on having a family any time soon.

Thirty miles outside of Las Cruces, he spotted a gas station, filled up his tank, and drove on down Highway 25. When he reached NMSU campus, he looked for a direction map of the campus so he could find Mervis Hall. He spotted a campus map, memorized it, and sped right into the parking lot of his new home for at least the next year. He only had two suitcases full of clothes – the dorm room was supposed to be furnished. And it was – two bunk beds, two small desks, and chests of drawers. Humble but sufficient for a freshman.

His roommate had not arrived yet so he chose the top bunk and the desk closest to the window. After unpacking, he ran out to meet his neighbors. It was an all-male dorm, so few kids were really interested in getting to know each other. A social dorm party was scheduled for that evening.

There he met a guy named Greg from California. Then he wanted to find the dorm's residence counselor. His name was Tim and he weighed well over three hundred pounds. He was a sincere, likable fellow though, and Trick knew he would become friends with him.

****

Study, study, study, play was Trick's game plan. He came to NMSU primarily to get an education, but he also wanted to have some fun. He declared his major as Biology because he thought he might want to be a forest ranger someday. So of course, he would have to take Cell Biology and Organic Chemistry and Physics, which meant he would have to study, study, study.

Things were going along fine and he started hanging out with Glen. He really liked Glen – he was your typical bubbly outgoing hunk-stud from California. Glen and Trick would go to the student union and play Ping-Pong for hours at a time. The student union was also trick's favorite place to study. He didn't like the library nearly as much because he couldn't take coffee breaks or get up and play pool. The student union had cushy chairs scattered throughout the building and he would move from one to another as the spirit moved him.

During Rush week, Glen and Trick had been invited to a "rusher" by Phi Kappa Omega fraternity. Trick liked the brothers who offered them the invite, so he decided to go.

It was on a Thursday night, and it was a huge success. About twenty freshmen showed up to visit the house and meet the brothers. Trick had already made up his mind by the time he left – he wanted to pledge Phi Kappa Omega.

13
CHAPTER

THE PLEDGE

The brothers of Phi Kappa Omega must have liked Trick and Glen because they wanted both of them to pledge, and they both accepted. The pledge process would take almost the entire semester, but Trick thought that it was worth it. He would have to wear his pledge ribbon everywhere he went, do whatever chore a brother asked him to do, and be on call 24/7. Trick didn't mind though. He knew he was pledging a decent band of brothers, and he could put up with a little humiliation to become a brother of Phi Kappa Omega.

After classes every day, Trick would go to the student union for two hours to study. As long as got his two hours in, he could keep on top of his classes and do whatever pledge duties needed to be done.

One week, the pledges were to serve as waiters during a dinner/mixer with a sorority. And the pledges were told they couldn't wear shirts, so they pinned their ribbons to their pants and served cocktails bare-chested.

The pledge class had started out with fifteen members, but by the second month, three had quit, leaving twelve.

For some reason, the pledge class did not like brother Sewinski, so on day four pledges kidnapped him and drove him south of the border, and left him stranded in Mexico. In retaliation, the brothers kidnapped two pledges and drove them all the way to Taos, and left them off.

Trick quietly performed his pledge duties while studying biology, and he couldn't wait to become a brother of Phi Kappa Omega. He couldn't wait for Hell Week to come and go. When Hell Week did arrive, it wasn't as bad as Trick thought it would be. On Hell night, the pledges were asked to drop trou and take ten whacks with a paddle. No big deal. After the initiation ceremony, Trick was in; he was now a brother of Phi Kappa Omega.

****

At least once a month, Phi Kappa Omega hosted a fraternity/sorority mixer. This month's mixer was with Gamma Delta Rho. Trick was put in charge of buying all the alcohol for the mixer, which included ten bottles of grain alcohol, ten gallons of Hawaiian punch, and three kegs of beer. After giving back the driver's license of the brother over twenty-one who gave it to him, he took all the alcohol down into the basement and made the grain alcohol/punch mixture and tapped the first keg, and put it on ice.

There was a young Delta Rho named Martha who Trick had his eye on. She had long brown hair and hazel eyes. Trick got up the courage to speak to her.

"How do you like NMSU so far?" Trick asked her.

"I like it fine, and the weather has been fantastic hasn't it?" she replied.

"I've been pretty busy studying so I guess I haven't noticed," Trick said.

"Are you a pledge or a full brother?" Martha asked Trick.

"I was made a full brother last semester," Trick replied.

"I just became a full sister last semester too," Martha responded.

"Can I get something to drink? Spiked punch or beer?" Trick asked.

"I could go for some punch," Martha replied.

Trick walked over to the punch table and ladled some into a cup. When he turned around, brother Tree was already talking to Martha. He walked up to her and gave her the drink.

"I see you've met brother Tree," trick said with a little hostility in his tone.

"Yes, he is a Biology major," Martha said. "I forgot to ask you what your major was," she added.

"Biology," Trick said.

"So it looks like you two have something in common," Martha said.

"Yes it does Trick smiled – you."

Martha laughed and said, "Well there's enough of me to go around."

Trick was giving Tree an evil eye and it was starting to work. Tree got the message and started to back off. "Well, nice talking to you Martha, but I've got to go upstairs and check on the food. Nice meeting you," he said as Trick's head nodded approval.

"Brother Tree is a Biology major too – kind of appropriate isn't it – brother 'Tree'", Trick said.

"He was very nice, but so are you," Martha said.

Trick was starting to feel the alcohol and his inhibitions getting loosened up. He wanted to kiss Martha.

"Do you want to see my room?" Trick got up the courage to say.

"O.K.," Martha said.

They climbed the stairs to the first floor, walked down the hall, and took the first door to the right. It was the biggest bedroom in the house. It was fifty feet long and twenty feet wide, with two bunk beds and one single bed. Trick's bed was the bunk bed on top. He climbed the ladder to the top and motioned Martha to join him. He couldn't believe his luck – she was climbing the ladder to get into bed with him. When she got to top, Trick pulled the blanket down and let her get under the covers with him. He didn't waste a second making his move. He brushed her brown hair back, leaned forward, and kissed her gently. She responded by giving him a little tongue. He was getting hard, and she knew it. She smiled and lay straight back in bed and stared at the ceiling.

Trick didn't want to push his luck and scare her away. He lay back in bed too and looked straight up. This was a nice beginning, and he didn't want to spoil it by jumping her bones.

14
CHAPTER

THE AFTERPARTY

After one sorority mixer, the "space cadet" crew had an afterparty. The group consisted of six or seven brothers who established good drug connections on campus. Their chief drug of choice was marijuana, but for this particular party, they also managed to purchase some mescaline powder and peyote buttons.

They invited five Theta Gammas to the third-floor party room where the ceiling and walls were painted black with stars painted in day-glow paint scattered about. It really looked like a planetarium when the black lights were turned on and the stars seemed to jump off the ceiling and walls. The game sorority girls were impressed.

"This is so cool!" one of them exclaimed.

Glen said, "Let's sit in a circle boy girl boy girl," and everyone agreed that that was a good idea. Sitting in a circle fifteen feet in diameter, black lights making the walls and ceilings phosphorescent, Rolling Stones playing in the background, brother John Kavka brought out a three-foot-long bong from the closet and proceeded to fill the one-ounce bowl with marijuana. Brother John said it was "Maui Wowi" from Hawaii.

Trick was sitting next to Suki, a foreign student from Lebanon. He watched the other brothers inhale deeply and then hold their breath so the drug would have the maximum effect. After inhaling, a few brothers and sorority sisters coughed because the smoke was so harsh and burned their larynxes. Trick took note of this and decided to inhale quickly to minimize the exposure of his larynx to the smoke.

Suki passed the bong to Trick. Suki evidently did not have a coughing reaction to the smoke. Trick inhaled quickly, held his breath, and passed the bong along to the sister on his left. He held his breath for just over a minute before exhaling. At first, he didn't feel anything and was disappointed. But by the time the bong was halfway around the circle his head started to spin. The stars on the ceiling were starting to move, and he felt as though his body was starting to move at the speed of light. And that was just from the marijuana. When brother bates pulled out the bags of mescaline and peyote buttons, Trick was wondering if he should leave the party, but he didn't because he really wanted to know how those other drugs would make him feel.

The mescaline powder was snorted, while the peyote buttons were to be chewed and swallowed. He took the mescaline first. He rolled up a dollar bill and then poured a small line of the blue powder from the bag onto his palm, and then he snorted half of the line into each nostril. He still hadn't noticed anything other than his high from the marijuana when the peyote buttons reached him. He grabbed one from the plastic bag and put it in his mouth and passed the bag along.

Then it hit him. The pure mescaline powder and the mescaline in the peyote produced a double-whammy effect. On top of that, he was already stoned on the marijuana. He started to feel like he was floating and the different colors of the stars became so intense he had to look away from them. He looked over at Suki to his right. She was giddy and cracking jokes with her sorority sisters.

Trick liked the way he felt. He felt like new dimensions were opening themselves up to him. He could sense alternate realities existing out there, but he wasn't ready to venture into them yet. He knew he still needed more wisdom before he could attempt to navigate these different worlds. As he regained control over his floating sensation, he had a much more concrete and immediate thought – he was still a virgin!

He looked over at Suki. She was giggly and more interested in what was happening to her sorority sisters than in what was happening to herself. Trick wondered if he could get her to have sex with him. He wanted to get this virginity thing off his mind; after all, probably all but one or two of his fraternity brothers were not virgins. He put his arm around Suki and said, "Let's go to my room."

To his surprise, she didn't resist. They walked down the stairs to Trick's second-floor bedroom and climbed the ladder to Trick's top bunk bed. Trick started kissing her and fondling her breasts. He could tell that she liked it. He was now as hard as a rock. He grabbed her hand and directed it to his shaft and showed her the rhythm he liked. He was kissing her and she was stroking him. He didn't want to come in her hand so he started pulling down her pants.

He climbed on top of her and inserted his shaft into her vagina. He started pumping and knew he wouldn't last long because had had almost come in her hand. She liked his rhythm and wet-kissed him back to show that she was really enjoying him. Trick could feel that the floodgates were about to burst, and he also knew that he was too high to hold back or control his orgasm. When he came, it felt like a bucket-full of sperm had left his ball sac, and he just gushed inside her.

He hadn't planned to lose his virginity to a foreign student, but somehow that didn't matter; what mattered was that he was no longer a virgin. He could now be a big stud on campus and chase pussy with confidence to his heart's content.

****

Trick was beginning to see the proverbial light at the end of the tunnel. He had just started his fourth semester of college and was looking forward to finishing his associate's degree so that he could enlist in the army and become a ranger in the eighty-first airborne division. He had heard the stories from his mother how some members of her tribe had become eighty-first airborne rangers during World War II and had helped to win that war. He was proud to be part Navajo when he heard that the Navajo code couldn't be broken by the Japanese, and that is why America was victorious on the Pacific Front.

But Trick still had to get through this fourth semester before he could think about joining the army. He knew he was partying too much and had better buckle down and improve his grades so that he could either transfer somewhere else to finish his bachelor's degree or finish it at NMSU.

It had only been your years ago that the Navajo's role in World War II had been declassified by the U.S. military. Now millions of Americans were finding out what he had already learned through word of mouth. Some of these Navajo warriors were invited to Washington to receive Congressional Medals of Honor. He had actually met some of them.

The Japanese code, codenamed Purple, had been a cinch for American cryptographers to crack. But the Japanese weren't so lucky when it came to breaking the Navajo code. Lieutenant Philips, who thought up the idea, was one of perhaps only twenty to twenty-five non-Navajo who could speak and understand their language. It worked beautifully – the Japanese never crack the Navajo code.

It was spring, 1971, and there were only three weeks of classes left. Trick had been dating Martha for almost a year, and he never did tell her about his one-night stand with Suki. Martha was a home economics major, which meant she had a lot more free time than Trick. Trick was busting his hump with five-hour-long organic chemistry labs while Martha was baking pies.

Trick felt a pang of guilt in not telling Martha about Suki, but he knew it would only hurt her and he knew it would never happen again so why not keep a little secret. Trick prepared for finals week by spending a lot of time alone studying in the student union. He'd really like to ace calculus and physics and just pass organic chemistry and zoology. He just wanted to take enough science to be able to become a forest ranger – either in Guadalupe or Los Alamos counties.

After finals week, he went to the science building to find his grades. He had aced calculus but not physics, and he did pull Cs in organic chemistry II and zoology. Oh well, he thought, at least he'd done well enough to receive his associate's diploma.

The day of graduation was a beautiful spring day in May, and students' parents were driving in from all over the West. The dean gave Trick his two-year certificate with a gold star in the top right-hand corner; he shook the hand of the dean as he took it, and then lifted it up to show his parents sitting in the back. They smiled at him and he gave them the thumbs-up signal.

15

CHAPTER

FORT BRAGG, NORTH CAROLINA

The first thing that Trick did after receiving his diploma was walk into the army recruiting center in the middle of Las Cruces. He told the recruiter that he wanted to be in the eighty-first airborne rangers. With an associate's degree, he might qualify for corporal or even sergeant rank, but not lieutenant or officer rank. But that was O.K. with Trick because he didn't really want to be an officer telling others what to do – he just wanted to be a soldier.

He was scheduled for a physical, and if he passed he was in. He couldn't imagine not being in good enough shape because he was as tough as nails. Nevertheless, he had experimented with drugs, and he wondered if some trace of them were still in his body.

Two weeks after his physical, he was declared fit for duty and was sent a letter telling him to report to Fort Bragg, North Carolina for basic training on July 26. It was already June 6, which left him with seven weeks to get ready.

****

When Trick arrived at Fort Bragg on July 25, 1972, his hormones were pumped, his body was solid as a rock, and his mind was willing, ready, and able to become a killing machine. He was given the rank of corporal thanks to his associate's degree. His commanding officer was a Lieutenant Thomas Harris from Long Island, New York.

He entered the officer's building to report to Lt. Harris. Trick found his office at the end of a long hallway. Lieutenant Harris was sitting behind a mahogany desk.

"Corporal Trick Hartland reporting for duty, sir," Trick said as he saluted his new commanding officer.

"At ease, corporal, have a seat," Lt. Harris said.

Trick sat down and stared at all the medals pinned on Lt. Harris' chest.

"You start basic training tomorrow," Lieutenant Harris said. "Report to building Q barracks and pick a bed," he said. "Your drill sergeant will be Sergeant Jerry Bernfeld," Lt. Harris added. "Report to him at 0700 hours tomorrow – you are dismissed."

Trick found Q barracks and walked inside. He picked out a locker and found a bed that did not appear to be taken yet. After storing his gear away, he decided to look for

Sergeant Bernfeld. He must have been out conducting drills because Trick was the only living thing in Q barracks. He decided he might as well go to bed because 0700 hours would come soon enough.

Trick awoke at 0500 hours, which left him two hours before he had to report to Sergeant Bernfeld. He hopped into the shower and turned the water on as hot as it would go to clean out the cobwebs. Once dressed, he started looking for Sergeant Bernfeld. Trick found him sitting behind an office desk.

"Corporal Trick Hartland reporting for duty sir," Trick said with a salute.

"Sit down Trick," Sergeant Bernfeld said. "Why did you want to be in the eighty-first?" Sergeant Bernfeld asked him.

"Because I have relatives who served in the eighty-first, sir. They were Navajo code talkers during World War II – I am half Navajo, sir" Trick said.

"Yes, your relatives were instrumental in winning the big one," Sergeant Bernfeld said. "You come from a distinguished line of warriors, Trick," Sergeant Bernfeld added. "I can see you're in tip-top shape; you shouldn't have any trouble with basic training. You'll be my right-hand man, Trick, my next in command. There's only one other corporal in our platoon, Corporal Smith, but I don't think he'll be as good as you. The rest of the platoon are privates," Sergeant Bernfeld said.

"I'll do my best to live up to your expectations," Trick replied as he stood up to go.

"Go get breakfast and report to barracks K at 1100 hours for a marching drill," Sergeant Bernfeld said.

"Yes sir," Trick said as he turned to go to the mess hall.

The platoon gathered outside barracks K at precisely 1100 hours and the marching drill began. Trick stood just behind Sergeant Bernfeld's left shoulder, and as he marched he let his gaze fall off to either side of the road. Trick had never seen such a lush environment. There was thick Spanish moss hanging from most of the trees and deep green fern plants covering much of the ground. The terrain was so lush it could have passed for tropical rainforest. Trick was glad to be training in such an environment because he knew that Viet Nam was probably even more lush than this. On and on they marched, over a bridge crossing a stream, past tobacco fields, and dairy farms. All in all, they marched ten miles in three hours. As they re-entered the gates of Fort Bragg, Sergeant Bernfeld said, "Tomorrow you're going to learn how to use an M-16."

The next day each soldier was given an M16 automatic rifle and told to report to the firing range at 0900 hours. Sergeant Bernfeld told his platoon to line up prone on the ground and start shooting at the practice targets about a hundred yards away. For a group of beginners, they were pretty accurate. When the M16 first came out about seven years ago, the gun jammed a lot, and soldiers in the thick of battle were getting killed. Just within the last year too so, improvements in the ammunition had been made, and there were far fewer jams, and the death toll declined.

In addition to the M16, each soldier above the rank of private was given a sidearm – a Colt 45 revolver. Trick knew that revolver could come in handy someday in close-quarters combat. He could take or leave the M16, but he learned how to operate it anyway, and pretend that it was his weapon of choice.

The weeks of basic training flew by, and the recruits were getting a little tougher each day and looking forward to battle. Trick had learned from Sergeant Bernfeld that his platoon was going to be deployed at a place called Phuoc Long. That's all he knew.

16
CHAPTER

WELCOME TO VIET NAM

It was mid-September, 1972, and Trick's platoon was sitting in the cargo hold of a C-130 transport on its way to Viet Nam. The battle of An Loc was ongoing, and his platoon was going to set down in the outskirts of Binh Long province to help recapture its capital – An Loc. Twelve more hours of airtime and his division would be on the ground. He polished his revolver with a cloth and put it back in its holster. Before he left Fort Bragg, he had also found a clever place for his bowie knife. He had found an ankle strap at the PX that held his bowie knife perfectly in place under his pants leg. Between his M16, his Colt 45, his knife, and two hand grenades he had strapped to his belt, he felt well-armed.

He was given direct command over a four-man squad. Corporal Smith had command over the other squad in the platoon. In his squad were privates Mike Fullerton from Kansas, Randall Miller from Erie, Pennsylvania, Tom Hoss from West Virginia, and Jim Pickens from North Carolina. They ranged in age from eighteen to twenty-six. Trick himself was only nineteen.

Trick looked out the window and saw types of clouds he had never seen before. Most of the clouds in the American Southwest were wispy, thin clouds that glowed red during sunset. These clouds looked like big white cotton balls that went on for miles in every direction. Some of them had a bluish-purplish color that he had never seen before. Most of his men were looking out the windows too wondering what their fate would be.

Touchdown occurred at 0600 hours on an airfield outside of An Loc. The C-130 required almost a mile of airstrip before it came to a complete halt just in front of the hangar. Air traffic control specialists waved their white flags to show the pilot where to stop.

The soldiers grabbed their gear and hit the tarmac. They still had a five-mile walk into the jungle before reaching their outpost. Trick formed his men into a single line to await marching orders from Sergeant Bernfeld.

The sun was rising and orange-red rays of light burst over the jungle forest treetops. It was an uncannily beautiful spectacle that Trick knew belied what was really happening in this country. He had already heard stories about how brutal the Viet Cong could be – torture, beheadings, POWs more often killed than put in prison camps. Trick was aware of the ferociousness of the Viet

Cong and would never take them for granted or think that Americans were superior to them.

President Nixon was trying to wind down the war, slowly replacing American troops with ARVN South Vietnamese troops. At the height of the war during the TET offensive of 1968, there were half a million U.S. troops in Viet Nam. Now there were only a hundred thousand.

An Loc had been besieged since May. The town had been bombarded every day since then, and it was only the U.S. air support that kept it from being swarmed and occupied by the Viet Cong. The eighty-first airborne rangers were being brought in to bolster the ground forces. The generals knew that if An Loc fell, it would only be a matter of time before Saigon fell too.

17
CHAPTER

VIET CONG
1/AMERICA 0

Lieutenant Harris set up command headquarters in a concrete bunker half submerged into the earth. His radio operator was a private from Corporal Smith's squad named Harriman. The rest of both squads were out digging foxholes and earth bunkers. The ground they decided to protect was on top of a hill maybe eighty yards high. Most of the trees had been cleared, and the stumps offered additional protection.

Trick was down at the bottom of the hill installing barbed wire around the perimeter. He spaced posts about ten feet apart, hammering them into the ground with a sledgehammer, and then stringing the curled barbed wire three rows high.

The heat was pretty unbearable. This heat wasn't like the heat of New Mexico; it was a humid heat, and the mosquitoes would eat you alive if you let them. The insects were a difficult adjustment that Trick was still learning to make. Sure there were gnats and flies in New Mexico, but not these green biting flies and bloodsucking mosquitoes. Fortunately, he had remembered to buy a whole case of bug repellant at Fort Bragg.

It took an entire week to properly secure the perimeter with barbed wire. The foxholes were fitted with machine guns, and land mines were buried outside the barbed wire perimeter. At night, Trick's and Corporal Smith's squad alternated duty as night watch. There were also night patrols just to ensure that the perimeter was clear. Trick only needed a little bit of moonlight to be able to "see" at night. He realized that his night vision was much better than anyone else in his squad. He kept this little secret to himself.

Lieutenant Harris had received intelligence that the Viet Cong were amassing some new divisions just over the Cambodian border, which was only seven miles from An Loc. Lieutenant Harris wanted assurance that additional reinforcements were on their way. He knew his position was undermanned and no amount of air support from Binh Long would save them if the VC decided to overrun them. Harris wanted the night patrols to venture out from base camp to make sure the VC wasn't within a ten-mile radius. That suited Trick just fine because what bothered him the most about this place was the humid heat, which was not nearly so bad at night. Sometimes a cool sea breeze would blow in at night, and that, combined with moonlight, put Trick at his peak. His senses became supersensitive; he could see through the underbrush and trees and hear a cricket from a hundred yards away.

That night, Trick could "feel" the danger out there somewhere. His squad was about seven miles west of the base, probably just over the Cambodian border. Then it happened: a single gunshot and a thud as Tom Hoss hit the ground. Blood was spurting from his neck. He stared up at the night sky with glassy eyes – he was already dead; the bullet had severed his carotid artery.

"Everybody down!" Trick yelled. He focused his eyes on the treetops to the west and spotted the sniper about three hundred yards away. He aimed his M16 and pulled the trigger – he hit the tree just next to the sniper who was climbing down. He didn't have time for a second shot.

"Let's get the hell out of here," Trick said. "Lucas, can you carry him?"

Lucas responded in the affirmative. They double-timed it back to their firebase. Trick told Sergeant Bernfeld what had happened. Score one for the Viet Cong.

18
CHAPTER

GERONIMO

Lieutenant Harris informed central headquarters about his unit's latest casualty. Trick reported to Lieutenant Harris that he thought his suspicions were correct – the VC were amassing troops just over the Cambodian border. Harris wanted reinforcements. He knew that one platoon couldn't hold back the oncoming onslaught. Without reinforcements, he knew that he couldn't hold on to An Loc.

Captain Longenecker in Binh Long couldn't make any promises. He assured Lt. Harris that his assessment was going up the chain of command, but right now he knew that the top brass had other concerns foremost in their minds. Captain Longenecker basically put Lt. Harris on hold. Lt. Harris relayed this status back to Sergeant

Bernfeld, Corporal Smith, and Trick. They had to accept their situation and deal with it as best they could.

Thus, An Loc became a waiting game. Whichever side got their reinforcements first would win An Loc, and aerial reconnaissance photos revealed convoys of Viet Cong coming down from North Vietnam were stopping a Kampong Cham, just twenty miles inside the Cambodian border.

The days went by and the night patrols continued, with instructions from Lt. Harris not to go past the Cambodian border. Lt. Harris didn't want any more casualties from snipers.

Sergeant Bernfeld pestered Lieutenant Harris every day about the reinforcements. Sergeant Bernfeld knew that they needed an entire division to hold on to An Loc. Even with air support from Binh Long, if the VC attacked now with a full division, it would be a massacre.

The days turned into weeks, and the weeks turned into months without change. No encouraging words except one came down from central command. There was a unit of Montagnards – part of the civilian irregular Defense Group (CIDG) – natives of the central highlands of Viet Nam, who were headed north from Saigon to help defend An Loc. The CIDG was part of the Vietnamization plan that Washington had been working on since Nixon took office to get America the hell out of Viet Nam and turn the war over to South Viet Nam.

Lieutenant Harris finally had something to be happy about. The leader of this CIDG unit, he was told, was a Colonel Tuan. Top brass in Saigon had heard of Colonel

Tuan's valor in battle, and if any unit could save An Loc it would be Colonel Tuan's.

Finally, one day in late November, Colonel Tuan's Montagnards unit arrived at An Loc. Colonel Tuan met with Lieutenant Harris in the concrete bunker. Through an interpreter, Lieutenant Harris told Colonel Tuan where he wanted him to station his men – on the hills just east of the village of An Loc. From that vantage point, they should be able to see the enemy coming and have the best possible defense position in the area.

The bad news was that Colonel Tuan only had a hundred or so men left in his unit. The rest had been killed or wounded in action and went back to their native hamlets to heal or be buried. Still, it was better than nothing, but Lt. Harris was still asking for more American troops every day.

****

The onslaught came on Pearl Harbor Day, December 7, 1972, at 02:00 a.m. in the morning. The VC were attacking Colonel Tuan's positions on the hills east of An Loc, and it was only a matter of time before they headed south and attacked Lt. Harris' position. At least by hitting Colonel Tuan first, Lt. Harris' rangers had time to hit their foxholes and bunkers. Lt. Harris called in air support from Binh Long before the VC had even reached his perimeter. Helicopter gun ships were on their way.

While the battle was still raging at Colonel Tuan's positions, the first VC to reach Lt. Harris' position had arrived; they had reached the barbed wire perimeter at the bottom of the hill. Through his binoculars, Trick could see them using wire cutters to get through the barbed wire. Trick called Jim Pickens, his best sharpshooter, to start picking them off.

Pickens didn't waste a bullet. One by one he picked them off, but by the fifth bullet they were now sending two at a time to shear their way through the barbed wire, and as Pickens picked off one, the other had time to breach the perimeter and move the barbed wire aside. They were in.

Lucas Troy and Mike Fullerton manned the machinegun nest closest to the bottom of the hill, and they opened up with a barrage that left at least a dozen VC dead. Further up the hill were Randall Miller and Greg Nolte. As the VC got in the perimeter, they veered left to avoid Troy and Fullerton's barrage, but then Miller and Nolte took over their left flank. Their job was to keep the VC out of grenade range, and so far it was working.

"Where the hell are my Chinooks?" Lieutenant Harris screamed into his radio transmitter. He knew that his platoon would not be able to withstand this onslaught much longer. Already a hundred VC lay dead around the perimeter of his hill, but they kept coming, and now there were several breaches of the perimeter.

Colonel Tuan was now taking heavy losses and wanted to retreat to the air base at Binh Long. Lieutenant Harris told him to stand his ground, that the Chinooks from Binh Long would be there any minute to provide air support, but Colonel Tuan did not think he could hold off the VC long enough for the Chinooks to make it there.

"I repeat: stand your ground Colonel Tuan; if you don't, we'll both be massacred," Lt. Harris insisted. Trick had positioned Pickens in the northeast bunker at the top of the hill to prevent another breach of the perimeter from that direction. Corporal Smith's men were in the machinegun foxholes on that side of the hill, and they were in just as intense a battle as his squad was.

There were countless VC inside the perimeter now, and they had been clever enough to breach the perimeter from three directions – the west, the northwest, and the northeast. It was the breach from the northwest that was the most dangerous, but the machinegun foxholes were not positioned close enough to that position to be effective.

And so the VC slowly made their way up the hill, hiding behind trees, their camouflage quite effective at night. The first machinegun nest to go was Troy's and Fullerton's. As Fullerton lifted his head up a little to feed a new magazine into the machinegun, he took a bullet in his upper right chest. Troy kept firing, but they were overrun. The VC shot Troy right between the eyes, and they finished the job on Fullerton with a bayonet through the heart.

"Sir, Colonel Tuan's on the horn," Corporal Smith said. The interpreter told Lt. Harris that half of Colonel Tuan's men were dead and that they were evacuating their position.

"Tell Colonel Tuan that if he doesn't hold his position we're all dead men," Lt. Harris told the interpreter. "The Chinooks should be over you any second now," he added.

"Colonel Tuan said that if you don't hear back from him, you'll know why," the interpreter said.

By this time, the VC had overrun Corporal Smith's lowest machinegun nest on the northwest side of the hill and were slowly making their way up the next one. Privates Miller and Nolte were holding their ground on the north face, having sent at least a hundred VC souls to their maker. Trick took Pickens with him to the west slope to make sure that the enemy wasn't trying to outflank them. But of course, they were. A new breach of the perimeter on the west face had already been made, and Pickens could only pick them off one at a time from the top of the hill.

Trick ordered Pickens to stay put and keep shooting. Sergeant Bernfeld was in a bunker at the top of the hill firing mortar rounds. "Feed me mortars and be my lookout," Sgt. Bernfeld screamed at Trick as he jumped into Bernfeld's bunker. Sgt. Bernfeld was aiming his rounds at the north perimeter, firing four shells a minute. The VC were getting better with their mortar fire aim too – a shell exploded just twenty feet outside Trick and Bernfeld's foxhole, sending earth cascading over them.

Corporal Smith's second machinegun nest had been overrun and he watched in horror as two of his men were shot close range and killed. Lieutenant Harris told him to take up a position fifty yards above that nest to prevent the hill from being overrun from the northwest. There was just one defensive position protecting the northwest face now, and Trick saw that he had to help Corporal Smith hold that position or it was all over.

"Sir, permission to join Corporal Smith, sir," Trick screamed at Sgt. Bernfeld.

"Go!" Sgt. Bernfeld screamed back.

Smith and Trick were all that was left to protect the northwest face. Trick had taken twenty hand grenades from the ammo bunker and was now pulling the pins and throwing them with all his might down the hill. Corporal Smith kept his finger constantly on the trigger of his M16 and stopped firing only when he had to reload.

"Sir, there's no report from Colonel Tuan," Corporal Smith's last surviving squad member, the radio operator, reported.

"Let's go help whoever's left," Lt. Harris told the radio operator. He drew his pearl-handled Colt-45 from his holster and started walking to Sgt. Bernfeld's position. Both he and the radio operator were hit with a spray of AK-47 fire. The radio operator fell to the ground dead. Lt. Harris took only one bullet in the chest. As he reached Sgt. Bernfeld's position, he slumped over and said "Looks like you'll be in command soon sergeant."

"Yes, Sir," Sgt. Bernfeld said, alternating between firing mortar rounds and spraying his field of vision with M16 fire. Blood was spurting out of Lt. Harris' chest, but as one VC soldier made it to the edge of the foxhole Lt. Harris shot him dead with his Colt-45. Another one took his place though and stabbed Lt. Harris with his bayonet. Sgt. Bernfeld knew he couldn't protect his right flank anymore, so he abandoned his position and ran full speed down the hill to Miller and Nolte's foxhole. He couldn't believe they were still alive.

They were down to five men now – Miller, Nolte, Bernfeld, Smith, and Trick, and they were trying to hold off an entire VC division. The machinegun fire was so loud they knew they would never hear the Chinook's engines until they were right on top of them.

Finally, the helicopter gun ships did arrive and were spraying the bottom of the hill with machinegun fire and cannon. Sgt. Bernfeld decided to make a run for it back to the ammo bunker for more hand grenades. He was about thirty yards from the bunker when he looked back and saw a new wave of VC come straight for Miller and Nolte. They mowed down twelve or fifteen before the rear of the surge was right on top of them pumping them full of bullets. Sgt. Bernfeld would have to make a last-ditch effort to save himself from the ammo bunker.

In the meantime, Trick asked Corporal Smith if he would try and make it to the ammo bunker to retrieve machinegun clips. He only got three steps before he took a spray of bullets in the back.

As he fell backward on top of Trick's legs he said "Sorry," and he was gone. Without more clips for his M16, Trick was left with only his revolver and his bowie knife to protect himself. He wasn't sure if he was the only one still alive or not.

He pulled out his Colt-45 and shot one VC who was getting ready to bayonet him, and he realized that his only chance was to play possum. He cupped a handful of Corporal Smith's blood in his hands and smeared the front of his uniform with it, then he pulled Corporal Smith's body over him to make it look like they had both been slain. Trick could hear Vietnamese voices getting stronger, and he tried to control his breathing so that there was no movement. He reached down to his ankle and pulled his bowie knife from its sheath and kept it ready in his right hand. After a few seconds, he heard a Chinook helicopter's gunfire almost directly above him. The Vietnamese voices were moving away. He squinted and saw one remaining Viet Cong who looked unconvinced. Trick saw him raising his bayonet and he knew he had to act fast. He grabbed the VC's ankle with his left hand, tripping him, and then he shoved the bowie knife into his chest as far as it would go with his right. He covered the VC's mouth with his left hand and watched his eyes as the life went out of him.

Meanwhile, at the top of the hill in the ammunition bunker, Sergeant Bernfeld was also fighting for his life. A pile of dead VC marked the entrance to the ammunition bunker and two dead VC had made it inside and put a bullet in Sgt. Bernfeld's left shoulder before Bernfeld could blow them away with his M16. Then the onslaught stopped as Chinook gunfire took care of the remaining VC near the bunker.

Hours went by before dawn. There was complete silence as the sun rose in the east. Rays of light shone on hundreds of dead VC and a scattering of dead Americans. Trick decided to take a peek outside his foxhole. He saw Sgt. Bernfeld, his left arm hanging limp to his side, walking around the top of the hill. He got up and waved to him; Sgt. Bernfeld waved back. They were the only two survivors.

19
CHAPTER

BLACK OPS

As Sergeant Bernfeld and Trick were looking at each other, the Fifth Calvary helicopter squads reached the top of the hill. They saw the two lone survivors and saluted them before loading them into a Chinook and flying them to Binh Long. Sergeant Bernfeld needed immediate medical attention, and the medic on the helicopter started bandaging him up. Trick looked down on the battlefield with hawk's eyes and saw the hundreds of bodies. A sergeant on the helicopter told him that none of Colonel Tuan's men survived. The battle of An Loc was "won" because Trick and Sergeant Bernfeld had survived.

Back at Binh Long airfield, Sergeant Bernfeld was whisked off to the field hospital to have that bullet taken out of his shoulder. Trick was told to report to Captain Longenecker.

As Trick entered, Captain Longenecker, two of his lieutenants, and a Green Beret saluted him. He saluted them back.

"I'm putting you in for the Congressional Medal of Honor, Trick," Captain Longenecker said. "I'm also giving you a field promotion to staff sergeant. I'm promoting Sergeant Bernfeld to second lieutenant. I'm also putting Sergeant Bernfeld in for the Congressional Medal of Honor," he added.

"Since you two were the only survivors in your platoon, I have to reassign you," Captain Longenecker went on. "Trick, the Special Forces Green Berets need a recognizance specialist who knows Cambodia. I know you've only been along the border, but you're more familiar with the territory than almost any regular Army soldier. Will you accept a temporary assignment as recognizance specialist with the Green Berets?" Longenecker asked.

Without hesitation, Trick answered, "Yes." He had always wanted to serve in the Special Forces and this was his chance. "What about Sergeant Bernfeld, sir?" Trick asked.

"Until he heals completely, he'll be working in the intelligence office of the Third Army," Captain Longenecker replied. "Trick, I want to introduce you to Captain Bystrom of the Green Berets," Longenecker said as he gestured for them to shake hands. "He will be your new commanding officer."

Trick saluted Captain Bystrom and then they shook hands. "Come with me," Captain Bystrom said.

A jeep and driver were waiting for them outside captain Longenecker's tent. Trick was asked to sit in the back seat as captain Bystrom got in the passenger seat. They drove off heading west toward Cambodia.

****

They were on old dirt roads for more than three hours. Finally, right around sunset, captain Bystrom turned around and said to Trick "This is it." The bivouac of this Special Forces Green Berets unit was on the outskirts of a hamlet named Krakor, about a hundred and twenty-five miles northwest of Phnom Penh.

Captain Bystrom said, "There will be a briefing in my tent at 1900 hours – go to the mess tent and get something to eat."

Trick asked a Green Beret where the mess tent was and was told that it was the last tent down the hill on the left. Trick entered and saw a small line of Green Berets waiting to get their food. The first thing that struck him was that these guys did not look like regular army. These guys looked like prime athletes getting ready for the Olympics, and their dispositions matched their physiques. They were the elite of the armed forces, and although they were friendly, there was a toughness about them that Trick admired.

After finishing his meal of beef stew and rolls, he found his way to Captain Bystrom's tent. He walked inside and Captain Bystrom motioned him to sit down in a wicker chair.

"Have you ever heard of the Khmer Rouge?" Captain Bystrom asked.

"No sir," Trick replied.

"Well, they are a group of communists from Cambodia who are helping the Viet Cong and North Vietnamese. They were only a minor nuisance a year ago – there were only a thousand or so of them then. Now, however, they are about thirty to fifty thousand strong, and they are helping North Viet Nam win this war," Captain Bystrom said.

"What is the game plan, sir?" Trick asked.

"We have to find a way to keep the Khmer Rouge from gathering steam, picking up new recruits from all parts of Cambodia," Captain Bystrom said.

"And how can we do that, sir?" Trick asked.

"By getting the people of Cambodia to see through the Khmer Rouge and to show them that their end goal is a Communist State dictatorship," Captain Bystrom said. "We've been keeping a record of the Khmer Rouge's atrocities, and they are even more brutal than the North Vietnamese," Captain Bystrom added.

"How can we achieve this sir?" Trick asked.

"There are resistance pockets amongst the people of Cambodia who want to see the Khmer Rouge go. We have been arming these resistance fighters and have provided them with intelligence, and we have also joined in on some of their missions," Captain Bystrom said.

"We have to keep moving and keep our forces small and under the radar, because any Americans caught by the

Khmer Rouge are shot on sight. We have suffered some casualties," Captain Bystrom added.

"Your role, Trick, will be to befriend the local resistance leaders and provide intelligence back to us so that we can assess what our best plan of attack will be," Captain Bystrom said. "You will live and travel as need be with these resistance leaders, and help supply them with arms," Captain Bystrom said.

"When will I meet them?" Trick asked.

"In a day or two," the Captain replied.

****

During his brief respite before meeting the resistance fighters he would be working with, Trick learned that what the Green Berets were doing in Cambodia was referred to as "Black Ops," another way of saying secret missions. He still wasn't one hundred percent sure of his mission here, and he thought that perhaps his commanders placed him here because of his ruddy-brown skin and some slight resemblance to the native population. Of course, not knowing the Cambodian language made him as awkward as the next American in trying to communicate with the resistance fighters. When they arrived at the temporary base two days later, Trick was introduced to Chu Hoa, resistance leader of the northern provinces, La Cao, leader of the southern provinces, Ly Khack, leader of the eastern provinces, and Vu Xuan Thong, leader of the western provinces. Along with them came Nguyen Van Lan, demolitions expert, Lai Dinh Hoi, intelligence expert, and Le Van Diep, bodyguard and driver.

Captain Bystrom brought two of his lieutenants, Trick, and a native interpreter with him. They all sat down in a circle on the ground inside Captain Bystrom's tent. After exchanging greetings they got down to business.

"Do you know the location of Duong Van Minh?" Captain Bystrom asked Chu Hoa. Duong Van Minh was the current overall leader of all the factions of the Khmer Rouge.

"Yes," Chu Hoa replied through the interpreter. "he is deep in the jungles of the Co Mi Forest," Chu Hoa said.

"And where is Vu Van Mau?" Captain Bystrom asked. Vu Van Mau was the number two man under Duong Van Minh.

"He is in the far western provinces, past the Chou Thoi Mountains," Chu Hoa said through the interpreter.

"Good, then their forces are separated," Captain Bystrom said. "Trick, I want you to go with Vu Xuan Thong to the western provinces and keep Vu Van Mau there, separated from Duong Van Minh. Ambush a few of his soldiers and then lead them further west toward Thailand. Go all the way to Bangkok and we will extricate you from there. Bangkok is about a hundred and twenty-five miles from the western Cambodian border. Your contact there will be your old staff sergeant, Lt. Bernfeld," Captain Bystrom said. "I'm sending my interpreter, Vo Van Hiep so that you'll be able to communicate with Vu Xuan Thong and his men, and my second lieutenant Roger Applethorpe will be your new commanding officer," Captain Bystrom added.

****

Vu Xuan Thong and Vo Van Hiep motioned for Trick to follow them. After picking up Trick's and Lt. Applethorpe's gear, they headed west in two beat-up jeeps. Van Hiep told them they were headed for Ban Hat Lak, a small hamlet on the border with Thailand. Vu Xuan Thong only had a renegade force of thirty or forty soldiers under his command, nothing compared to Chu Hoa's forces in the north, but the resistance fighters he did have were dedicated and would follow him without question.

A dozen or so thatched huts on the outskirts of Ban Hat Lak made up the encampment of Vu Xuan Thong's men. A nearby stream provided water, and food was plentiful in this agricultural area. Trick was shown to his hut, and a man pointed to the straw bunk that would be his bed. Trick nodded to show his appreciation, but inside he knew his existence here would be austere.

The only thing that made Trick's existence here a little less austere was Xuan Thong's two daughters, Lian and Lela. Trick learned from Van Hiep that Lian was nineteen and Lela eighteen. They were considered by the other resistance fighters to be their equal, and their unquestioning loyalty to their father was admired by the entire camp. Lian and Lela were instructed by their father to watch out for Trick. They both knew a little English and were able to communicate the basics with Trick in broken English.

Trick admired their courage and resolve to take back their country, and he wanted to help Xuan Thong in any way that he could. He explained the importance of night patrols to Vo Van Hiep, and Vu Xuan Thong responded by taking Trick's advice. Nightly patrols of five or six men were sent out into the jungle to make sure there was no Khmer Rouge in the area. It was thought that Van Mau's Khmer Rouge was currently near Batdambang, two hundred miles north of Ban Hat Lak.

Lieutenant Applethorpe, Xuan Thong, and Trick planned to traverse the two hundred miles, ambush one or two squads of Vu Van Mau's men, then lure the rest of his men west toward Thailand. Batdambang was only fifty miles from the Thai border, and the ambush party would have to travel quickly over mountain trails to get out of Cambodia alive.

They would wait until Christmas week to make their move. Xuan Thong knew some of the mountain paths between Batdambang and the Thai border; he knew they would have to cross the Moi River before reaching Thailand.

It would take Xuan Thong's men ten days to reach Batdambang. They covered twenty miles a day, heading due north into Vu Van Mau's territory. They reached the Chou Thoi Mountain Range to the west of Batdambang on January 5. From the top of a ridge, they could finally see Van Mau's encampment, which was run like some sort of agricultural concentration camp, where the people worked hard all day in the rice paddies and were under guard at night. Since Van Mau's men were only out in the daytime, a night ambush would be impossible. The resistance fighters would have to pick one field, preferably one of the more isolated ones, and attack during sunlight. That meant they would have to scramble like hell back into the relative safety of the mountains where vehicles couldn't follow them.

Each of the fields being worked was guarded by fifty to sixty Khmer Rouge soldiers. There were thirty-five resistance fighters under Xuan Thong's command, including his daughters. Lieutenant Applethorpe only had Trick under his command. All that they had on their side was the element of surprise. It was decided that the field farthest north from Batdambang would be the target. Sleeping on his bedroll, waiting for the battle the next day, Trick at least felt more secure in the mountains. These jungle mountains were nothing like the Rockies, but at least the altitude felt good to him.

****

Before sunrise, Xuan Thong roused his men. He wanted them in position before the Khmer Rouge ever herded their captives into the rice fields. They formed a single file and walked down out of the mountains to the northernmost rice paddy. Spacing his soldiers out about twenty yards apart, Xuan Thong commanded his men to lie down and cover themselves in the field grass.

Xuan Thong and his daughters, Trick, and Lieutenant Applethorpe made up the very northern tip of the phalanx. The sun was just beginning to rise over the rice fields in the east. Streams of red and orange colored the sky, and under those colors came the peasant farmers in round straw hats, being guarded by a platoon of Khmer Rouge. Closer and closer they came, now only about a half-mile away. Xuan Thong's orders were to not start shooting until he gave the signal.

The Khmer Rouge guards were walking in two lines on either side of the column of peasants. At five hundred yards away they started branching off into different fields. The field furthest west and north, where Xuan Thong's men were hiding, was guarded by about forty soldiers – even odds.

Xuan Thong waited until all the guards were in position, then he waved his yellow handkerchief – the signal. All at once, all the resistance fighters rose up out of the field grass and started firing. Fifteen to twenty Khmer Rouge were dead in the first ten seconds. Only the guards furthest east had time to point their guns and start shooting back. One of his resistance fighters was shot and fell dead. Xuan Thong ordered his men to close in. They marched straight for the remaining guards, picking them off one at a time. It was all over in less than five minutes. Xuan Thong had lost one man, while thirty to forty Khmer Rouge lay dead on the ground. Now the chase would begin across western Cambodia. Xuan Thong ordered his men to fall back and double-time it to the mountain path. The race was on.

20

CHAPTER

THE ARMISTICE

About ten thousand miles away from the mountains of western Cambodia, the Paris Peace Accords were being signed. It was January 23, 1973. William Rogers, the U.S. Secretary of State, Henry Cabot Lodge, leader of the U.S. delegation, Tran Van Lam, the Minister of Foreign Affairs of South Vietnam, and Nguyen Thi Binh, the Minister of Foreign Affairs for North Vietnam were the signatories.

The Accord called for an immediate cease-fire from both sides, and the withdrawal of all American troops from Vietnam within 60 days. In addition, all prisoners of war were to be freed within the 60-day withdrawal period. In addition, there were to be peaceful negotiations on establishing normal relations and reunification of the country.

Finally, it looked as though peace would be given a chance. Secretary Rogers flew back to Washington with high hopes for peace and the good news that prisoners of war would be returned. Tran Van Lam flew home to Saigon knowing that President Thieu would not be very content; he suspected that soon after the American forces withdrew, North Vietnam would ignore the peace accords and invade the South, and this basically is what happened.

****

Trick and Lian, who could climb over rocks like a mountain goat, were at the front of Xuan Thong's men and were already more than halfway up the mountain in less than thirty minutes. Trick looked back and saw at least a hundred now unguarded peasants scurrying up the mountain trying to catch up to Xuan Thong's men. Trick saw several of the resistance fighters telling the peasants they couldn't come with them; they had to find their own way back home.

The Khmer Rouge from the other fields was just starting up the mountain range. The resistance fighters only had a half-hour lead on the Khmer rouge. Trick and Lian were aware of the gap and kept the pace as quick as they could without losing anybody.

At the top of the Chou Thoi Mountain Range, Trick and Lian waited for the rest of the resistance fighters to catch up. Trick looked down at Batdambang through his binoculars. He could see Khmer rouge scrambling into jeeps and trucks. Only a handful of them was following them on foot.

Trick asked Lian if there were fewer roads to the south or to the north. She said there were fewer roads to the north. With that information, Trick told her "Let's move," and proceeded to turn right and follow the ridge of this mountain to the north. Trick knew that a thirty-minute lead translated into only a three-mile lead. Xuan Thong and his men would have to travel through the night if they weren't to be caught. A three-quarters moon like the previous night would help them accomplish that.

Trick and Lian kept up a blistering pace heading north up the Chou Thoi Mountain Range. They saw a gap in the range of mountains to the west and decided to head for it. They came to a trail narrower than the one they were on, but it headed to the west where they wanted to go so they took it. It headed down the western slope of the range they were on until they reached a creek at the bottom of a gorge. They stopped at the creek only long enough for the fighters to re-supply their water. Then the trail headed upwards again towards the top of the second ridge. This second range was higher elevation than the first ridge and was a rigorous climb. But Trick and Lian were up to the challenge and did not slow down. They knew their lives depended on outrunning the Khmer Rouge on foot and avoiding the Khmer Rouge who had taken to vehicles to pursue them.

Xuan Thong, Lieutenant Applethorpe, and Lela made up the rear of the cavalcade. Xuan Thong commanded his daughter to go catch up with her sister and Trick. Lela was carrying the best maps they had of the region, and perhaps they could help Lian better navigate her way through these mountain passes. Trick and Lian knew from the sun that they were headed west by northwest, but now from the maps, they knew they were headed for the village of Wang

Nam Yen, which was about ten miles past the Cambodia-Thailand border. From there, it was still a hundred and twenty-five miles to Bangkok.

Xuan Thong was sure that the Khmer Rouge would chase them to Wang Nam Yen, even though it was over the border, but he wasn't sure if they would chase them any further west than that. In other words, if they could outrun them in the next 24 hours and make it to Wang Nam Yen, odds were they were home free.

What was going through Trick's mind was whether or not these men could keep up with him for 24 hours. If they could, odds were that they would make it to Wang Nam Yen unscathed; if not, there would be a fight and undoubtedly some casualties. Trick would have to discuss this with Xuan Thong, and Xuan Thong would then have to discuss this with his men. It was pretty clear that their fate would be decided by whatever happened within the next 24 hours.

****

Meanwhile, in the northern provinces of Cambodia in the Co Mi Forest, Duong Van Minh was growing stronger by the day. The Paris Peace Accords had actually put North Vietnam in a better position than ever, knowing that the Americans were withdrawing, and this made many Cambodians willing to take up arms with the communists in their country – the Khmer Rouge. There was no staunching the flow now; thousands of Cambodians signed up with Duong Van Minh's communist forces in the Co Mi Forest, and most people in Cambodia knew that it was only a matter of time before they would seize complete control of the government. Duong Van Minh and his mentor, Pol Pot, were already in the planning stages of overthrowing the current U.S. puppet leader of Cambodia – General Lon Nol, who had ousted Prince Sihanouk from power in a coup d'etat in 1970.

While General Lon Nol was in power, the U.S. felt free to move throughout Cambodia, which became an extended battlefield of Vietnam. B-52 bombers pummeled Cambodia during these years trying to eradicate the Viet Cong, but more civilians were being killed than Viet Cong. America realized too late that they had a failing strategy.

Because of the disaffection with the U.S., during 1973 the Khmer Rouge had grown by several hundred thousand soldiers, and in some ways, they were even more ruthless than the Viet Cong.

****

Captain Bystrom was aware of the situation in western Cambodia. He was proud of Applethorpe and Trick and hoped they would make it to Bangkok. His own orders were to assassinate Duong Van Minh. The National Security guys in Washington and the CIA thought that eliminating Duong Van Minh would undermine Pol Pot's credibility. By taking out the number two man of the Khmer Rouge, perhaps down the road, President Thieu of South Vietnam could convert the Cambodians to democracy. All of this was hypothetical, of course, and the only thing Captain Bystrom was focused on right now was how to kill Duong Van Minh.

21
CHAPTER

THE RACE TO WANG NAM YEN

Trick and Xuan Thong's two daughters led the resistance fighters westward onward into the Chou Thoi Mountains. They were hoping to make it to the Cambodia-Thailand border by dusk. Trick couldn't believe that the dozen or so Khmer Rouge soldiers who were chasing them by foot were slowly gaining on them, although they were still out of shooting range. By high noon, Xuan Thong's men were halfway to the Cambodian-Thailand border, but the dozen or so Khmer Rouge chasing them by foot were only two miles behind them now. At this stage, a firefight seemed inevitable. At least by staying to the north they had avoided the Khmer Rouge searching for them in vehicles.

Trick was beginning to admire Lian more and more. She showed no sign of weariness even after scrambling up and down the mountains of western Cambodia for six hours. Of course, she was only nineteen, but she still showed amazing endurance. As Trick admired her physical ability more and more, he began to realize that he was also sexually attracted to her. She had long brown hair twisted into a braid in the back, not the black hair of the Japanese and Chinese. She had a cute upturned nose, nice white teeth, and olive-colored skin, just a shade darker than his own. Her eyes were brown, but they were a light brown that seemed to have flecks of hazel in them. But what turned Trick on most about her was her speaking voice, a mellifluous voice that was pleasing to listen to.

Unfortunately, they were in a race of their lives, and Trick realized that he had better put his sexual thoughts about Lian aside. It was now 1500 hours; the resistance fighters had made it to the top of the third mountain range of the Chou Thoi Mountains, and about twelve miles from the Thai border. The Khmer Rouge on foot was only a mile behind them now, and Xuan Thong wanted to face them now and use the elevation of the third range to their advantage. Lieutenant Applethorpe convinced him, however, that it would be better to face them after they crossed the Thai border, because there may be government or independent friendlies in the area who would be willing to help them. Xuan Thong agreed and told his men to move out.

****

To the east, Captain Bystrom was planning his attack on Duong Van Minh. He realized that he would have to ask for volunteers because this was basically a suicide mission.

He figured he'd need six men to try and get the job done. Of course, it would have to be a night ambush. All of his Special Forces had the latest in night-vision technology – goggles that used infrared light to see in the dark. He had the latest satellite photographs from the CIA, which showed that Duong Van Minh's forces were fortifying their position around Phumi Phaang, near the northwestern border with Thailand. This was approximately 300 miles to the north and west of his current position near Krakor.

****

Moving down the westward slopes of the third range of the Chou Thoi Mountains, Trick could finally see the river valley of the Moi River out in the distance. On the other side of the Moi, River was Thailand, and ten miles from there was Wang Nam Yen.

****

Lieutenant Applethorpe and Xuan Thong left the rear of the cavalcade and moved to the front with Trick, Lian, and Lela. There were twenty-nine other resistance fighters under Xuan Thong's command. There would have been thirty had not one died back in the rice paddy at Batdambang. Still, Xuan Thong felt confident that he could defeat the Khmer Rouge foot patrol if need be. But he saw the logic in Lieutenant Applethorpe's argument that they would have an even better tactical advantage if they waited until they were into Thailand.

****

Xuan Thong was fairly certain that Vu Van Mau was in one of the vehicles looking for him. Lian had done her job well in keeping the resistance fighters away from any roads. They made it to the Moi River by 1800 hours as it was just turning dark. Fortunately, the river was only three feet deep and they were able to wade across it. Once all the men were across, Trick looked through his binoculars and found the Khmer Rouge foot patrol still coming after them. They were still a mile behind as they climbed down the westward slopes of the third range of the Chou Thoi Mountains. Trick wondered if they would stop their pursuit when they reached the Moi River.

****

Captain Bystrom had assembled his team. It consisted of himself, four other Green Berets, and a CIA operative named Jimmy Belgium. It was Jimmy Belgium who had put an end to the life of a renegade CIA operative who went AWOL and had established his own little kingdom in Laos. This operative, known as "Kurtz", had given rewards to anyone who delivered the heads of any Pathet Lao, the communist equivalent in Laos of the Cambodian Khmer Rouge. By accomplishing his mission, Jimmy Belgium had become a legend within the CIA.

****

Nightfall was almost complete as Trick looked through his binoculars and saw Route 3395 about a mile away.

Looking back, he saw that the Khmer Rouge foot patrol did not follow them past the Moi River. They had avoided one threat, and the only one remaining was the vehicle caravan carrying the main body of Khmer Rouge troops. At least they were not visible on the stretch of road that Trick could see with his binoculars. From Route 3395, Wang Nam Yen was only five more miles. To make sure that they would be safe once they reached Wang Nam Yen, Xuan Thong had radioed some friends amongst the Hmong tribesmen, who were America's allies against the Pathet Lao. Some Hmong had bases in eastern Thailand, and even though none of them were this far south, they were willing to send a platoon to Wang Nam Yen to help protect Xuan Thong's resistance fighters.

From a little knoll, Trick could see the hamlet of Wang Nam Yen about a mile away, and to his relief, the platoon of Hmong tribesmen was already there waiting for them. Trick passed the news along to Xuan Thong, who in turn informed his troops. Spirits rose as they knew they now had at least a fighting chance if Vu Van Mau's main force did find them.

They greeted their Hmong allies with pats and handshakes. All told, there were approximately fifty Hmong to greet them. The locals welcomed the soldiers into their huts and offered them food. Most of the soldiers were exhausted and spread out their straw bed mats on the ground and went to sleep. Lieutenant Applethorpe walked up to Trick and said "Good job, Trick, you saved our lives today."

"We were lucky, sir," Trick replied. Lieutenant Applethorpe and Trick walked to a thatched hut on the north end of the hamlet, threw down their foam bed mats, and got ready to go to sleep. Lian, Lela, and Xuan Thong were in the next hut to their left, while the Hmong remained on the southern edge of the hamlet. If they made it through the night without a firefight, odds were they would make their rendezvous in Bangkok.

22
CHAPTER

FAILURE AT PHUMI PHAANG

Captain Bystrom received word that Lieutenant Applethorpe and Sergeant Hartland had accomplished their mission and made it to Wang Nam Yen. He thought this was a good omen for his own mission. Certainly, having Jimmy Belgium on the mission gave him a further sense of security. Still, the odds against them were staggering. Duong Van Minh had a team of bodyguards who watched him twenty-four hours a day. Getting past them to get to Duong Van Minh would be difficult if not impossible.

Captain Bystrom's team was handpicked for the skills that each team member brought to the mission. Lieutenant Doug Price was one of the best sharpshooters in the Green Berets, Sergeant Allen Pope was a martial arts expert and a black belt in karate, Lieutenant Jack Shirley was the Huey pilot for this mission, Lieutenant Nguyen Van Lan was the South Vietnamese officer who would be their language expert, and Jimmy Belgium was a small arms expert and intelligence officer for the CIA. The mission was set to take off at 0100 hours.

The plan called for the Huey to set down at 0400 hours ten miles southeast of Pak Charang, just over the Cambodian-Thailand border. The pilot, Lieutenant Shirley, was to remain there to await the five-man assassination team's return. The assassination squad was then to make their way to the compound at Phumi Phaang about five miles away. The command headquarters was right in the middle of the compound. They would have to slip past all the night watch guards and make their way to the central command headquarters. Once inside, Duong Van Minh was to be disposed with by knife – a silent kill. The assassination team was then to slip out of the compound and return to the landing spot by 0700 hours. That was the plan, and the best-laid plans of mice and men often go awry.

In the pitch of blackness at 0100 hours, the team converged at the Huey pad and boarded the chopper. It was three hours to the landing site southeast of Pak Charang. Lieutenant Shirley flew the Huey at a high altitude to avoid attention from the ground. Two hours into the flight he started a slow descent. He had flown almost due north for two hours until he thought he was on top of the Thailand-Cambodia border, and then he turned west and flew directly over the border for another hour. At 0330 hours, Captain Bystrom asked his men if they were ready. They all gave the thumbs-up sign.

The Huey set down as planned at 0400 hours just a mile inside the Thai border. They were about one mile south of route 214. The five men had blackface covering their faces and black fatigues for this mission. They crossed a creek that served as the border between Thailand and Cambodia and they knew that they had only three more miles to traverse. Captain Bystrom took point as they walked through the jungle. Nguyen Van Lan was next, followed by Doug Price, Allen Pope, and finally Jimmy Belgium.

They made it to the perimeter of the compound by 0445 hours. Allen Pope began snipping the barbed wire with wire cutters. When he was done, he pulled a three-foot section of wire away and signaled that the coast was clear.

The assassin squad ran for cover to the nearest building. From where they were, the central command headquarters was still at least a half-mile away. The next closest building was about fifty yards away. No guards were in sight, and Captain Bystrom made a run for it. He gave the signal for his team to follow. One by one, they all sprinted the fifty yards to the second building. They advanced one building at a time until they finally saw the central command headquarters building with a large antenna on the roof. Two guards on night watch were guarding the central command headquarters and would have to be taken out. Captain Bystrom gave that duty to Nguyen Van Lan and Jimmy Belgium.

Jimmy Belgium snuck up behind his guard and slit his throat while cupping his hand over the guard's mouth. It was all over in three seconds. Nguyen Van Lan lunged at his guard and stuck his knife into the guard's back. But this guard did not die right away, and he was able to pull the trigger of his AK-47, waking up the whole compound. Captain Bystrom made a mad dash for the entrance to the central command headquarters with his Colt-45 revolver cocked and ready. But the warning burst of gunfire had awakened Duong Van Minh who was standing ready with a 38-caliber inside his command headquarters. As Captain Bystrom ran in he couldn't see through the darkness, and Duong Van Minh put a bullet right between Captain Bystrom's eyes.

When Bystrom didn't come out of the command headquarters, the remaining team knew the mission was a failure and now they had to run for their lives. They started running like hell the 500 yards to the hole in the barbed wire. Guards started pouring out of their barracks like disturbed ants pouring out of their anthill. AK-47 fire started lighting up the night sky. About fifty yards from the opening in the barbed wire, Lieutenant Nyugen Van Lan took ten rounds into his back and staggered forward then fell dead. Sgt. Pope, Lt. Price, and Jimmy Belgium made it through the barbed wire and were sprinting like hell through the jungle back to the helicopter. If they could reach the helicopter in less than thirty minutes, maybe they had a chance. Meanwhile, an entire division of Khmer Rouge was converging on the jungle north of Phumi Phaang. Sergeant Pope, Lieutenant Price, and Jimmy Belgium crossed the creek that separated Cambodia and Thailand and knew they only had a mile to go.

Lieutenant Shirley had heard the gunfire from six miles away and knew the mission was a bust. The only question in his mind was how many, if any, were going to make it back to him by 0700 hours. When he saw Sergeant Pope,

Lieutenant Price, and Jimmy Belgium emerge from the jungle to his clearing, he started his engines and prepared for lift-off. The moment all three were aboard, he lifted off and headed west.

23
CHAPTER

WESTWARD HO TO BANGKOK

The sun rose at 0645 hours. As the first beams of daylight touched Wang Nam Yen, Xuan Thong's men were already out of their huts preparing breakfast. That night, Trick had dreamed of making love to Lian. He put those half-remembered images to rest, however, when he focused on his present reality.

Lieutenant Applethorpe and Trick met Xuan Thong for breakfast. Xuan Thong was going to take his men south along Route 317 for about fifty miles before turning east and entering Cambodia. The Hmong platoon was headed back north and west towards the Cambodia/Thailand/Laos nexus. Lieutenant Applethorpe and Trick were on their own to reach Bangkok, which was about a hundred miles away.

After morning radio contact, Trick and Applethorpe were informed of Captain Bystrom's failed mission and his death. Trick was sorry that Captain Bystrom was killed and wondered if he had been on that mission if he would have survived. Their new commanding officer in Krakor was Lieutenant Colonel Mike Sheets, a career soldier whose subordinates sometimes referred to him as "Iron Mike". "Iron Mike" grew up in the Bible Belt in the South and sometimes his soldiers thought he sounded like a religious zealot. Their orders were to make it to Bangkok, and make contact with Lieutenant Bernfeld, who would have their next orders.

As the three groups parted ways, Trick was angry at himself for not making a play for Lian. He cut himself a little slack, though, when he realized that Lian had shown no interest in him. He tried to see through her, but there was something about the oriental character that was inscrutable to him, a mystery, and Trick still hadn't found the key that unlocked this mystery's door. Trick watched her walking away with her father and her sister, and he wondered if he would ever see her again.

There were no roads that ran west from Wang Nam Yen, only Route 317 that ran north and south. Trick and Lieutenant Applethorpe would have to walk on small footpaths through the jungle for almost a hundred miles. One of Xuan Thong's men had given Trick a machete to hack his way through the jungle. Trick thanked him by giving him an extra pack of cigarettes he had been saving.

The trail that Lieutenant Applethorpe and Trick were on was windy and sometimes barely detectable. They crossed several creeks, and the surrounding areas were marshes full of leeches. After wading through one creek, several leeches attached themselves to Trick's pant legs, and he picked them off one by one when he got to the other side. Then there were the mosquitoes. These weren't your garden variety of mosquitoes, but massive swarms of mosquitoes that would cover you from head to toe if you let them. The insect repellant that Trick and Lieutenant Applethorpe had only went so far, as if the stuff merely dazed them for a few seconds before they realized the stuff really wasn't that bad.

All day Trick thrashed his way through the jungle with Lieutenant Applethorpe following behind him. They wanted to travel at least twenty miles a day before setting up camp for the evening. It was difficult to tell how far they had gotten by dusk because they had had slow spells and fast spells. They found a spot where the underbrush wasn't quite as dense, laid down their bed mats, and fell instantly to sleep.

The next day they were up at dawn and started west on the trail. The second day on the trail, the land became marshier than the first day. Patches of the trail were flooded by marsh waters, and the trail became Trickier and Trickier to follow. The marsh waters kept getting higher and higher until the water reached the tops of Trick's and Applethorpe's boots. And just in a flash, it happened – Lieutenant Applethorpe tripped over a half-submerged log, and something long and green that had blended in perfectly with the log flew into mid-air and bit Applethorpe on the right thigh. Trick looked back just in time to see the Malayan pit viper slither away into the water. Applethorpe stood there like a deer caught in the headlights. He knew the venom would soon be pumping throughout his body.

"Take off your pants!" Trick yelled. Applethorpe was starting to sweat as he threw his pants to the ground. Trick saw the two bloody puncture wounds just above Applethorpe's right kneecap. Trick took his knife and made a wound about an inch above the puncture marks. He put his mouth to the wound and started sucking. Trick could taste the venom mixed with blood as he spit it out. He spent five minutes trying to head off the venom that was flowing into Applethorpe's bloodstream. He then took his first-aid kit out of his backpack and bandaged up Applethorpe's entire thigh. Only time would tell if Trick's intervention had worked or not. Beads of perspiration formed on Applethorpe's brow as he started to move forward.

"Let's see how far we can make it before dusk," Trick said. They both knew that they weren't even halfway to Bangkok, so if Applethorpe was going to survive, he'd have to do without anti-venom.

Applethorpe could only continue at half his previous pace. With each step forward, his thigh throbbed with pain and was swelling rapidly. The bandage that Trick had put on had to be loosened. Within an hour, the size of Applethorpe's right thigh was more than double the size of his left.

By dusk of their second day on their westward trek to Bangkok, Applethorpe's face was the color of white chalk. He was fairly certain he wouldn't survive this journey.

"Trick, I have a letter here for my wife back in Florida. Please mail it if you make it and I don't," he said as he gave Trick a stamped envelope.

"Sure thing," Trick replied in sympathy.

Trick awoke at dawn as usual on the third day of this jungle walk to Bangkok. He looked over at Applethorpe who didn't move. Fearing the worst, Trick moved closer and looked again. Applethorpe's mouth was gaping open but he wasn't breathing – he didn't make it through the night.

Trick knew he would lose a half-day, but it was his duty to bury Applethorpe. He found a flat twelve-inch stone and started digging into the soft earth of a small clearing about twenty yards from the trail. He knew he couldn't make the grave that deep with the tool he was using, but he thought three feet deep would do. By 1000 hours he was done with the grave, and he pulled Applethorpe's body into it. He covered him in dirt and made a cross at the head of the grave with the nearest stones he could find. When he was done, he took off down the trail toward Bangkok.

****

Trick marched on alone wondering if he should read the letter in his pocket and then reseal it, or do the right thing and not open it. He decided to do the right thing and not open it; after all, it was none of his business. Good for Lieutenant Applethorpe to find a woman who loved him before he died.

Trick followed the trail and watched each step to be sure he wasn't trouncing on some snake. Besides the pit vipers, other poisonous snakes indigenous to Thailand included the King Cobra, the coral snake, and the water snake. All of these were deadly. Trick felt sorry for Applethorpe's widow. Fifty more miles to Bangkok and everything would have been O.K. By the end of his third day on the trail, Trick knew he had covered at least twenty more miles that day and had to be within fifty miles of Bangkok.

By mid-day of the fourth day of his westward trek through Thailand, Trick made it to the village of Khok Pho. When the local villagers saw the lone soldier emerging from the jungle, they knew he had been through quite an ordeal. Trick knew from the maps that Lian had given him that the rest of his journey to Bangkok would be relatively easy. There were roads from this village that led directly to Bangkok. He could either walk the roads and hope to get a lift or walk to one of the villages on the Gulf of Siam and take a ferry into Bangkok. He decided to walk Route 344 to Chon Buri on the coast, and take a ferry from there into Bangkok. He knew he could make Chon Buri by nightfall if he left Khok Pho now.

He arrived at Chon Buri by 1800 hours and went directly to the dock. He found that there was not a ferry that left at night and he'd have to wait until the following morning. He walked down the main strip of town and came across what looked like a boarding house. He walked inside and saw a countertop with a little bell on it. He rang the bell and from some back room, an elderly Thai man came to the counter.

"You want room?" the old man asked in a thick accent.

"Yes," Trick replied.

"Five hundred baht," the old man said.

Trick fumbled through his pockets and found his billfold. He only had about 5,000 baht on him, the equivalent of about a hundred U.S. dollars. Five hundred baht was around ten dollars.

"No, no, too much," Trick knew he was being overcharged.

"Two fifty," the old man managed to mouth out.

"O.K.," Trick said as he handed the old man the money.

The old man led him down a hallway until he came to a door on the left at the end of the hallway. He opened the door and Trick set his backpack and rifle down on the floor. The room only had a twin bed, a dresser, a window, and a chair, but after sleeping on a foam mat for more than a week, it looked inviting.

"You like girl?" the old man queried.

"No, no, too tired," Trick said as he pressed the back of his hand against his cheek and angled his head.

It was true. Trick was exhausted. He had just walked over a hundred miles through the jungle, buried an officer, and gave up potential romance with a Cambodian girl, all within the last week. He had, at last, reached an outpost of civilization, and his body, mind, and spirit needed rest.

He slept ten hours, and when he awoke he realized he had already missed the first ferry that left at 0700 hours. The next ferry left at 0900 hours, and it was already 0800 hours. He'd have to get cleaned up, eat breakfast, and get down to the dock in less than an hour. After buying some fruit for breakfast from a small stand on the street, he made it to the dock by 0830 hours.

The "ferry" was actually a small motorized junket. There were only a handful of other passengers and a three-man crew. The trip across the Gulf of Siam took half a day, and the boat was scheduled to dock at Pom Phra Chunlachomkiao at 1300 hours.

There was a stiff southerly breeze that blew across the Gulf of Siam, and Trick leaned against the port rail of the junket and tried to put the horror of the last few weeks out of his mind. It would be good to see Bernfeld again. As he stared out over the Gulf of Siam, he tried to let his mind float free of the images of the last few weeks. Going to Bangkok was going back to civilization again, and he knew he would have at least a few days to enjoy being with Lieutenant Bernfeld and getting to know Bangkok a little bit.

It was now early February 1973, and most of the regular U.S. military was in the process of packing it in and getting ready to go back to "The World" by the end of March. For Special Forces, it was different – they had their own timetable that didn't conform to any rules or agreements.

As scheduled, the junket docked at Pom Phra Chunlachomkiao at 1301 hours, and as he stepped onto the dock, he started looking for a water taxi to take him up the Chaophraya River into the heart of Bangkok.

24

CHAPTER

THE REUNION

Bangkok, or Krung Thep as it is known in the Thai language, sits ten miles north of the Gulf of Siam in the Chaophraya River Valley. American military intelligence officers and CIA operatives had made it their base of operations since the early 1960s.

Trick's instructions had been to find the Madrid bar on Patgong Street and just hang out there until Lieutenant Bernfeld found him. He got out of the water taxi at Thonburi and went looking for the nearest kiosk to buy a map. He found Patgong Street on the map and started walking. The boat ride across the Gulf of Siam had reinvigorated him, and he was getting excited to see Bernfeld again.

He found the street he was on on the map and only had a few blocks to go to get to Patgong Street. When he got there, he didn't know which direction to turn, so he asked the nearest passerby "Madrid?" A Thai man pointed left so that was the direction in which Trick took off. His heart felt a little more buoyant when he saw the sign about fifty yards ahead of him.

The Madrid was an Americanized bar, comfortable, with dark mahogany walls and tables. Servicemen from just about every conceivable branch were scattered around. He scanned the room but didn't see Lieutenant Bernfeld. He would have to find a cheap hotel in the area and just hang out until Bernfeld showed up. He didn't see any other Green Berets in the bar either, so there was no one to approach to ask about Bernfeld.

Trick sat down at a table and ordered a pint of beer. He was only twenty years old and couldn't legally drink back home, but no one in uniform was refused a drink here. There were some Navy guys at the bar, some Marines at a table near the front, some "civilian" Americans at another table – probably CIA – and at least one Air Force officer that he could see sitting in a booth. He thought about checking in with the CIA men, but they didn't have jurisdiction over him and he decided he would just wait it out until Bernfeld showed up.

After waiting in the bar for two hours, Trick decided to call it a day and go look for a hotel. He found one practically across the street from the Madrid, the Rama 4, so he took it. It was only twenty-five baths per night. He lay down on the single bed and before he knew it he was asleep, fully uniformed and booted up.

****

Uncharacteristically, he slept until 0900 hours. He looked down and couldn't believe he was so tired that he forgot to take his clothes and boots off. He got out of bed and walked across the room to the window that looked out over the street. The Madrid was already open for business. Trick was hungry and figured he may as well eat all three meals there while waiting for Bernfeld.

Trick walked across the street and entered the bar. It dawned on him that he should ask the barkeep if he knew a Lieutenant Bernfeld and if he did when he would be coming in again. He felt stupid that he hadn't thought of this yesterday.

He walked up to the barkeep. "Do you know a Lieutenant Bernfeld?" Trick asked. "He's expecting me to meet him here," he added.

"Ah, ya, ya, wutenen Bunfen," the barkeep said in broken English.

"He alway come hare," the Thai barkeep said. "He be hare soon," he added.

Trick felt relieved that he wouldn't have to wait much longer. He was anxious to get his new marching orders and to get resituated in Bangkok. He knew that Special Forces must have some kind of accommodations around this city, and he liked the idea of having a "base of operations" to return to. He wondered what kind of accommodations Bernfeld had set up for himself by now.

Trick's eyes shifted to the door as an oriental man in a South Vietnamese officer's uniform walked through the door. Then his eyes lit up when he saw Lieutenant Bernfeld walking in behind the South Vietnamese officer.

Trick!" Bernfeld exclaimed as he saw his protégé and walked over to give him a hug.

"Good to see you, too, Jerry," Trick said, returning the embrace.

"Trick Hartland, let me introduce you to Colonel Huynh Son Phuony of the South Vietnamese army," Bernfeld said. Trick extended his hand and was impressed with the strength of the diminutive man's handshake. They went to go sit down in a booth at the quietest side of the room.

"Where's Lieutenant Applethorpe?" Bernfeld asked and then knew the news wasn't good when he looked at Trick's expression.

"He's dead, sir," Trick replied. "Bitten by a pit viper on our second day out from Wang Nam Yen. He died that night, and I buried him just off the trail the following morning," Trick replied.

"I'm sorry he didn't make it," Bernfeld said.

"I have a letter to mail to his wife," Trick said. "I was thinking of opening it, but I'm glad I didn't," he added.

"You can mail it from Special Forces command headquarters," Bernfeld said.

"By the way, where is command headquarters?" Trick asked.

"It's about five miles north of the city, near Bang Yai," Bernfeld replied.

"How long have you been here?" Trick asked.

"Since right after An Loc," Bernfeld said.

"How is it here?" Trick asked.

"If there's a heaven on earth, this place is it," Bernfeld smiled as he answered Trick's question.

"You'll have to show me why," Trick retorted with a wry smile.

"I think Colonel Phuony and I can do that," Bernfeld said as he downed a shot of Jack Daniels.

Trick couldn't put his finger on it, but there was something different about Bernfeld. He looked the same, and his personality was the same, but there was definitely some intangible difference that had Trick guessing. He was the same, but at the same time, he was more ebullient, more full of life – happier. Trick knew that something had changed Bernfeld, and he knew it must have something to do with this new environment, Bangkok.

"By the way, do you know why you survived An Loc?" Bernfeld asked. "It's because fate often saves an undoomed man when his courage is good – Beowulf. Now, let's get you situated at headquarters," Bernfeld said.

****

Special Forces Command Headquarters at Bang Yai resembled a MASH unit without the surgical equipment. There was an on-base still making whiskey, a football field, and tropical flowers and shrubs all around made the base seem like an attempt to duplicate Bali Hai. No wonder Bernfeld was so happy here.

Trick was assigned to a barracks near the western border of the compound, about a half-mile away from

Bernfeld's quarters in the officer's barracks. Bernfeld had promised Trick that he would give him a proper tour of Bangkok that evening, which he was really looking forward to. He put his personal belongings, which didn't amount to much, in the steel trunk at the bottom of his bed. He received a new uniform, so he put it on and folded up his old uniform, and put it in his trunk.

Bernfeld came by at 1800 hours, without Colonel Phuony, to pick Trick up. Trick hopped into the passenger seat of the jeep, and Bernfeld stepped on the gas and headed south.

"Where we headed?" Trick asked.

"Rama Five Street," Bernfeld replied.

"What's there?" Trick pushed for a little more detail.

"I want to show you that even amongst the misery, there is still some fun to be had," Bernfeld replied.

At the south end of Rama Five Street, Bernfeld parked the jeep and jumped out. "Welcome to paradise," he said as he gestured with his hands as if to say Behold.

The strip was filled with bars as far as the eye could see, but Trick could tell that Bernfeld had one joint, in particular, picked out. They entered The Sumi Club and found a table near the dance floor. Half-naked Thai women were dancing with servicemen from all branches to the beat of rock and roll music. There was more than a little bump and grind going on here, and Trick enjoyed the eye candy.

"See one you like?" Bernfeld asked. "She's yours for ten bucks," he added.

Trick, like any red-blooded American twenty-year-old, was getting excited. He knew he was attracted to Thai women because he had had several wet dreams about Lian. He looked around the room and saw several real beauties.

"More than one," Trick finally answered. Bernfeld laughed and with a wave of his hand, two Thai women joined them at their table.

"You buy us drinks?" the woman closest to Bernfeld asked.

"Yes, what would you like?" Bernfeld asked her.

"Singapore sling," she said with a giggle.

"That sounds good to me; I think I'll have one too," Bernfeld said as he put his hand on the thigh of the woman closest to him. "How 'bout you Trick?" he asked.

"Sounds good," Trick said.

The waitress returned with four Singapore slings, with a miniature umbrella jutting out of each glass. This concoction originated from the Raffles Hotel in Singapore. The five liquors in this drink could put lightweights on the floor within minutes. Bernfeld took out his umbrella, and as he lifted his glass to his lips he toasted "To paradise!"

The Thai woman next to Trick moved over and sat on his lap at the same time that the woman closest to Bernfeld sat on his lap. This was definitely the beginning of a party.

"You wanna date?" the Thai woman on Trick's lap asked.

The thought crossed Trick's mind that he hadn't had sex since his last semester at NMSU. He felt the Singapore sling loosening his inhibitions, and he wondered what Bernfeld's next move would be.

"O.K.," Trick said.

"Ten dolla," the Thai woman said.

"O.K.," Trick said again.

They didn't have to go far. Upstairs from the club was a row of doorways, each leading to a little room. The woman walked down the hallway to the fifth door on the left and opened it.

"Ten dolla," she repeated.

Trick gave her the money and sat down on the single bed.

"Take off clothes," the woman said.

Trick started unbuttoning his shirt while the woman unzipped her floral print dress and stepped out of it. She had a nice, curvaceous body with size C breasts. She had slender hips and a round face. Trick was getting an erection, and when he pulled off his underwear his penis sprang out into to air in its full glory. The woman giggled and grabbed Trick's penis with her hand and started stroking it. Trick put his hand on her right breast and started fondling it. Then she leaned over and started sucking Trick's cock. It was as if she intuitively knew the right rhythm to achieve. Trick lay back on the bed and let himself enjoy the blowjob. God bless Bernfeld, he really knew what a soldier needed.

Trick wanted the feel of pussy around his cock so he pushed the woman's shoulders back onto the bed, mounted her, and starting thrusting. He was already warmed up from the blowjob and knew he was getting ready to come after a minute of thrusting. To prolong his ecstasy, he slowed down, and to his surprise, the woman reached down and grabbed the base of his penis with her hand and started stroking it while he was still inside her. The effect of this move was a prolongation of Trick's orgasm, with the pressure from her hand controlling the amount of ejaculate from each spurt so that in total his orgasm lasted over thirty seconds. She was worth every penny of the ten bucks. Pipes unclogged, Trick got dressed and went back downstairs. He felt like a new man.

25
CHAPTER

THE OPIUM DEN

Bernfeld came down from the upstairs five minutes later grinning from ear to ear. He spotted Trick, walked over to his table, and sat down.

"How'd it go?" he asked.

"I had a good time," Trick replied.

"That was just the appetizer," Bernfeld said as he got up and motioned for Trick to follow him. They walked out onto the street and headed north along Rama Five Street. They turned right onto a little side street. After a couple of blocks, Bernfeld stopped at a house and rapped on the door. A peephole in the door opened, and a pair of eyes scanned the two soldiers. The door opened and as he stopped inside, he said to Trick, "Welcome to Fang Wu's place."

There were thick oriental rugs on the floor and batik-dyed tapestries on the walls. The chairs in the front room were soft and cushy, and a cloud of white smoke hovered a foot below the ceiling. An old oriental man appeared in the doorway whose corneas were almost pure white.

"This is Fang Wu," Bernfeld said to Trick. Fang Wu bowed his head a little bit and Trick returned the gesture. Fang Wu was only about five feet two inches tall. He was bald on top, but he had long gray hair down to his shoulders from the back and sides of his head. Trick wondered how he could see through those white corneas.

Fang Wu ushered them into the next room which was a little bigger than the first room. He motioned for them to sit down on the floor and then disappeared into another room. He came back holding a brass hookah the size of a Scottish bagpipe. He sat down next to Bernfeld, struck a fireplace match, held the flame to the bowl, and started inhaling. After a few tokes, he passed the hookah to Bernfeld. Bernfeld took one long inhale, then passed the hookah to Trick.

"What is it?" Trick asked.

"Opium," Bernfeld said. "Smoking opium," he added. Then he held his lighter to the bowl and inhaled. After he exhaled he said, "I'll never Mainline heroin, but I will chase the dragon. Over here, smoking opium is called chasing the dragon."

Trick had smoked some pot and hash, and he had tried mescaline and peyote, but he knew that that stuff was minor league compared to opium. He decided to take a small toke to test the waters, then handed the hookah to

Fang Wu. As he did this, he noticed Fang Wu's fingernails were three to four inches long, and curlicued at the ends. The opium must have started to take its effect on Trick because this image of Fang Wu's fingernails lingered in his mind and didn't want to go away. Trick knew he wasn't thinking or seeing right because those pinkish, translucent nails of Fang Wu's reminded him of seashells. Then he remembered seeing seashells at Pom Phra Chunlachomkiao when he stepped off the ferry from Chon Buri. There had been beautiful seashells all over the beach at Pom Phra Chunlachomkiao, but he didn't go pick any of them up because he was in a hurry to get to the Madrid. Trick looked over at Bernfeld who was fixated in some kind of soporific stare. He looked over at Fang Wu, this time focusing on his face and not his fingers. He now looked truly ancient. The whites of his eyes distracted one from seeing the lines and wrinkles on every square inch of his face. Trick thought he had to be at least ninety.

Trick knew that he had had a minor hallucination, so when Bernfeld handed him the hookah again, he just passed it on to Fang Wu. Trick liked the feeling of being a little stoned, but he knew that with opium, he was playing with fire.

Bernfeld crawled on his hands and knees to a chair and lifted himself up into it. Fang Wu disappeared with the hookah to another room.

Trick wondered if Bernfeld was addicted to the drug. He knew enough about opium to know that it was extremely addictive, and he could understand why – he felt absolutely no pain. He felt like superman like his body could do anything.

Bernfeld roused himself from his stupor long enough to focus on Trick's eyes.

"Trick, did you know that right now we are only two hundred miles south of some of the most fertile land in the world for growing poppies?" he said with a smile. "They call it the Golden Triangle. It's where Burma, Thailand, and Laos meet, and it's more than two hundred thousand square miles of the best poppy-growing land in the world. In Thailand, it's in the Chiang Mai Province. Colonel Phuony and I have a little business venture up there. I want to take you up there soon so you can see it for yourself. It's like Shangri-La."

Trick could feel Bernfeld's enthusiasm and wanted to go up there with him. However, he didn't want to become an opium addict, and he would have to be careful that Bernfeld didn't turn him into one.

26
CHAPTER

SHANGRI-LA

Growing poppies in eastern Burma, northern Thailand, and western Laos was a CIA-sanctioned operation. The profits from the drug trade helped fund and arm some of the military groups who were fighting against the communists, in particular, the Laotian Hmong and the Nationalist Chinese in Burma. The CIA condoned the growing of poppies and the selling of opium because the drug profits financed their allies much better than they ever could.

Operating with this kind of cooperation from the CIA gave Bernfeld a lot of leeway. Bernfeld's connections with the CIA, with Colonel Phuony, and with the Special Forces put him in the unique position of being a major dealmaker, a role that he loved.

Trick's report of the Batdambang success had reached Colonel Sheets' desk, and he promoted Trick to full staff sergeant and made Lieutenant Bernfeld Trick's commanding officer, an act that made both of them very happy. Colonel Sheets was in the loop concerning Bernfeld's activities up north, and now he was given official sanction to bring Trick into the loop as well.

Bernfeld wanted Trick's promotion to be a public spectacle, so he told every Green Beret in his unit to come to the ceremony at 1700 hours in the officers' command room. When the hour rolled around, they all shuffled in and sat down in the folding chairs.

"In recognition of valor in the performance of duties, Sergeant First Class Trick Hartland is hereby promoted to Full Staff Sergeant. Congratulations, Trick," Bernfeld said as he gave him his new patch with three stripes instead of two.

"Thank you, sir," Trick replied as the audience starting clapping. Trick had gone from corporal to sergeant first class to staff sergeant in less than a year. He was now the highest non-officer rank; even so, most staff sergeants were treated like officers.

Bernfeld planned to show Trick Chiang Mai Province the next day. After all, there were no guarantees over here, and if anything happened to Bernfeld, he wanted somebody who could take his place. He liked Trick so much he chose him even though he wasn't an officer and he was only twenty years old. So what? He was, after all, just a mature kid, with most kids his age studying something in college.

Trick was anxious to see Chiang Mai Province too. Here he had an opportunity to learn a business literally from the ground up – the opium business, and he felt grateful to be the sorcerer's apprentice.

****

They arrived at Nakhon Sawan by 1200 hours and still had two hundred miles to go to reach Chiang Mai, where Bernfeld's "office" was. After filling up on satay and Thai beef noodle soup, they were off again headed for "Shangri-La".

From the passenger seat, Trick noticed the change in the terrain. The geography south of Nakhon Sawan had been lush, flat jungle. Now they were driving on a slow, inclining upgrade. Ever since Nakhon Sawan, the hills were becoming bigger hills and the bigger hills were becoming mountains. Everything two hours north of Nakhon Sawan was mountains, and Trick guessed they were somewhere between 7,000 and 10,000 feet above sea level. He felt the altitude change and liked being at the same altitude as his home in New Mexico. Here the climate was quasi-tropical but at the same time quite temperate, which made the land extremely arable.

They passed beautiful mountain lakes and mountain streams, and each new mountain ridge that came into sight was more beautiful than the last. They passed Lampang, which meant they only had an hour to go and got on Route 11 which ended at their destination – Chiang Mai.

With three-quarters of an hour left to drive, Bernfeld told Trick that he had called a meeting for 1900 hours that evening, between Colonel Phuony, some Hmong leaders, some growers, and himself. He told Trick that the growers were becoming dissatisfied with their share of the profits. Colonel Phuony kept telling them that their product would be worthless without a market and distribution system, which his network provided, and to be satisfied with their share. He kept telling them how much better off they were compared to their brethren in the south. But the growers suspected that it was the middlemen like Colonel Phuony who were getting rich and not them.

The meeting tonight had been called to placate the growers and to tell them how great their contribution was in the war against the communist invaders. The Pathet Lao, the Khmer Rhouge, and the Viet Cong were all aware that drug profits from the Golden Triangle were helping to arm their enemies, and sporadically they conducted missions to disrupt the drug chain, but often with little real effect. The Americans were keeping them so busy they didn't have the resources to really stop the drug trade.

Bernfeld pulled up to the entrance of a guarded compound. The guards evidently knew him and let him through the checkpoint. The dirt road led to a huge wooden building of approximately five thousand square feet. Part of the building was a storage area for the opium, and a smaller section of the building looked like some kind of laboratory. As they walked past it, Bernfeld told Trick that this warehouse mostly shipped out pure opium, but some of it was converted to morphine in this laboratory, and then the morphine into heroin. Bernfeld told Trick that he would explain the basic chemistry to him tomorrow after tonight's meeting.

Poppy-farm workers had sent their best negotiators to the meeting. As a precaution, Colonel Phuony had brought a platoon of South Vietnamese soldiers with him to maintain the peace, if need be. The farm workers were not militant, and they knew where the bulk of the monies from their work was going and didn't disapprove of it; they only wanted to better their own lives. They wanted schoolhouses for their children, hospitals for their sick, and better equipment to do their job.

Bernfeld wanted more productivity from these Thai workers. His estimates were that only one-fifth of the opium coming from the Golden Triangle was coming from Thailand, with another one-fifth coming from Laos and three-fifths coming from Burma. He wanted to increase that proportion.

Colonel Phuony was working closely with the growers in both Laos and Thailand, and he would like to see Thailand's and Laos' production combined equal to that of Burma's. The growers weren't stupid. They knew that their cut was about one one-hundredth of the street value of the drug. They wanted to make that figure about five one-hundredths. They weren't on the brink of revolt just yet, but they wanted to let their middlemen know that they weren't satisfied. Through Colonel Phuony's interpreter, Phan Van Huan, Bernfeld promised the growers' representatives that their efforts were appreciated at the highest levels in the American government and that they would be duly rewarded. That seemed to placate them a bit, and the dialogue became less bitter and more jubilant. Bernfeld became more and more jovial as though he were the sultan of Chiang Mai. For now, his promises were enough to keep the growers happy.

****

At 0700 hours the next morning, Bernfeld stood next to Trick's bunk and said, "Let's go." Trick roused himself and remembered that today he was going to learn the "science" behind opium. He grabbed his uniform and boots and threw them on and followed Bernfeld to the kitchen.

"Today, you're going to see something beautiful," Bernfeld said. After a rice and noodle soup breakfast, they hopped into the jeep and drove off to the poppy fields.

Bernfeld was in his element. Trick could sense Bernfeld's excitement and pride in a being a CIA-approved drug merchant. A few miles out into the country, he told Trick with a smile on his face, "I'll never leave here."

Bernfeld pulled the jeep onto a dirt road that led to a plateau. On that plateau, as far as the eye could see were poppies. The breeze brought an odor of what Trick thought smelled like roasted nutmeg. It reminded him of that scene in *The Wizard of Oz* where Dorothy finally gets out of the forest and comes to the poppy fields and promptly falls asleep.

For miles upon miles, the bluish-green seedpods swayed with the breeze. Bernfeld started walking into the field with the air of an ancient Buddhist monk contemplating the cosmos. He signaled Trick to come to him. He pulled a pocketknife out of his pants pocket and freed the blade. He started making incisions into a poppy seedpod. A milky yellowish-white fluid started oozing out of it.

"This, my boy, is the nectar of the gods. Some farmers use eight incisions, and some use ten. I personally think eight incisions are sufficient to get all of the opium out. This milky juice is dried, and both opium and morphine are extracted from it. You can also isolate codeine, papaverine, and thebaine from the extract. Heroin starts with morphine. All you have to do is add two acetyl groups to morphine and you have heroin."

"Opium poppies are annuals and have to be replanted every year. The poppy seeds are also collected and sold as a spice, and the farmers also make poppy oil for cooking. Ninety-five percent of what we export from here is opium. The main laboratories for converting the opium to heroin are in Indonesia, Malaysia, and Burma."

Trick was beginning to understand the vastness of the empire. He was also beginning to see how protecting this empire was important to the U.S. war effort. He felt small, almost insignificant when he envisioned how many people were involved in the drug trade and the complex geography of the empire.

"So what exactly are our orders?" Trick asked Bernfeld.

He looked back at him with surprise. "To help these people, of course," he said.

27
CHAPTER

CHEMISTRY 101

Trick was glad he had gotten through a year of general chemistry and a year of organic chemistry in obtaining his associate's degree in Biology. He knew he could understand the chemistry of heroin production much better having had all this chemistry under his belt.

It was also Valentine's Day, February 14, 1973. He thought about Martha and wondered if she had found a new boyfriend. Little Dove had been out of the picture for a long time and he wondered if she was happy.

Today was Science day in North Thailand. Lieutenant Bernfeld was going to teach him the science basics of the opium trade. Trick couldn't wait. He had gotten up at 0600 hours and went for a walk. There was a little knoll about a hundred yards from the compound, and he wanted to see if he could see the poppy fields from there. He could. For mile after mile, there were poppy fields, with blue-green seedpods swaying in the breeze. Soon he would learn their secrets.

Bernfeld must have seen Trick standing on top of the knoll from the compound because he was walking up to greet him. When he got there he said, "You ready?"

"Yes sir," Trick replied.

"Here's what I know," Bernfeld said. "The growth cycle of the opium poppy is only four months. The fields are burned in March before the rainy season starts. We call this slash-and-burn; the Thai have their own word for it. This burning produces potash, which opium plants love. The rainy season then lasts until late September. The farmers use long-handled hoes to trim up the soil and break clumps. Stones and weeds are discarded and the ground leveled. Planting is completed before the end of October. By late December, the plants are about two to three feet tall. The opium poppy flowers bloom in late January into February. They have four pedals, and the color ranges from white to pink to crimson. When the pedals drop after a few days, all that is left is the seedpod, which is about the size of a chicken egg. Only the seedpod contains the opium alkaloids. Two or three weeks after the flower pedals fall off, the seedpods are ready to be harvested. Most plants produce three to five seedpods."

"When the points on the seedpod's crown stand straight up or curve upwards, the seedpod is ready to be incised. If they still point downward, the seedpod isn't mature yet. Most harvesting blades are made with three or four pieces of glass bound together on a wooden handle. If the blade cuts the seedpod too deep, the opium flows too quickly and drips onto the ground. If the incisions are too shallow, the flow will be too slow and the opium will harden inside the seedpod. After centuries of perfecting the technique, the farmers know that the best depth for the incisions is about one millimeter."

"The best time for making the incisions is in the late afternoon so that the opium latex can ooze out of the seedpod and coagulate on the surface overnight. If the incisions are made too early in the afternoon, the sun will cause the opium to coagulate over the incisions and block the flow. The next morning, the opium gum is scraped from the seedpods using a flat iron blade three or four inches wide. On average, a seedpod can be scraped five or six times before all the raw opium oozes out. By then, more than 95% of the gum has oozed out of the seedpod."

"The average yield of one seedpod is about eighty milligrams of opium. For an acre, the dried opium weight can be between eight and fifteen kilograms. Good raw opium is sticky in texture and brown, not black. The raw opium is then dried in the sun then wrapped in banana leaves until ready to export."

"After the seedpods are harvested, they are cut off the stems and allowed to dry. After they are dried, they are cut open and the seeds removed and dried in the sun, then stored for next year's planting. It only takes one pound of opium seed to sow an entire acre of land. It usually takes one farming family to cultivate and harvest one acre of poppies."

"The beauty of this land is that this climate is so good for poppies that irrigation, fertilizer, and insecticides are unnecessary. Most farmers have found that poppies grow better on western slopes because they get more sun, with gradients of twenty to forty degrees best for water drainage."

"O.K. That's the basic biology," Bernfeld said. "Are you ready for the chemistry?"

"Hit me with it, sir, my two years of college chemistry is only a year behind me," Trick said.

"That's about as much as I had, and I didn't have any problems," Bernfeld said. "By the way, did I ever tell you that I have a nursing degree from NYU?" Bernfeld asked.

"No, you never did, sir," Trick replied.

"Well, I do, and it's come in handy a few times over here too," Bernfeld said as he pumped out his chest a little. "How far in college did you get? Associates?" Bernfeld asked.

"Precisely, sir. I plan to finish when I get back home," Trick answered.

"Well, let's see how much chemistry you can remember," Bernfeld said with a smile.

"Opium contains more than thirty-five alkaloids, and morphine is only one of them, which accounts for about ten percent of raw opium by weight. Morphine is extracted from opium by dissolving it in hot water, adding lime to precipitate out the non-morphine alkaloids, and then adding ammonium chloride to precipitate out the morphine from the solution."

"The farmers use 55-gallon oil drums to "cook" the morphine out of the opium. They stack bricks about a foot high, start a fire under the oil drum, and bring about thirty gallons of water to a boil. They add ten to fifteen kilograms of raw opium to the boiling water. The opium dissolves in the boiling water while impurities like soil, twigs, and leaves float to the top. These get scooped out. Then they take a chemical fertilizer with a high concentration of lime, or calcium hydroxide from a chemical factory and put it in the boiling solution. The lime converts the insoluble morphine into water-soluble calcium morphenate. The other alkaloids do not react with the lime to form calcium salts, except for codeine, which is slightly water-soluble. The other alkaloids become sludge at the bottom of the oil drum."

"When the water cools, the brown solution is scooped out of the drum and passed through some kind of filter, usually a burlap rice sack. The liquid is then reheated until the water is evaporated as steam; what is left is a dark brown paste called "cooked" opium. Cooked opium has a putty-like consistency and is about eighty percent by weight morphine; thus, it sells for a higher price than raw opium."

"Sometimes the process stops here because cooked opium can be smoked or eaten. What we had at Fang Wu's was cooked opium. Did you get high enough from it?" Bernfeld laughed.

"If you want to make heroin, you have to go a further step. Very little heroin is made by the farmers – they usually stop at the cooked opium. The cooked or uncooked opium gets shipped to a heroin lab where the heroin gets made."

"To make heroin at the labs, ammonium chloride is added to the heated morphine solution to get the pH up to 8 or 9. Then the solution is cooled for an hour or two. By then, the morphine base and the codeine base precipitate out of the solution and settle at the bottom of the pot. The contents are then filtered through a cloth and the solid chunks of morphine and codeine remain on the cloth. The morphine base is then wrapped and left to dry in the sun. When it is dried, it looks like a coffee-colored powder."

"The morphine powder is wrapped in cloth or paper and formed into small five by four by two-inch bricks which weigh around three pounds each. The bricks are then dried and readied for transport to the heroin labs. It takes about a hectare of poppies to produce one of the bricks."

"Well, that's the hard part," Bernfeld said as he made a big exhale.

"Converting the morphine bricks into heroin is the easy part."

"At the labs, the morphine bricks are pulverized and the powder put in cooking pots. Then, acetic anhydride, which smells like pickles by the way, is added. The pots are then heated to about a hundred and eighty degrees but not to boiling. This gives us diacetylmorphine or impure heroin."

"Next, water, at three times the volume of acetic anhydride, is added along with activated charcoal, and the solution is stirred. The last step is adding sodium carbonate at two and a half pounds for every pound of morphine. This precipitates out the heroin base, which then gets dried in a steam bath. You get about eleven ounces of heroin for each pound of morphine."

"That's it. That's the making of heroin in a nutshell," Bernfeld said as he surveyed the beauty around him.

28
CHAPTER

THE TWO WARLORDS

While the details of the science of opium production under his belt, Trick became a keen observer. Each day, he would drive out to the fields to watch the farmers. There was a rhythm and serenity to their work. This work was in their blood. The only analogy he could think of in America were the steelworkers around Pittsburgh, where one generation after the next filled the steel mills to make steel. But even that analogy paled in comparison to what he was witnessing. This work wasn't centuries old but <u>millennia</u> old, thousands of years not hundreds.

Then he thought about Lieutenant Applethorpe. He was one of the nicest officers he had ever met. He wondered if his widow back in Florida had received his letter yet. God was he unlucky, to survive the chaos of a gunfight in

Cambodia only to die of a snakebite in Thailand. Trick wondered if it was his destiny. And then he thought about all the others who died at An Loc. Only he and Bernfeld had survived – why? Was that destiny?

Trick got in the habit of waking up at 0600 hours and driving out to the poppy fields for an hour or two before coming back for breakfast. He loved to watch the farmers work. Their short, stringy-muscled bodies were perfect for opium harvesting. All day they would work in the fields, their heads covered by cone-shaped straw hats, working in perfect silence to an ancient rhythm. He was transfixed.

Every day during the harvest, Bernfeld would also drive out to the poppy fields – after breakfast. He would be gone all day, and he never informed Trick where he was going.

By the end of February, most of the raw opium had been harvested and the farmers were starting to "cook" their opium. The smell of almonds filled the nostrils of everyone in North Thailand.

Near the end of the harvest, one evening at dinner Bernfeld sat across from Trick and looked at him as if he had something important to tell him. Trick looked back at him wide-eyed, letting him know that he wanted in on the sorcerer's secrets. When Bernfeld saw this look, he knew Trick wanted to know everything.

"Only a fifth of the opium coming out of the Golden Triangle comes from Thailand," Bernfeld said. "Another fifth comes from Laos. That means that about sixty percent comes from our neighbor to the north – Burma. There are two warlords up there who control all the opium production in Burma. One is named Lo Hsin Han, and the other is named Khun Sa."

"About nine years ago, both of these men were given money and arms by the Burmese government to keep the communists out of eastern Burma. What they really did was form their own armies to protect their burgeoning drug empires. As we speak, in a little village just inside the Thai border called Mea Hong Son, Lo Hsin Han is getting ready to be arrested. The DEA had been putting pressure on the Thai police to take him into custody. If this happens, it will make Khun Sa the king of opium in the Golden Triangle," Bernfeld went on.

"We will know in the next twenty-four hours if this arrest attempt is successful or not," he added.

"Let me back up a little bit," Bernfeld said. "The opium empire wasn't always in the hands of Lo Hsin Lan and Khun Sa. In the beginning, the whole opium empire was under the control of the Nationalist Chinese who got kicked out of China and headed for Burma when the People's Republic of China took over in 1949. These Nationalist Chinese calls themselves the Kuomintang now, or KMT, and they have always been our allies. Just five years ago, a CIA operative reported that ninety percent of Burma's opium harvest was carried by KMT mule caravans based in northern Thailand, only seven percent was controlled by Shan armies, and three percent by Kachin rebels. For the last three years, though, the Shan armies have taken over the bulk of the trade from the KMT, and Lo Hsin Han and Khun Sa became the two biggest drug warlords in history."

"Do you want to be a part of history and go with me to Mea Hong Son and witness the capture of Lo Hsin Han?" Bernfeld asked Trick.

"Yes I do, sir," Trick replied.

"O.K. We leave in an hour," Bernfeld said.

29
CHAPTER

THE CAPTURE OF LO HSIN HAN

"**B**y the way, Colonel Sheets is flying in from Krakor for this one – for political reasons I guess – so we'll have to wait for him before we leave," Bernfeld added before heading for the mess hall.

Trick was amused. He could sense Bernfeld's excitement and he did want to be a part of history. Perhaps someday his obituary would just read "present at the arrest of Lo Hsin Han"; he didn't know. All he knew is that he was looking forward to the event.

Colonel Sheets' helicopter landed a half-hour later and Bernfeld and Trick walked out to greet him. They could tell that he was pretty excited too. They walked back to the bungalow where Colonel Sheets filled Bernfeld and Trick in on the details.

A few months ago, one of Lo Hsin Han's top officers approached a CIA operative – Jimmy Belgium – with a proposal to sell five tons of morphine base to the United States for twelve million in cash plus the promise of foreign aid. Apparently, Jimmy Belgium had played his role well as though the U.S. might seriously consider the offer. He promised Lo Hsin Han that he would take the proposal back to the powers that be and he would get a decision. After discussions between the DEA, the State Department, Special Forces, and Thai military intelligence, it was decided that they would pretend to accept the plan, but in reality, bring Lo Hsin Han out of hiding and arrest him instead. After all, he wasn't the Kuomintang, he was a renegade opium lord running a rebel Shan army.

The plan, then, was to give him the impression that the U.S. had accepted his proposal, and then lure him into Thailand to "sign" the deal. Instead, half a dozen Thai police and half a dozen Thai military intelligence officers, and Special Forces would put him under arrest once he was on board the helicopter headed for Bang Yai.

The news came in that the Thai police helicopter was on its way and would be at Mae Hong Son within the hour. Colonel Sheets, Bernfeld, and Trick hopped into their jeep, with Bernfeld at the wheel, and sped off heading north.

Most of the poppy fields had now been completely harvested, and the farmers were starting to slash and burn their fields to make potash for next year's planting. As they drove through one valley to the next, the smoke hovered like a thick fog where above the poppy fields. The smoke burned their nostrils and Bernfeld tried to avoid the lower-lying roads and stick to the mountain roads.

From a mountain top about five miles outside of Mae Hong Son, the three Special Forces men saw the Thai police helicopter land in a field next to a wooden bungalow. The Thai police were under orders to wait for the three Special Forces soldiers before making their arrest. They got there in less than ten minutes.

Trick got his first look at Lo Hsin Han. He was a small-framed man, very much Chinese-looking in appearance, but he had piercing eyes that commanded authority. The Thai police told him through an interpreter that he had to fly with them to Bangkok to sign the official papers on the deal, that the U.S. ambassador to Thailand and he had to witness each other's signatures. Incredibly, he actually bought that.

Colonel Sheets was sent on this mission because he was to be present during the interrogation of Lo Hsin Han, which would take place at Bang Yai. He wanted to get a feel for the man who had the audacity to try to sell twelve million worth of heroin directly to the U.S. government. Lo Hsin Han boarded the helicopter with one of his officers and the twelve Thai officials. Within five minutes of lift-off, he was told that he was under arrest.

****

On the drive back to Chiang Mai, Colonel Sheets told Bernfeld and Trick that he wanted them present at the interrogation of Lo Hsin Han, as he may impart information that might be useful to them later on. The state of politics in Burma was a mess that the U.S. couldn't get a grip on. The DEA was in conflict with the State

Department and they were both groping at a useful strategy in dealing with the Burmese military junta.

At Chiang Mai, Colonel Sheets' Huey was waiting for him. He told Bernfeld and Trick to be ready for take-off within the hour. They went back to their respective rooms, collected their gear, and headed to the Huey.

It was a two-hour flight to Bang Yai. Colonel Sheets, Lt. Bernfeld, and Sgt. Hartland headed to the POW barracks where the Thai police had taken Lo Hsin Han. When they got there, they couldn't believe it. Instead of treating Lo Hsin Han like a criminal, they were treating him like a celebrity. The quarters he had been given were more like a saloon than a prison, and they had all been drinking whiskey and scotch.

Trick guessed that the Thai police were treating him this way because they could get more information out of a tough hombre like Lo Hsin Han by lubricating him with alcohol than by torture. And it was working because Lo Hsin Han was telling them everything they wanted to know: what his troop strength was, where his heroin factories were located, his relationship with the Burmese military dictatorship, his relations with the Kuomintang, and his relationship with Khun Sa. He knew the jig was up, and that he was going to spend several years in prison, so he may as well cooperate.

The POW barracks continued to be a bar/entertainment salon even into the late evening. The Thai police had recently gotten a hold of the reel of an American Western movie called *A Man Called Horse* starring Richard Harris. They played it for Lo Hsin Han and he enjoyed every minute of it. There was a scene in the movie where incisions were made into Richard Harris' pectoral muscles, wooden stakes driven through them, and then ropes were attached to them and he was strung from a tree by the ropes. Lo Hsin Han exploded with laughter and said through his interpreter-officer – Nguyen Van Bo – that he would have to use that torture technique on his Burmese militia prisoners if he ever got out of prison.

Bernfeld had learned the Shan dialect and told Lo Hsin Han that his staff sergeant was a Navajo American Indian. Lo Hsin Han looked at Trick with awe in his eyes, and then he signaled Nguyen Van Bo to come to him. He whispered something in his ear. The Thai police told Nguyen Van Bo that they were not going to prosecute him, that he would be free to go. The Americans didn't understand this, but they let it pass.

It became apparent to Trick how different the oriental mindset and the western mindset were through Lo Hsin Han's behavior. He realized he had been duped by the U.S., in collusion with the Thai police, and that there was nothing he could do about it now, so he may as well make the best of it. What the U.S. didn't predict was the respect and tolerance his official Thai captors would show him. The U.S. missed the boat on that one. Bernfeld knew, and Trick was starting to realize, that all that this arrest had accomplished was the handing over of the reigns of the drug trade to Zhang Qifu, alias Khun Sa. Zhang Qifu had been defeated in 1967 at Ban Howay Xay by the Kuomintang for control of the opium traffic. For his failure, Zhang Qifu was imprisoned. In prison, Zhang Qifu transformed himself into Khun Sa and it would take him six years to make a comeback. But when he did, he would go on to become the biggest drug warlord in the history of the world.

30
CHAPTER

KHUN SA
REIGNS SUPREME

Within a few months of the arrest of Lo Hsin Han, Khun Sa had consolidated his position, while still in prison, as the most powerful opium lord of the Golden Triangle. He formed the Shan United Army (SUA) from prison, which over the next few years would grow from four or five thousand men to forty thousand soldiers. Later, this private army became known as the Mong Tai Army. In time, he would control more than eighty percent of the entire opium trade in the Golden Triangle. The CIA let this happen because the SUA fought against the Communist party of Burma (CPB), and even a drug lord was better than a communist in the CIA's eyes. The government of Thailand tolerated him as long as he was fighting the communists. Thailand's military intelligence actually protected Khun Sa's base camp at Ban Hin Taek from other guerilla armies.

It was the geopolitical chaos around him that allowed Khun Sa to become "The King of Opium". Like Lo Hsin Han, Khun Sa was half Kokang Chinese and half Burmese Shan, and he had learned from Lo Hsin Han's mistakes.

It was now nearly the end of March, and almost all regular army American soldiers had been evacuated from Southeast Asia. All that remained were the Special Forces, including the Green Berets, the CIA, the DEA, and, of course, the top brass.

Intelligence sources had confirmed that there was a major heroin epidemic going on. The availability of the drug, thanks to the Golden Triangle, made it so easy and cheap that many American soldiers succumbed to its charms. U.S. Army medical officers estimated that between 10 and 15 percent of all lower-ranking enlisted men were addicted to heroin. After officers started coming down hard on the marijuana smokers, the GIs just switched to heroin because it was odorless, small in volume, and hard to detect. Everyone in Vietnam was selling the stuff, from fifteen-year-old girls standing in the streets to high-ranking Vietnamese military officers. The burgeoning use of heroin coincided with the ouster of Prince Sihanouk in March 1970. Once Phnom Penh opened up, hundreds of commercial, military and private flights flew contraband narcotics all over Southeast Asia. The Vietnamese navy became specialists in importing the drug, and the Vietnamese army became the specialists in distributing and selling the drug inside the country.

On June 22, 1971, the U.S. military command ordered every GI leaving Vietnam to submit to a urinalysis that could detect morphine or heroin if taken within the last four or five days. Many addicts got around the test by bringing a buddy's "clean" urine to the test facility. Many other addicts were capable of refraining for a week to pass the test.

Back home, the Veterans Administration hospitals did nothing to help the addicted GIs. Out of twenty to fifty thousand GI heroin addicts who returned to the "World", only three were treated.

In mid-1971, President Nixon declared war on the international heroin traffic. But the antinarcotics campaign did more harm than good because the crackdown and closing of Vietnam's hundreds of opium dens made life difficult for the average opium-smoking drug users. So they turned to heroin. Opium smoking isn't necessarily healthy, but it's not heroin, which is made with acid and can kill an addict within a year.

Trick understood its appeal, and he had only had a taste of it. He suspected that Bernfeld was a regular user, but he wasn't sure because he handled it so well. Of course, any officer hooked on drugs had better be able to handle it well.

After March 1973, because no Americans were supposed to be in Vietnam, everyone in the Special Forces and CIA was given a codename. For some reason, some genius high up in the chain of command decided to use the colors as codenames. Colonel Sheets was now Agent Green, Captain Longenecker was now Agent Yellow,

Lieutenant Bernfeld was now Agent Black, Jimmy Belgium was Agent Orange, and Trick was now Agent Blue. Who had decided these colors was unknown, just that they had been issued from on high from Binh Long.

For months, Bernfeld had secretly been helping Khun Sa organize his Shan United Army; he wasn't doing anything wrong by doing this; those were his orders. He would visit Khun Sa in his Mandalay prison cell every couple of weeks, and it was clear to Trick that Bernfeld was pleased with his progress. Bernfeld was not only keeping communism out of Burma, he was getting some wampum on the side for his efforts. He would have to make trips to the Bank of Thailand at least once a week for some reason. Bernfeld's relationship to Khun Sa was evidently a mutually symbiotic one.

There was only one fly in the ointment – Jimmy Belgium. Apparently, Jimmy's (Agent Orange's) orders from the CIA and Bernfeld's from Special Forces were the same – become Khun Sa's collaborator and ally. It was becoming apparent to Trick that Bernfeld and Jimmy were starting to get in each other's way. It was only logical that Khun Sa could have only one American majordomo.

By the end of April, it was clear that Bernfeld (Agent Black) was very unhappy with Agent Orange. Bernfeld had established relations with the Shan State Army under General Jau Nhu, the Kachin Independence Army (KIA) under General Zau Seng, and the Kokang Revolutionary Force (KRF) under Jimmy Yang, and was in secret luring soldiers of these guerilla armies away to join Khun Sa's Shan United Army. Jimmy Belgium, to his credit, had lured away soldiers from the Mon Liberation Front (MLF) and the Kayah New Land Revolution Council (KNLRC) to join the Shan United Army.

Behind the scenes, Khun Sa was playing the two Americans against each other. He benefited from being in cahoots with both the Special Forces and the CIA, but he knew in the end he could have only one American collaborator.

31
CHAPTER

AN INCURSION OF PATHET LAO

s spring rolled into summer, Bernfeld's progress in becoming Khun Sa's chief American collaborator became stronger and stronger. Whether it was because he had learned to speak fluent Shan Burmese or his Armenian-Jewish heritage in good business acumen, Bernfeld was becoming a star within Special Forces.

In June, the Pathet Lao made an incursion into Burma and took over one of Khun Sa's refinery labs at Na Yao. Evidently, they wanted more of the action in the opium trade.

Colonel Sheets himself was going to lead the mission to route the Pathet Lao. He arrived at Chang Rai on a Tuesday and held a briefing that evening. The attack was planned for Thursday, and to get the troops psyched up for it, he used his Bible-thumping Baptist upbringing.

"Just remember, men," he said as he pulled a Bible out of his back pocket and laid it on the lectern. "I read from Ephesians, Chapter six, verses eleven through thirteen, 'Put on all the armor that God gives you so that you will stand up against the Devil's evil tricks. For we are not fighting against human beings, but against the wicked forces in the heavenly world, the rulers, authorities, and cosmic powers of this Dark Age. So take up God's armor now! Then when the evil day comes, you will be able to resist the enemy's attacks, and after fighting to the end, you will still hold your ground.'"

The briefing room was silent as the men looked around at each other to see if anybody had any questions. Finally, a new Green beret recruit got up the courage to ask Colonel Sheets "How many Pathet Lao are there, sir?"

"We don't know their numbers, son; we won't know until we get there," Colonel Sheets replied.

Trick got up the nerve to ask, "Which direction will we be attacking from, Colonel?"

"We'll come straight up from the south, son" Colonel Sheets replied.

Bernfeld spoke up, "Do they have tanks and armed personnel carriers?"

"We don't know," Colonel Sheets replied. Then he flipped through his Bible until he found what he wanted. "Just remember, and I quote from Philippians, Chapter four, verse thirteen, 'I have the strength to face all things by the power that Christ gives me.' And from Romans, Chapter eight, verse thirty-seven, 'In all these things we have complete victory through Him who loved us.'"

Bernfeld spoke up again, "Do we have the firepower without heavy equipment to win this battle sir?" he asked.

"I quote from Hebrews, Chapter four, verse twelve, 'The word of God is sharper than any double-edged sword. It eats all the way through to where soul and spirit meet, to where joints and marrow come together.' "

"O.K. sir, thank you, sir," Bernfeld said as he looked at Trick with a knowing look. Bernfeld realized that Colonel Sheets' screws were starting to come loose. But he was still his commanding officer and he had to show him some respect. He would humor Colonel Sheets, realizing it would fall upon him to make this attack a success. He sent word to Nguyen Van Bo and to all his friends up north in the Shan United Army for their help.

****

The platoon of Special Forces rolled out of Chang Rai at dawn on Thursday morning. They would be at Na Yao in four hours. With any luck, if they met with only light resistance, they should be able to take the hamlet in a matter of minutes. It depended upon what they found when they got there and what kind of help they would get from the Shan.

Colonel Sheets, Colonel Phuony, Bernfeld, and Trick rode in the same jeep. About two hours into the ride, Bernfeld finally got up the nerve to ask Colonel Sheets if he believed in an afterlife.

"Yes, I do, lieutenant. I guess it was how I was raised. I was also taught to believe in the Second Coming of Christ.

I was taught that if we can love him hard enough, He will come," he said with a serious expression on his face.

"I was raised Jewish, sir," Bernfeld said looking for his reaction. Colonel Sheets pulled his Bible out of his back pocket and gave it to Bernfeld.

"Only those who believe in Jesus will see the kingdom of heaven," Colonel Sheets said.

"Thank you, sir," Bernfeld said as he put the Bible in his inside jacket pocket.

The convoy crossed the Thai-Burma border and rolled up to Mae Sai, where a platoon of Shan United Army soldiers were waiting for them. As they approached Na Yao, the only question was where to get off the road. Unfortunately, the caravan didn't get off early enough and they were spotted by a perimeter guard. A mortar round exploded twenty yards in front of the lead vehicle.

The soldiers scrambled from their vehicles and were divided up into two flanks. They would have to advance the last mile through mortar fire.

They were only two hundred yards away from the hamlet and none of the soldiers had been hit. Then, as Colonel Sheets started running forward, a mortar round landed right next to him and he was blown to smithereens. The Green Berets looked on in horror as fragments of his uniform caught the wind and blew upward towards the tops of the trees.

Bernfeld was now in command. He ordered a charge and Green Berets from the right flank and Shan Army from the left flank converged on the village. The gun battle didn't last long; the Pathet Lao had no tanks and they tried to make a retreat through the north end of the village, but they were mowed down by M-16 fire. About twenty of them lay dead in the streets of Na Yao.

Bernfeld called headquarters to report that Na Yao had been retaken and Colonel Sheets' death. He looked up from the receiver at Trick and said, "I guess if you love him hard enough, he will come to you, ... or you will go to him. Gives a whole new meaning to the expression 'three sheets to the wind'. "

32
CHAPTER

COMRADES IN ARMS

In the aftermath of Colonel Sheets' death, top brass at Bang Yai decided to promote Captain Longenecker to Major, and Lieutenant Bernfeld to Captain, with Major Longenecker being Captain Bernfeld's new commanding officer. When Captain Bernfeld returned from Bang Yai, he told Trick that he had recommended to Major Longenecker that he be promoted to first lieutenant. Bernfeld felt that Trick had what it took to be an officer. The recommendation was already sitting in Major Longenecker's "in" box.

Captain Bernfeld was planning an extensive sweep of eastern Burma, traveling from hamlet to hamlet recruiting for Khun Sa. He carefully arranged his itinerary so that he would always be able to get to Ho Pong within a day's notice.

Trick could tell that something else was also brewing in Bernfeld's head. It wasn't clearly perceptible just yet, but there was definitely something there, slowly changing Bernfeld's countenance. Trick wasn't sure yet if he wanted to know what it was.

After Colonel Phuony arrived at Chiang Mai with the blessings of his commanding officer, General Vang Pao, Bernfeld pulled out his maps and showed Colonel Phuony where he wanted to go. Trick was to be the driver for this expedition, leaving Bernfeld and Colonel Phuony free to survey the landscape.

It was already August and had they been on the coast of Thailand instead of the northern mountains, the heat would have been sweltering. Instead, the mountain air felt cool on their skin as they headed north in the open jeep. This journey would last several weeks and take them to farthest northernmost regions of Burma.

They made it to Mae Sai, sitting right on the nexus of Thailand, Laos, and Burma by high noon. They stopped and ate their lunch that had been prepared by the chef at Chiang Mai. As they rolled into Na Yao twenty miles up the road, they stopped to talk with the Shan platoon that had helped them defeat the Pathet Lao incursion. They praised Colonel Sheets for his heroism and said they would never forget him. They showed Bernfeld and Trick a little marker noting the place where he had been killed, and Bernfeld thanked them before heading back to the jeep.

Bernfeld had his first meeting late that afternoon in Mong Hoayak with a leader from the Kokang Revolutionary Force (KRF), Major Lao Chung. They acted as if they were long-lost friends. Bernfeld told Trick they were spending their first night there and to get the sleeping rolls from the jeep and put them into the far hut on the right. After that was done, he could rejoin them for the rest of the meeting.

At the meeting, Lao Chung made it clear that he and the men under his command were willing to defect from Jimmy Yang's KRF and join Khun Sa's Shan United Army. Bernfeld was very pleased. He gave instructions to Lao Chung how and when to defect and his assurances that he would be helped by the American Special Forces in any way that they could.

Lao Chung and Bernfeld had one more thing in common than working for the same team. They also both liked to chase the dragon. Lao Chung had his assistant bring in a hookah and a sealed bag of opium. Bernfeld motioned for Trick to come over and he nodded in the affirmative. He thought the smoke would help his muscles after driving all day. Colonel Phuony made it a foursome.

Bernfeld lit the hookah and inhaled deeply before passing it to Colonel Phuony. Colonel Phuony took a quick inhale and passed the hookah to Trick. This opium hit Trick up much more than his experience at Fang Wu's. He looked at Bernfeld with a beseeching look, but Bernfeld was deep in conversation with Lao Chung. This opium sent Trick's head spinning and for some reason, visions of a feathered god-like Quetzalcoatl swirled in his head. He hadn't felt this good in a long, long time. He felt alive for the first time in months. He was able to put those images of battle out of his mind and simply enjoy the crazy adventure he was on.

After the bowl of the hookah was exhausted, Lao Chung left the room and was gone for about five minutes. He returned with a prisoner who had his hands tied behind his back. Lao Chung pulled a chair to the center of the room and sat the prisoner down in it. After a few words between Lao Chung and Bernfeld that Trick didn't understand, it was still clear to Trick that this prisoner was in for a world of hurt. Bernfeld told Trick that the prisoner was a government militia soldier who was secretly helping the Pathet Lao. In other words, he was a double agent. Bernfeld told Trick to watch and learn some oriental interrogation techniques.

Lao Chung started off his questioning in a soft voice. He circled the chair, leaning in occasionally to speak directly into the prisoner's ear. Then he stood motionless for a few seconds and finally nodded to his assistant. Lao Chung's assistant left the room for about a minute and then came back with a syringe in his hands, which he gave to Lao Chung. Lao Chung pointed the needle of the syringe straight up as if inspecting for bubbles, and then he injected the prisoner with its contents. The prisoner's head rolled back and his limbs became limp, but he was still conscious. He was now ready for interrogation. Bernfeld translated everything for Trick and told him the syringe was full of pure China White heroin.

"What is the name of the Pathet Lao leader who ordered his men to overtake Na Yao?" Lao Chung struck the man across the face with a backhand.

"Why did you become a double agent for the Pathet Lao? Wasn't the Burmese army paying you enough?"

Lao Chung was now punching the man with his full fists all over his face and in the stomach. A cut over one of the prisoner's eyes was oozing blood that Trickled down his face and neck and into his clothes. Still, the man refused to speak. Lao Chung nodded at his assistant again. This time the assistant came back with a syringe the size of a turkey baster – with a needle. There must have been at least twelve ounces of pure China White heroin floating around in that syringe. Lao Chung looked down at his victim without pity. Once this syringe was administered, it would be all over in a matter of minutes.

Do you have anything to say?" Bernfeld translated for Trick.

After the man said nothing, Lao Chung emptied the entire syringe into the man's left bicep. Lao Chung kept punching the man as long as he was conscious. It was difficult to tell if he was conscious or not at this point. White bubbles of foam started to appear in the corners of the man's mouth that mixed with the blood running down his face to form pink bubbles. The corneas of his eyes disappeared somewhere into his head and only white showed from the sockets. Finally, his chest stopped moving and his breathing stopped. It was over. Lao Chung and Bernfeld knew that they were going to kill him whether he talked or not, and so did the prisoner so why give them the satisfaction of breaking him.

The dead man's hands were cut free from behind his back and Lao Chung's assistant carried him out over his shoulder. The party was over and it was time to go to bed. They had many miles to travel tomorrow.

33
CHAPTER

A MURDER
NEAR MANDALAY

In the early morning hours, Bernfeld, Colonel Phuony, and Trick set off heading north towards Loi Mwe. Even though Trick was driving, he couldn't help but notice the incredible landscape. The morning fog was still hovering over the valleys, and the mountains peaked through to reveal their glory. Northern Thailand was beautiful, and Trick could understand why Bernfeld considered it to be Shangri-la, but for a rugged American westerner, Burma was even more beautiful. The land was as untamed as its inhabitants were, and Trick revered that intangible feeling of something not quite conquered yet.

Bernfeld interrupted his reverie while driving to tell him to drive straight through Loi Mwe and keep going. They would stop in Keng Tung for lunch, the MREs they had brought with them from Chiang Mai. Bernfeld's contact in this town was a Shan State army captain named Ly Kohach. Captain Kohach told Bernfeld that Khun Sa had requested a meeting with him before he headed up any further north. When pressed for a reason why Captain Kohach just said it pertained to a matter that needed immediate attention.

So instead of heading north, Trick drove west. They arrived in Ho Pong by the middle of the afternoon. They drove straight through Taunggyi, even though it was a beautiful provincial capital. They drove on through Kolon at about five o'clock and arrived at the outskirts of Mandalay at around six o'clock. Bernfeld directed Trick to the prison compound where Khun Sa was being held. Bernfeld made it clear to Trick that only Colonel Phuony and himself would be present at the meeting. Trick's job was to find more fuel. It was Trick's job to buy fuel from the fuel depot at the base and sit out in front of the prison compound until Bernfeld and Colonel Phuony returned. Trick filled the jeep up with fuel and drove to the front of the prison. After some two odd hours, he saw Bernfeld with Colonel Phuony coming through the prison gates, and even though he had difficulty reading Colonel Phuony, Bernfeld definitely did not look happy. Bernfeld's look was stern and somber at the same time.

"We have a job to do," Bernfeld said in an expressionless tone. They drove all around the Buddhist temples around Mandalay and they were absolutely beautiful. They stopped at the temple at Amarapura and looked around. There were images of Buddha all over the place, and Colonel Phuony bowed his head each time they passed one.

Finally, Bernfeld confided in Trick the nature of his chore. Jimmy Belgium was in Mandalay alone negotiating with an officer of the Mon Liberation Force, Lieutenant Colonel Than Aye, in essence bribing him to let more of his men join the Shan United Army.

Bernfeld said "Khun Sa wants to put an end to Jimmy Belgium for two main reasons: he is skimming too much money off the top and sooner or later he will be caught by his own people and will be an embarrassment; second, Khun Sa knows he can never completely trust the CIA. Khun Sa said he didn't like him either. We are going to his meeting this evening, and then we're going to drive him far out into the country and eliminate him."

Trick didn't know what to think. Eliminate a CIA operative who had a lot of friends back in Bang Yai? Dangerous.

"Don't you think if you do that you're signing your own death warrant?" Trick asked.

"There will only be five people in the world who will know the truth," Bernfeld replied. "You, me, Colonel Phuony, Lieutenant Colonel Than Aye, and Khun Sa," he added. "It needs to be done."

Trick looked at Colonel Phuony and knew that it would be him who pulled the trigger. No matter how much Bernfeld hated Jimmy Belgium, he wouldn't be the one who pulled the trigger on a fellow American.

****

Bernfeld gave Trick directions to a house near the top of Mandalay hill, the center of the city. Trick, Bernfeld, and Colonel Phuony walked in to find Jimmy Belgium drinking Sang Li beer with Lieutenant Colonel Than Aye. They were both in a jovial mood, but Bernfeld knew that Lt. Col. Aye knew the real reason for Bernfeld's visit.

They decided to let him enjoy his last evening on the planet. They wanted Jimmy to keep drinking so that he would be easier to dispense with.

"Tell me again Jimmy how you eliminated Colonel Kurtz," Bernfeld requested.

"Well, I crept up to his cave, my machete behind me so that when he saw me he wouldn't be suspicious, and when he was off his guard, I chopped off his head with one stroke," Jimmy replied.

"Didn't any of his men see you leaving the cave with the bloody machete?" Bernfeld pressed on.

"No, it was a pitch black moonless night and I was out of there in less than a minute," Jimmy replied.

"That's amazing," Bernfeld said with a smile as he refilled Jimmy's glass.

After a while, the conversation turned to the present. Jimmy was trying to get a promise from Than Aye for a certain amount of soldiers to join the Shan United Army. What brought Jimmy to Mandalay was Khun Sa's request to him to meet with Than Aye, who had already promised Khun Sa some soldiers. The negotiating points were how many soldiers, the time frame, and the pay. Or so at least Jimmy was told.

Than Aye was enjoying the pretense a little too much and Bernfeld was starting to get angry. He wanted to bring the charade to an end and get the real work of the evening over with.

"Thank you, Colonel Aye, for your hospitality," Bernfeld said in Burmese. "But we must get going."

"It is good to finally meet you," Colonel Aye replied. "I wish you safety on your journey."

"Jimmy, we'll give you a lift to your hotel – overdid it a little bit, didn't you?" Bernfeld asked.

"Thanks guys, I guess I did," he replied.

Bernfeld sat in the passenger seat beside Trick while Colonel Phuony put Jimmy in the rear driver's side seat. Trick knew his job was to keep quiet while he drove according to Bernfeld's directions.

They were at the bottom of Mandalay hill and Bernfeld told Trick to head east. Jimmy was finally getting suspicious because they were not heading in the direction of his hotel.

"Where we goin?" Jimmy asked.

"Oh, we want to show you something really special," Bernfeld replied.

About twenty minutes later, they arrived at the temple of Kuthodau Paya, which houses the largest book in the world. They climbed to steps to the top. The view of Mandalay was breathtaking, and finally, Jimmy realized why he was here. He stood motionless scanning the horizon. Bernfeld walked over to Trick and motioned for him to start walking down the steps with him, leaving

Jimmy alone with Colonel Phuony. Bernfeld and Trick had just reached the jeep when they heard the single gunshot. The sound reverberated around the temple halls. They waited until Colonel Phuony jumped into the back of the jeep and they took off.

"We killed a real monster," Bernfeld said.

34
CHAPTER

IT'S A MAD, MAD, MAD, MAD, WORLD

There are some actions for which there are inevitable consequences, and one of those actions for which there are inevitable consequences is killing a CIA operative. The punishment for this action is death. There are no ways around this consequence; it is an inviolable rule of life. The scales of justice will be balanced; the only variable is time.

Bernfeld must have realized this as his protégé drove the jeep through the night without a word spoken towards the Kachin State to the northeast. Bernfeld's brother back in the States had written him a letter forewarning him that he had had a vision of his death. Bernfeld wrote back saying that he had never felt better in his life.

They reached Zigon by three a.m. in the morning, and Bernfeld asked Trick if he was tired. When Trick said no, Captain Bernfeld told him to keep going so Trick continued to drive through the night, and they reached Bhamo in the Kachin State at dawn.

Bhamo was where General Zau Seng had set up temporary headquarters for his Kachin Independence Army. The general was expecting Bernfeld and his associates. When they found the camp, they were stopped at the perimeter by guards, but when they found out who it was, they let them through.

General Zau Seng was in a jovial mood when he met them. He had met them outside of his command headquarters bungalow, shook their hands, then asked them through an interpreter to follow him inside.

The KIA had always been at the periphery of the drug trade, even though the Kachin State in northeastern Burma was home to some of the best poppy-growing soil in the world. Yes, the opium trade did help in supplying their troops, but it was not their main focus, unlike the Shan State.

The general was calling for an inspection of his troops, which was appropriate for a visitor of Bernfeld's stature. Evidently, Bernfeld's reputation was spreading throughout Burma as well as Thailand. Out on the inspection grounds, the soldiers looked eager to please their leader. They high-stepped into position and then stood at attention. General Seng looked at his troops with approval and then walked back to where Bernfeld was standing.

Through his interpreter, he asked, "What do you think?"

Bernfeld replied, "Do you need them all? Khun Sa would like to add to his Shan United Army," he said.

"And what would I get in return?" General Seng asked.

"Enough money to replace twice the number of troops that you lose," Bernfeld answered.

"I will give you my answer by tomorrow," General Seng said.

They spent the remainder of the day eating and drinking in General Seng's command headquarters. Bernfeld was on the radio for a little while, but he never told Trick who he was talking to or what the communication was about. Trick assumed Bernfeld had relayed the message to someone that they didn't have to worry about Jimmy Belgium anymore.

The next morning was a bright and beautiful summer's day. It was so beautiful that the strong sunlight brought the jungle foliage to life in Technicolor. There were more shades of green here than Trick had ever thought possible.

General Seng had given Bernfeld his answer: he would give him one hundred men, and Bernfeld was satisfied with that because he knew that when he asked him for more he wouldn't be refused. It was clear that General Seng had heard from somebody that Bernfeld was Khun Sa's number one majordomo and that he was owed some respect. As the two Americans and the South Vietnamese Colonel drove out of the camp followed by their one hundred recruits, they were saluted.

****

Bernfeld wanted to find out the strength of the Burmese Communist Party along the Burma-China border, so he ordered Trick to drive south along the border. They didn't encounter any communists until they reached Mong Yu. There, two miles from the Chinese border was a squad of about fifteen BCP soldiers. When they saw the one hundred Kachin soldiers coming down the road, they made a run for the Chinese border through back jungle trails. Several of the men given to Bernfeld must have been sharpshooters because from the road they picked off a few of the BCP before they made it into the deep jungle. The rest weren't worth chasing into China and risking their necks.

They decided to stay at the BCP encampment and make it their base for the night. Bernfeld sent out two Kachin soldiers each to the four directions as perimeter guards and set up command headquarters in the abandoned largest building. He called Nyugen Van Bo and told him to tell Khun Sa that he had recruited one hundred soldiers from the KIA. He knew that Khun Sa would be pleased.

They were gathering their supplies from the jeep when Trick noticed a copy of Mad magazine sitting at the bottom of the rear compartment. He pulled it out and looked at the picture of Alfred E. Neuman with an army helmet on his head on the cover. He thought it must be Bernfeld's so he decided to walk to the command headquarters and give it to him.

"I found this at the bottom of the rear compartment," Trick said. "I guess it's yours."

"Yeah, thanks," Bernfeld said. "I thought I'd bring it along to lighten things up. Sometimes I feel like I'm living the white spy versus black spy cartoon," he added.

"Pretty silly cover, isn't it?" Trick asked.

"Don't laugh, this world is so crazy someday Alfred E. Neuman will be President of the United States," Bernfeld replied.

Trick took that one in and decided not to press on. They placed a howitzer in a machine gun nest facing north just in case the BCP decided to come back with reinforcements to take back their base. After they were finished they went back into the command headquarters to let Major Longenecker know where they were. After several conversations on the radio, it became apparent to Trick that Bernfeld was a little agitated.

"What's the matter, Jerry?" Trick asked.

"Nyugen Van Bo warned me that the CIA is investigating the disappearance of Jimmy Belgium," Bernfeld replied.

Now Trick was worried about the safety of his CO. If they ever connected Bernfeld with Belgium's death . . .but for now other matters weighed more heavily, and their current focus might mean the difference between their survival and death.

35
CHAPTER

THE TWO
GOOD DOCTORS

When they awoke the next morning, everyone was surprised that there was no counterattack during the night. Evidently, BCP reinforcements were not in waiting just across the Chinese border. That was good luck, but Bernfeld decided not to tempt the war gods and hang around. He ordered an evacuation within the hour, and the recruits scampered around gathering their supplies and arms. They were on the road heading south about an hour after dawn.

"Where we heading, Jerry?" Trick asked.

"Ho-Pang," Bernfeld replied.

Trick pulled a map onto his lap while driving and saw that Ho-Pang was about one hundred and fifty miles away. They'd be there within two hours.

"Any destination in particular in Ho-Pang?" Trick asked.

"Yes, there's a hospital there – that's where we're going," Bernfeld replied.

"We'll be meeting Captain Nyugen Van Son of the Shan State Army. He should have some more soldiers for us, too," he added.

There were some unidentifiable soldiers straggling on the road to Ho-Pang, but they offered no resistance. It was unclear which army they belonged to, and Bernfeld ordered his Kachin soldiers not to shoot.

They rode into Ho-Pang and looked around for the Shan State Army camp, and finally found it near the east side of the hamlet. Trick drove the jeep straight up to the largest building and parked. Captain Nyugen Van Son walked out of the building, and Bernfeld walked up to him and greeted him in Burmese.

Then Colonel Phuony bowed and stood behind Bernfeld. As Trick moved up to greet him, Bernfeld said something to the captain in Burmese and he smiled. They walked into the large building together and sat around a long table. Food was brought in and they all ate.

"We need to go to the hospital this afternoon," Bernfeld told Trick.

"We have a chore to do," he said.

Colonel Phuony had a knowing look on his face and then smiled.

"We're going to meet some French doctors," Bernfeld added.

After lunch, Captain Van Son led Bernfeld, Colonel Phuony, and Trick across some rice paddies, then some poppy fields to the International Red Cross hospital with its universally known flag flying overhead. Once inside, Bernfeld asked a nurse for Drs. Guy LaForge and Roland Chrétien. They came out to see who wanted them.

"Doctors, I'm Captain Jerry Bernfeld of the American Special Forces. Finish treating your patients and when you're done, please follow Colonel Phuony to our command headquarters," Bernfeld said.

Both doctors said "Non" at the same time. Bernfeld and Colonel Phuony pulled their revolvers and pointed them at the doctors.

"We don't want to, but we will kill you if you don't cooperate," Bernfeld said in French. Trick knew just enough French to understand the threat. The two doctors looked at each other, spoke a few soft words, and left.

On the way back to the Shan State Army's camp, Trick asked Bernfeld, "What's going on?"

Bernfeld smiled and said, "We're going to take these doctors hostage for the release of Khun Sa," Bernfeld said.

"Trick looked at him incredulously. "You mean you're gonna kidnap these doctors and hold them as ransom for the release of Khun Sa?" Trick asked.

"These doctors have saved the lives of thousands of Burmese militia soldiers, and the honchos in Rangoon owe them a debt of gratitude. It's the only way Khun Sa will ever get out of prison," Bernfeld replied. "Also, they're getting a bargain – two doctors for one warlord," he added.

Trick walked away because he knew he needed time to think. He respected men of medicine and wasn't sure if he could show his CO much enthusiasm for this mission. He started walking the perimeter of the camp to clear his head. He realized that Bernfeld was in many ways a renegade officer who was using the war to his own ends. If ever there was a "Heart of Darkness" this was it, and Bernfeld, marching to his own drummer, was now completely sync with it.

Trick decided he was going to show Roland Chretien and Guy LaForge the ultimate respect and do everything to protect them and make them as comfortable as possible.

The two doctors arrived at the base with Colonel Phuony who showed them inside the command headquarters. Trick could tell they were hot under the collar as they hissed at each other in French. Finally, Bernfeld came out of another room and addressed them in French, another language he had somehow mastered.

When he was done he said, "I told them they wouldn't be harmed and the reason for their captivity. They're angry but know that anything can happen during a war."

"How long do you think it will be before the Burmese let us know if they'll take the deal or not?" Trick asked.

"It'll probably take a week or so before they make a decision and another week to arrange the exchange," Bernfeld answered.

With that, Bernfeld led the two good doctors to their new quarters where they would always be under the watchful eye of Colonel Phuony. Bernfeld's negotiations with Captain Van Son for recruits to join the Shan United

Army were not going well. Bernfeld was holding out for another hundred men to join the hundred Kachin soldiers he had negotiated for from General Seng. Captain Van Son said he could only give him fifty. The stalemate lasted several hours until captain Van Son finally relented and upped his number to seventy-five. Bernfeld was a little disappointed, but he knew it was a marginal victory to get Captain Van Son to budge at all.

36

CHAPTER

THE DEATH OF
AGENT BLACK

Bernfeld knew that the government would send militia to Ho-Pang in an attempt to rescue the two doctors, so Bernfeld ordered an evacuation. He decided to take his one hundred and seventy-five man army to Mong Yai, about a hundred miles east of Mandalay, to await the government's decision. He figured that the government would never think he would be so bold as to be sitting practically on their doorstep as the decision was being made.

Mong Yai was in the heart of rebel territory, and Bernfeld thought he might be able to pick up even more recruits there. Thus, there were three good reasons for going there: to be within three hours of Mandalay and to be able to make the hostage exchange within one day of the go-ahead, the possibility of more recruits, and the relative safety of the area. He explained all this to Trick, adding that he wished Trick spoke Burmese. Even Colonel Phuony couldn't speak Burmese, so if ever something happened to Bernfeld, he was worried about the chain of command.

They were headed west towards Hsenwi by 0900 hours. The two French doctors were put in the back of a medical supply truck so that they could inventory the supplies. Even though they were hostages, they had agreed that they would treat any wounded soldiers.

They rolled into Loi-lawn at 1100 hours and decided to stay there for lunch. There were a few rebel army soldiers who greeted their Kachin cousins with open arms. They were exchanging war stories and the plot to free Khun Sa. After the meal, at 1200 hours, they headed south towards Mong Yai. Bernfeld figured they'd be there by 1500 hours. He stopped about fifty miles out and radioed Major Longenecker and Nguyen Van Bo to tell his position, and then he jumped back into the jeep and ordered the convoy to move out.

Just outside of Mong Yai, there was a radio call from Nguyen Van Bo. Good news – the deal was on. The only negotiating points left were where and when. Bernfeld decided that the exchange should take place the next day at the Kathodau Paya temple, just outside of Mandalay. The French doctors were elated with the news.

Secretly, in the back of Bernfeld's mind, he had always been a little worried about the disposition of Jimmy Belgium's body. Who had found it? What did the authorities do with it? Were there any leads? He thought that by doing the exchange there, he might be able to keep ahead of the investigation.

****

It was a crisp, clear September morning, and Bernfeld left Colonel Phuony in charge of the men at Mong Yai. He wanted only himself, Trick, and the two doctors present at the exchange. They drove off at 0700 hours and expected to reach the temple by 1200 hours.

As Trick, Bernfeld, and the two doctors sped towards Mandalay, Trick could feel something in the wind. He couldn't put his finger on it, but it gave him a very uneasy feeling. The closer they got to Mandalay, the stronger he felt it. He finally decided he had better say something to Bernfeld.

"Jerry, I don't know what it is, but I have a very uneasy feeling about this mission," Trick said.

"Just nerves, forget about it," Bernfeld replied.

Trick knew it was more than just nerves, but Bernfeld evidently didn't want to discuss it anymore. They had just passed through Kyawkka and were within ten miles of Kathodau Paya. Bernfeld thanked the doctors for being good hostages and said he was sorry for what he had done to them.

The minarets of the temple finally came into sight, and within a few minutes, they were at the eastern base of the temple. The prison guard truck was already parked at the western base of the temple. Khun Sa was to walk up the western steps of the temple just as the two doctors were to be walking up the eastern steps of the temple; they were to pass each other at the top and then come down the other side.

It was 1500 hours, time for the exchange. Bernfeld told the two doctors to start walking up the steps. Within minutes, they had disappeared. Khun Sa was nowhere to be seen. Bernfeld radioed Nyugen Van Bo to find out if he had been double-crossed. Van Bo said no, the guards had instructions not to let Khun Sa go until they saw the two doctors walking down the eastern steps first. The guards had just spotted him, and Khun Sa was starting up the eastern slopes.

"Let's go!" Bernfeld said to Trick when he heard from Van Bo that Khun Sa was starting up the western steps. Bernfeld and Trick started running up the eastern steps, two or three at a time; Bernfeld wanted to reach the top before Khun Sa did.

The closer Trick got to the top, the more he sensed danger. His blood was filling up with more and more adrenaline with each step he took. They reached the top of the temple where there was a myriad of pointed columns, and they started running faster on the flat top surface towards the western edge. When they got there, they looked down and saw Khun Sa halfway up the steps. Off to his right, Trick heard a noise. He scanned the columns to his right but didn't see anything. He decided he better go investigate while Bernfeld stood at the top western edge of the temple waiting for Khun Sa who was now almost to the top. In a split second, Sergeant Allen Pope (Agent White) and Lieutenant Doug Price (Agent Red) emerged from behind a column, and Pope caught Trick with a karate chop right across his forehead which knocked him to the ground in a daze. Trick was only able to look up from the ground in time to see them assault Bernfeld, who sent Khun Sa running towards the eastern edge of the temple.

The conflict only lasted a few seconds, but in Trick's eyes, it occurred in slow motion. Using his Kung Fu training, Pope attacked Bernfeld straight on with a plum flower punch to Bernfeld's throat while Price maneuvered behind him.

"Fucking Jew," Pope said as he slammed his fist into Bernfeld's throat. "Did you really think you could get away with it?"

For insurance, Price, standing right behind Bernfeld, pulled the trigger of his service revolver from about two feet away.

"Here's one for Jimmy," he said.

Bernfeld was somehow able to reach down, pull out his bowie knife, and thrust it into Pope's sternum. Pope looked surprised as he watched the blood starting to spurt out of his chest. In a daze, Trick got up and ran over to Pope and stuck his knife into his back. Pope and Bernfeld stood there, one foot apart, staring into each other's eyes, dying from mortal wounds. Trick pointed his Colt-45 at Price to let him know if he didn't retreat he would be dead too. Price realized it was over and stepped back and started walking away. From the edge of the top of the temple, he yelled, "You're a dead man too."

Bernfeld was able to stumble over to the nearest column and sit down. Pope was already dead. Price's bullet had gone straight through Bernfeld and blood was pouring out of the exit wound in his chest. He pulled a notebook out of his jacket pocket.

"I want you to have this book, Trick," he said in a whisper. "It contains all my contacts, their radio frequencies, and directions to their bases. With this, you'll be set for life."

"That's not my destiny, Jerry. Who do you want me to give it to?" Trick asked.

"Just leave it with Fang Wu if you don't want it," Bernfeld said barely audibly. A second later, the life went out of him, and Trick closed his eyes. His life was done. He had lived a long life for a soldier – he was forty-five years old, and he was right; he would never leave the Far East.

Trick picked up Bernfeld's body and started carrying him back to the jeep. Khun Sa was already waiting for him at the bottom of the steps. As he laid Bernfeld in the back of the jeep, Khun Sa jumped into the passenger seat. Then Trick jumped into the driver's seat and took off for Mong Yai. There was no communication between Khun Sa and Trick; they didn't speak each other's language.

37
CHAPTER

DAYS OF MOURNING

Back at Mong Yai, the first thing trick did was look in Bernfeld's little black book for Major Longenecker's radio frequency. He told major Longenecker that Bernfeld had died in a BCP ambush at Ho-Pang. He bought it and asked Trick when he could bring the body to Bang Yai. He told him he would be there within three days.

"What happened?" Major Longenecker asked.

"We were trying to secure the perimeter of Ho-Pang, when a division of BCP moved in. We had picked up about a hundred soldiers up north, but we were outnumbered and had to retreat westward. As he was giving fallback orders, Bernfeld took one in the back, sir," Trick explained. "He died a hero, sir; he was the last one to fall back," Trick added.

"O.K.," Major Longenecker said. "By the way, your paperwork went through – Lieutenant Hartland. I'll see you in three days."

Trick knew he had to make up a story about Bernfeld's death and he thought he had come up with a pretty good one. He wanted Bernfeld to be remembered as a war hero, not a mercenary drug majordomo.

Trick shouted out to the troops asking if there was anyone among them who spoke English. One soldier with thick glasses said he could speak English, Vietnamese, and Burmese. Trick asked him to be his interpreter.

Trick found Colonel Phuony and told him what happened. Colonel Phuony was very sad and said he had never served with a better man than Bernfeld. Trick needed to tell Khun Sa about the book that Bernfeld had given to him, and who Bernfeld thought he should give it to. Khun Sa didn't agree with Bernfeld about giving it to Fang Wu. Khun Sa said he wanted to pick his own new chief of operations. Khun Sa asked Trick for the book, and after some resistance, he gave it to him. After all, Trick reasoned, wasn't the whole purpose of the book to expand Khun Sa's empire, and who better to pick a new chief of operations than the king himself.

Trick started planning his route back to Bang Yai, Thailand. It would be a full day's drive if not more. He was leaving first thing next morning. Some soldiers had found some body bags in the back of the medical supplies truck, and they put Bernfeld's body in one. Trick would have liked to have held some kind of memorial service, but he knew nothing about the Jewish religion, and it would have just made it sadder anyway. Instead, he just went to bed early because he wanted to be fresh for his long drive the next day. He went to bed realizing that now he was the only American soldier still living who had survived An Loc.

****

Trick awoke the next morning at 0600 hours and wanted to be on the road by 0700 hours. He figured he had at least a twelve-hour drive. He was thinking about what he would do if he encountered any checkpoints. He drove the jeep to the fuel shed, filled it up, and walked over to the mess tent. He filled up on bananas and kiwi fruit and walked over to Khun Sa's makeshift command headquarters building to say goodbye. The interpreter told Trick that Khun Sa wished him a happy, long life and that he would always be grateful to him for helping him regain his freedom. Trick bowed and said thank you, and then he walked over to Colonel Phuony and bowed. The thought crossed his mind that most probably he would never see either one of them again.

As he drove off heading south he held his right arm up in the air and made a fist; it was his way of showing that he thought they were men of courage. Within an hour, he came to the hamlet of Man Kat, and then he headed southeast towards Mong Ping. He didn't take any main roads because he knew there were roadblocks, so he stayed on the back country roads. Sometimes patience is the better part of valor. The windy back country roads weaved through the mountains and valleys and the scenery was beautiful; if only there wasn't a war going on this place would be one of the most serene places on earth.

The dirt road he chose was rocky, and the fastest he could go was thirty-five miles an hour. Still, he figured he could reach Mae Sai before 1700 hours. Up and down and up and down, the dirt road followed the contour of the geography, and the bumpiness was starting to give him a sore backside. Finally, from the top of one mountain, he could see the hamlet of Mae Sai maybe fifteen miles to the southeast. He got off the dirt road about a mile from the village and started driving straight through the jungle just in case there were any border patrol guards there.

He pulled his jeep in between two palm trees and stopped. Ahead, he could see the main street through the village. There were Thai border patrol guards there, but surely they would see that it was an American in the jeep and let him pass. He pulled up onto the main street and waved at the Thai soldiers. They were surprised, but instantly they identified him as an American and let him pass by unscathed. Trick held out his forefinger to show them which direction he was headed in and they started nodding their heads. He still had a three-hour drive to Chiang Mai, and he reconciled himself to the fact that he couldn't make the whole journey in one day. He got on Route 110 and he knew he would make good time, but that he would have to stop at Chiang Mai for the night. Even from Chiang Mai, he still had an eight-hour drive to Bangkok.

He stayed on Route 110 for about an hour then pulled off onto a smaller road that headed southwest towards Chiang Mai. He figured he should reach there around dark.

He kept thinking about Lieutenant Price's threat. His two-year tour of duty was over in nine months, and he knew he had had enough of war and wouldn't re-enlist. He wondered as he saw the outskirts of Chiang Mai if he would live to complete his tour of duty.

38

CHAPTER

FAREWELL TO THE GOLDEN TRIANGLE

Trick arrived at Chiang Mai at dusk. He drove up to the bungalow that used to be their headquarters and found only a few Thai military officers there. He asked in sign language if he could spend the night there, and they said yes. He was offered some food, which he gratefully accepted, and then walked back to his jeep to get his sleeping gear. On the way to the jeep, some of the farmers he had met before smiled and waved at him, which made him feel a little more comfortable.

Back inside the bungalow, he asked if there was anyone there who could speak English. They said there was one, but that he hadn't come back from the mess hall yet. He motioned for them to show him which bunk he could have, and they took him into an uninhabited room and pointed to the bunk. He thought to himself that at least he should be able to get a good night's sleep. He put his bedroll down on the bunk and was unconscious within one minute.

Trick awoke at dawn and watched the first rays of the sun strike the landscape. He was glad he had awakened this early. He knew he had an eight-hour drive, which meant he could leave as late as noon and still be at Bang Yai by dusk. He wanted to take one last walk alone on the southern fringes of the Golden Triangle.

It was a brilliant September day, and he wanted to walk into the fields and say his goodbyes to all the peasant farmers he had met. In sign language, he showed the farmers that he wanted to smoke some opium. It wasn't clear to him why he wanted to do it, whether it was to pay homage to Bernfeld or because it was his way of saying goodbye to the Golden Triangle. He just felt that it was the right thing to do.

Two farmers brought him a pipe and a pouch of smoking opium, and then they left. Trick found a knoll that looked out over the poppy fields. He lit the pipe and inhaled. Nothing happened at first. Then, slowly, as he took another puff, the landscape started to change. The mountains in the distance were now a deep purple. The sky, which started out a beautiful pink and blue, was becoming lavender-blue, and the fields were becoming a golden-yellow. He knew such colors weren't real in a normal world, but he didn't care and took another toke. Now the clouds in the sky were forming into white feathers and the background sky was becoming more lavender than blue. The feathers started to dance, at first in an incoherent way, and then, as he looked harder, he could see the pattern. It was the Navajo rain dance! At first,

Trick wondered if Bernfeld's spirit was putting on some kind of magic show for him. Then he realized that wasn't it – this had nothing to do with Bernfeld. This was his own destiny, and he knew his future would somehow be involved with the Navajo rain dance.

He put the pipe down and closed his eyes. He knew he had to stop hallucinating before his long drive to Bang Yai. He sat there and he felt pretty sure that he would live through this war to find his true destiny back home in the mountains of New Mexico.

****

He walked back to the bungalow and said goodbye to all the Thai military officers and took all his supplies and put them in the jeep. With a salute, he took off to the south toward Bangkok.

39
CHAPTER

THE GREAT FALL

Two hours from Bangkok, Trick thought back to his medieval literature course at NMSU. He saw how in the story of Beowulf he was Wiglaf to Bernfeld's Beowulf. But instead of accepting the treasure (the little black book), he had refused it. He didn't want to be Bernfeld's successor. He felt he had done enough for his country already and wanted to go back home. One of the few men he respected over here was gone, and he didn't feel like fighting anymore.

When he reached the compound at Bang Yai, he drove straight to the MASH building and gave them Bernfeld's body for processing. Again he had to lie and say he had died in a skirmish with the BCP. His next job was to report to Major Longenecker.

As he pulled up to the officer's headquarters, he went over his story in his head again, so that there were no details that could be questioned later. He walked into Major Longenecker's office and saluted.

"At ease, soldier," Major Longenecker said. "Tell me again what happened."

Trick went through his whole story again, neither adding nor subtracting a single detail. He asked Major Longenecker what he wanted him to do now.

"Trick, I'm assigning you to Tactical Operations. Now that you're an officer, we need a bright young mind in our Strategic and Tactical Operations staff. You won't be seeing any more front-line action, son," Major Longenecker said.

The news gave Trick an overwhelming sense of relief. He didn't want to be on the front lines anymore; this was the perfect post for him.

"Thank you, sir," Trick finally managed to get out. He had also been assigned new digs in the officer's quarters.

****

By mid-October, Trick had his new duties down pat. He put pins on maps, went to intelligence briefings, stayed in shape by running five miles a day, and kept his mouth shut. He reread all the letters his parents had sent him over the last sixteen months, imagined what kind of beauty Little Dove had become, and kept his uniform crisp and clean and his boots polished. Let the tougher men do the killing, he thought; he had had enough.

It became more and more clear to Trick with each passing day that all the Americans were doing now was planning a decent exit strategy. They weren't going to win this one; they weren't going to keep South Vietnam out of communist hands. Back home, it was learned, Nixon had bungled his re-election campaign by spying on the Democrats – and he got caught and was forced to resign in disgrace. The soldiers over here couldn't believe it – what a loser. Gerald R. Ford had assumed the Presidency of the United States on August 9, 1974.

As October passed into November, he thought about all the peasant farmers planting their next poppy crop. All over the Golden Triangle, farmer families were planting their poppy seeds and irrigating their fields. This was the kingdom that Bernfeld wanted to rule, but God took it away from him. Maybe he aspired to too much.

Trick kept a low profile and did his job. He said as little as possible and never asserted his opinions too strongly. He knew his survival depended on Lieutenant Price never finding out where he was.

One day, he went to Fang Wu's and told him about Bernfeld's death. Fang Wu was saddened, but he had some news of his own. He had heard through the grapevine that Khun Sa had found another number two man, a Shan native named Farang. They discussed it for a while and came to the conclusion that eventually Bernfeld probably would have been replaced by a Shan native no matter how much Khun Sa trusted him.

Back at Bang Yai, Trick heard of a man who was working for the U.S. Defense Attache's Office in Saigon, and the rumors were that that was just a front and that his real job was the head of the CIA in Southeast Asia. His name was Richard Armitage. He had moved from the Defense Attache's Office in Saigon and was now working out of the U.S. embassy in Bangkok. Trick hoped that he would never have to meet the man.

By the start of 1975, the writing was on the proverbial wall. The North Vietnamese were winning in Viet Nam, the Khymer Rouge had all but conquered Cambodia, and the Pathet Lao were going to take Laos. Trick's job was to help plan a retreat with the least loss of life.

The war was over by April 1975. The day was April 30, 1975, to be exact. The North Vietnamese had surrounded Saigon and were demanding the surrender of the South Vietnamese Army. The American embassy was evacuating the few Americans still there and as many South Vietnamese as they could fit onto the last few helicopters. It was chaos. Thousands of screaming South Vietnamese were left behind as the last Chinook took off.

Major Longenecker called a briefing. His superiors had told him that even the Special Forces were going home. The war was over and we had lost.

Major Longenecker had known for months that this day was coming and had been preparing reassignments during this time. He started handing out the reassignments after the briefing. Trick opened his up. He was being reassigned to Fort Lowry Air Force base outside of Aurora, Colorado. This made him very happy because it was only a hundred or so miles away from his hometown. In his mind, he was already packing.

40
CHAPTER
RETURN TO THE WORLD

By mid-May, Trick was in the passenger compartment of a giant C-130 cargo plane on its way to Dover Air Force Base in Dover, Delaware. His term of enlistment was over in about a month and his soldier days would be over. Major Longenecker had told him that he would have the option to stay on once he reached Lowry, but Trick had already made up his mind. He wanted to finish college, settle down, start a family, and work in his father's business until he could start his own.

From Dover, he was scheduled on a smaller cargo plane that would take him directly to Lowry. Once at Lowry, he was granted a 48-hour pass to visit his parents in Galileo, and during that time he also planned to fill out some college applications – he wanted a four-year college degree.

The flight he was on was twenty hours, and Trick found himself reminiscing about his experiences in Southeast Asia. Would Lieutenant Price ever catch up to him? Would his lies to major Longenecker ever be found out? If they were, would he lose his GI Bill financing to finish college? All of these questions swirled around in his head as he tried to put them out of his mind. He was only twenty-one; he had his whole life ahead of him to put these ugly queries to rest. For now, he just wanted to sleep.

****

The arrival in Dover was uneventful. There had been a few coffins on board, draped with a flag, and on his way to the hangar, he looked back just long enough to see them being unloaded from the plane. The marines who did the job were silent and stern. They showed no emotion on their faces as they put the coffins into a convoy that headed back up the tarmac to another part of the hangar. Trick started to realize how lucky he was that he wasn't in one of those coffins.

He only had a two-hour wait before his ride to his final destination arrived. Six hours from now, he would be on Colorado soil, a hundred miles from home. He watched the clock on the wall tick off the minutes one by one; he couldn't believe how slowly this clock moved. Finally, it was time, and he boarded the smaller cargo plane bound for Colorado. Three more weeks in the military and his life would be his own again. All he had to do was keep his mouth shut, act sincere, and obey orders, and he would be on the threshold of a new life.

On board the plane were a few other soldiers and officers, mostly Air Force men. Some of them wanted a Green Beret to tell his story, but he said he was sorry but he was under orders not to. They bought it and left him alone. When the plane landed in Colorado, Trick jumped from the cargo hold to the ground and knelt down, and kissed it. A few of the other soldiers knew where he was coming from and did the same. Then he picked up his duffel bag and headed towards the officer's headquarters. He was to report to a captain Thomas Grissom.

Trick entered the officer's building and asked an Air Force private if he knew where Captain Grissom's office was. Third door down the hall on the left. He entered, saluted, and said "Lieutenant Trick Hartland reporting for duty, sir."

"At ease, Lieutenant," Captain Grissom said. "I see you only have three weeks left, and a forty-eight-hour R & R for this coming weekend. We can find something for you to do for three weeks, lieutenant. In the meantime, I'm sure your family will be happy to see you."

"Thank you, sir," Trick said. "I haven't seen my family in two years. I hope they remember me, sir," he added.

"I'm sure they will," Captain Grissom said. "In the meantime, I'll try to make your time here as pleasant as possible," he added.

Trick felt gratitude. He knew his last CO was an O.K. guy. When he got to his barracks, he got his mother on the phone and told her he was coming home this weekend.

41

CHAPTER

HOME ON THE RANGE

The drive from Aurora made Trick feel nostalgic. These were the mountains he had grown up with. This is what he had fought for. He started thinking again how lucky he had been to survive.

He reached Pueblo, Colorado, and saw the Wet Mountains to the west. He knew that just past the Wet Mountains would be the Sangre de Cristo Mountains, which would be on his right all the way to New Mexico.

As he crossed the state border, he started wondering how much of his experiences did he want to tell his parents. Should he tell them about his real role for his first year in Vietnam? That he was an undercover operative helping a drug warlord? Or should he make them believe that everything he did in the Far East was noble. He opted

196 | GARRET GODWIN

for the latter. Maybe if he stuck to his story long enough it would become true.

He pulled up his parent's house driveway, got out of the jeep, and walked to the side door. As he entered he yelled, "Hi Mom, Hi Dad, I'm home."

Running Deer came running from the den and hugged her son. "Welcome home, Trick," she said as she cupped his face with her hands. "We're having a special dinner for you tonight," she said.

"Geeze, it's great to be back home," was all Trick could say.

"Your Dad should be home in about an hour," Running Deer said.

Trick carried his duffel bag into his bedroom and put in down. Nothing in the room had changed; the same bedspread as when he left was still on the bed, his bookshelves looked like they had never been touched, and his desk was still in the same corner of the room. As he came back out to the kitchen, his mother gave him a large glass of iced tea.

"Well, tell me what your orders are and how long you're going to stay in the army," Running Deer said.

"I'm finishing up my tour of duty at Lowry Air Force base just outside of Aurora, Colorado. Once that is over and the summer is over, I want to go back to college and finish my degree," Trick said.

"I'm so excited for you," his mother said. "You went away a boy and have come back a man," she added.

"Can we eat as soon as Dad comes home?" Trick asked. "I'm starving."

"Of course. I bought some steaks and I thought we could cook them on the grill outside," his mother said.

Trick walked into his bedroom to take off his uniform. His clothes were still in his closet. He picked out a pair of jeans and a polo shirt, put them on, and then put on the pair of sneakers sitting at the bottom of his closet. The new clothes made him feel more like a kid again, and he liked that feeling.

He walked back to his iced tea in the kitchen and then walked out onto the deck and sat down in a deck chair. The deck had a northern exposure and a view of the Jemez and San Dea Mountains in the distance. He would think about his future plans tomorrow. For now, he just wanted to enjoy this reunion with his family.

****

Jackson's car pulled into the driveway behind Trick's jeep, and Running Deer came out onto the deck to light the grill. Jackson stepped out onto the deck and Trick walked over to him and gave him a hug. "Did they make a man out of you?" Jackson asked with a smile.

"Pretty close," was all Trick could think of.

"I want to hear all about it," Jackson said as he beamed from ear to ear with pride.

The steaks were done and put on the plates and Trick knew his father wanted the whole story. He told them about An Loc, his trek through Thailand, and his reassignment to the Green Berets. He just told them he was fighting communists in north Thailand, and eastern Burma, and western Laos. He told them he had a CO who got killed fighting the communists in eastern Burma, and that after that he was put in military intelligence. He told them that tomorrow he wanted to sit down with some college catalogues and pick out a school where he could finish college. His parents asked if the GI bill would cover any of his expenses and he said it should cover most of them. They looked relieved when he told them that and he smiled. He knew his parents didn't have much money, which was one of the reasons why he joined the service in the first place.

They sat up talking until ten o'clock at night. Running Deer filled Trick in on the little information she had about the neighbor's kids and Jackson told him how the business in Galileo was going.

Finally, Trick said he was tired and wanted to go to bed. He'd tell them more details about his experiences tomorrow. Jackson and Running Deer said they thought that was a good idea, turned off the lights, and headed for their bedroom.

****

Trick awoke at seven o'clock and he never felt more full of energy. He felt the need to be outdoors, so he walked into the kitchen, poured himself a bowl of Grapenuts cereal, ate it, and left a note for his parents saying he was going for a hike.

He headed west towards the San Deas. As he headed up the street, he noticed a few more homes had been built along the road his parent's house was on. One was a very big adobe house surrounded by flower gardens. On one side, the weigela were in bloom, and green and purple hummingbirds were flitting about the flowers.

Another house had blue climbing clematis covering a whole side of the house and butterflies were all over it. He finally reached the dirt road that headed up into the mountains. About a mile up the road he started to notice the native New Mexico wildflowers in the fields on either side of the road. The red Indian paintbrush mixed in with the Scottish bluebells, each about a foot tall, as far as he could see on either side of the road. He had forgotten about the wildflowers and their beauty. The white Achillea punctuated the red and blue landscape, and Trick had a crazy notion that if he could fly he wondered what the landscape would look like from a thousand feet up in the air.

He sat down on a rock and stared out over the fields. It came to him that what he really loved was trees and plants and that he should become a botanist. He liked plants better than people, so maybe that's what he should study when he went back to college. The more he let the idea simmer, the more it felt right to him. Botany, where could he study botany?

He had a new mission. When he got home he wanted to look in those college catalogues on his bookshelves for schools that taught botany. He started back down the mountain with a new purpose. He knew what he wanted to do. He couldn't wait to tell his parents.

42 CHAPTER

BACK TO SCHOOL

As he was driving back to Lowry, Trick was thinking about what his father had said. "Why don't you apply to St. Johns College in Sante Fe to finish your degree? With a degree from there, you can probably get into any graduate program in the country, no matter what you want to study. Besides, it's only a hundred miles from home."

Trick thought about that the whole way back to Lowry, and the more he thought about it, the more he liked the idea. There were all kinds of scholars there, many of whom could give him life-long connections. Besides teaching the classics there, they also taught science. Why not throw it in the mix, he thought.

He kept a low profile at Lowry and tried to avoid conversation. Captain Grissom was very nice to him and he let him finish out his remaining days with a minimum of duties. His fellow officers treated him like royalty, having served with the Green Berets, and they wanted him to reveal more of his story, but they respected his wish not to.

The day finally came and he was honorably discharged. He had sent in his application to St. Johns and the University of New Mexico and was waiting to hear back. He'd have to take a bus back to his parents' home after his discharge, and he asked his parents to keep a lookout for a good used car to purchase after he was home.

The day finally arrived and Grissom had a Private drive him to the bus depot. He bought his ticket and walked over to the kiosk and put his duffel bag on the ground. He was now a free man, an experienced war veteran, and anxious to resume life in civilian mode. The bus came, he got on, and he walked to the back and sat down. He knew he would never forget the men he knew who had died overseas.

****

In mid-July, Trick received a letter from St. Johns College – he got in! He had been leaning towards this school ever since his father had recommended it, and Trick thought he was right.

For the rest of the summer, he worked as a maintenance man for his father's old west amusement park. He picked up the trash every night after the business of the day was over, he polished the wood of the saloon bar, and he picked up everything in the streets that wasn't supposed to be there. He was only making minimum wage, but that was better than nothing, and by living at home he was able to save some money.

The rest of the summer flew by, and the next thing he knew it was the day before he had to take off for Sante Fe and St. Johns. His father was very proud; Trick had done an excellent job for him and Jackson could tell the military had taught him some discipline.

The evening meal on the day before Trick's departure, Jackson gave his son a three hundred dollar bonus. "You might need this for books," Jackson said as he dug three one hundred dollar bills out of his wallet.

"Thanks, Dad," Trick said. "I probably will need this," he added.

Trick finished his dinner and went back into his bedroom to finish packing. He was already more than half finished, but he had written up a checklist and wanted to go through it again before stuffing everything into the suitcases. When he completed the checklist, he felt relief that he was finally getting to finish his education. He was luckier than fifty-five thousand other boys who had served in Vietnam.

43
CHAPTER

THE COLLEGE

When Trick arrived on campus, he took his map, found his dorm, and walked into his dorm room. His roommate had evidently not arrived yet. He started unpacking his suitcases, taking over one of the dressers and one of the desks. He loved his room. From out of his window he could see the peaks of the northern San Dea Mountains. The College was located at an altitude of about 7,000 feet, and the peaks were only another 1,000 to 1,500 feet higher. When he finished unpacking, he decided to go for a run.

In shorts and a T-shirt, he started running on a dirt path that went up one of the mountains. It was about a thirty-degree incline, and he started huffing and puffing after a half-mile or so. He knew he could reach the top without stopping so he kept going. The trail curved to the left and then to the right, and he kept hammering out his steps, and suddenly he found himself on the top of the ridge. Sweat poured off him, and he leaned over and put his hands on his knees to catch his breath. After a minute, when he was no longer huffing and puffing, he looked out over the town of Sante Fe. He was happy that this would be his home for the next two years.

He walked back down the mountain toward his dorm, and as he entered his room he saw his new roommate.

"Hi, I'm Sam Newell," his roommate said as he extended his hand.

"Nice to meet you; I'm Trick Hartland."

"I'm from California, but I wanted to go to school here," Sam said.

"This is about a hundred miles away from home for me," Trick said.

They both could tell immediately that they were going to like each other.

"What part of California are you from?" Trick asked.

"Big Sur," Sam replied. "Near the giant redwood forests," he added.

"That's cool. I've heard about them and definitely want to go there someday," Trick said.

"Hungry?" Sam asked.

"Yep, I just did a run and my body wants to put the calories back," Trick answered.

The dining hall was full of students. They were going over their class schedules, eating, and socializing. After getting their food, Sam and Trick sat down next to two Arab-looking students. At first, Sam and Trick just talked to each other, but after a lull in the conversation, Sam looked over at the two foreign-looking students and said "Hi, I'm Sam."

"I am Mustafa and this is Omar," the taller of the two said.

"Hi, I'm Trick," Trick said with a smile.

After talking for a while, it became apparent that these two Arab students were no ordinary people. It turned out that Mustafa's father was the King of Morocco and Omar's father was the last monarch of Egypt, that both royal families had been friends for years, and Mustafa and Omar became such good friends they wanted to go to college together in America. Trick immediately liked them as much as he liked Sam and he realized that these foursome could have a really good time together.

As he met brilliant scholar after brilliant scholar in class after class, Trick knew he would have to buckle down and study hard to keep up with his studies. He was thankful that he was a year or two older than most of his classmates because that extra maturity gave him a little edge when it came to classroom discussion. And at St. John's, classroom participation made up more than a third of your grade in most classes.

He settled into a routine, where he had classes between nine a.m. and four p.m., then he would either run or play ping pong with Sam, hit the dining hall around six, and then settle in at the library for study. It was pretty close to heaven for Trick after what he had been through. On weekends, he would get together with Sam, Mustafa, and Omar and hit the Sante Fe bars scouting for cute chicks.

By the middle of his first term there, Trick had mastered his discipline for study, and because of this, he was able to devote more time for fun. Since he was the native New Mexican, he led trail hikes in the Kit Carson and Pecos National Forests.

By the middle of his first semester, he had a 3.5-grade point average and he knew his professors were excited by his abilities. Sam, Trick, Mustafa, and Omar all became fast friends and descended upon Sante Fe every chance they got.

There were other students there too whom Trick befriended. There was Tom, a Jesuit priest from Brooklyn, New York who wanted to bone up on his classics, Maggie, an elementary school teacher from Ohio who was pursuing a graduate degree here, and Roland, a nice kid from Maine.

The school hired local tour guides for most of the organized wilderness trips, but Trick was considered by most of the students to be on par with the tour guides because of his knowledge of the local terrain and because of his physicality. Everyone knew he had been a soldier, and he had the sculpted body of a Marine.

Maggie, in particular, noticed this and Trick could tell that she was interested in him. He wasn't ready to make his move just yet, however, as there were plenty of other girls on campus.

In late November, Trick turned 22, and he had enough time to go home to visit his parents for a day. He said goodbye to his friends, jumped into his Ford Rambler, and took off for Galileo.

He went over everything in his mind of what he wanted to tell his parents. His two new Arab friends, Sam, his professors. He arrived home just in time for dinner. His mother was setting the table and his father was reading the newspaper when he walked in. They could tell in a second that he was happier than he had ever been. After they sat down to a meal of enchiladas, Trick gave them the scoop. They ate up every word. They were so happy for him.

Trick's mother told him that Little Dove had taken off for California and her parents haven't heard from her in months. They were extremely worried about her. Running Deer told Little Dove's father that she would keep his daughter in her prayers. Trick couldn't believe Little Dove would run off like that; she didn't have a rebellious bone in her body when he last saw her.

Although that news tempered the joy of the evening a little bit, Trick's overall happiness tipped the scales for it to be a jubilant evening. His parents asked Trick if he had any career plans yet, and he had to admit that he didn't, but that he would like to work in the field of botany eventually. With that, his parents were satisfied and realized that their son wasn't wasting his time in college.

44
CHAPTER

PRECEPTORIALS, SEMINARS, AND TUTORIALS

Trick finished out his first semester with a 3.75-grade point average. His intellect was on fire, and he had plunged into his studies after the trip home for his twenty-second birthday with a new zeal and passion.

There were only three kinds of classes at St. John's: seminars, tutorials, and preceptorials. The seminars were the largest classes, with fifteen to twenty students per class. These were the equivalent of a "survey" course at other colleges. The tutorials were classes with only five or six students per class, and the professor acted as a tutor who could give students individualized attention. The preceptorials were the equivalent of lab work, where each student worked on an independent project. Trick learned how to excel in all three types of classes, but his favorite was the preceptorial, where he could work on his own independent projects.

For the spring term, Trick enrolled in all the required math and science courses. He wanted to study Euclid, and Newton, and Einstein in his math classes, and he wanted to study Lavosier, Plank, and Einstein in his science classes. These were men who had left their mark on the world, and the world would not have been the same without them.

As he became more efficient with his study time, he had more time for social activities. Sam, Mustafa, Omar and he always did something every weekend, and Trick enjoyed every minute of it.

One weekend they all decided to go to a bar on Washington Street called the Bull Ring. They got a little carried away and started doing shots of tequila. Everyone got drunk. Trick came up with a great idea. He would drive up the dirt path that led to the top of the San Dea peak that looked out over the town. Since he knew they were too drunk to walk it, he would drive. They all concurred that this was a fabulous idea and they all climbed into Trick's Ford Rambler. Trick drove back up the mountain, past the end of the paved road, and onto the dirt road that led straight up the mountain. There were ruts in the dirt road and the car rattled and rolled its way up the mountain, shaking its riders like some kind of amusement park ride. Trick was doing his best to stay on the road with all that tequila coursing through his blood. Finally, after ten or fifteen minutes, they reached the top. Everyone got out and looked at all the little lights that shown from the town; they looked like little stars.

"Well guys, we made it," trick said as he stumbled over a rock.

"It is beautiful up here," Omar said.

By some mysterious cue, they all turned around and faced the opposite direction. There was only a small glow of light in the far distance, which must have been Albuquerque. It wasn't much to look at so they all turned toward Sante Fe again.

"I don't think I've ever seen a more beautiful sight," Mustafa said.

"I think we should stay away from the Bull Ring," Sam said.

Everyone laughed and then climbed back into the car. Trick had sobered up a bit and the drive down the mountain was much easier than the drive up. They reached the College in twenty minutes.

****

This semester, Trick was maintaining a 4.0-grade point average. He had aced every test and every paper he had submitted. His paper on how Lavosier had discovered oxygen had received an A++. Mustafa and Omar gave him their papers to edit before they turned them in because English was their second language and they made many grammatical and usage errors. Trick was happy to help them because on the whole, their papers were quite good, except for the grammar and spelling. Sam helped them out too by typing their papers for them and putting them in binders that made them look "professional".

Trick never met a professor at St. Johns that he didn't like, unlike some of his professors at NMSU. The professors here were dedicated to teaching and learning, and they weren't interested in teaching a class with more than twenty students in it.

One of the professors Trick liked best was Dr. Richard Brown, a philosophy professor on loan from Yale University. Dr. Brown was teaching a history of science course that Trick just loved. Dr. Brown had given Trick an A for his first paper of the course entitled "The Influence of Isaac Newton on Modern mathematical Thought." Trick was given special dispensation in the class, and Dr. Brown almost treated him like his teaching assistant.

Outside of the classroom, Dr. Brown and Trick developed an easygoing friendship. They ate together many times in the dining hall and discussed scientific books when they happened to meet in the library. Their conversations could go on for hours and only once or twice did they disagree on something. Dr. Brown told Trick that he had an absolutely incredible mathematical mind and that perhaps he should consider a career in statistics. Trick told Dr. Brown that he was more interested in botany and was thinking about a career in the biological field. Dr. Brown told Trick to "follow your bliss" and he would be successful at whatever endeavor he attempted.

As the spring semester came closer and closer to an end, Trick never felt more confident in his life. He secured a job in the library and decided to take required courses all summer long so that he could finish up his degree in the fall semester. On his job at the library, he could study eighty percent of the time, and he realized he was killing two birds with one stone, learning and getting paid at the same time.

45

CHAPTER

A MAN OF DESTINY

It was the summer of 1976. Mustafa, Omar, and Sam had gone home for the summer. Trick was looking forward to being in their company again in the fall. Subconsciously, Trick realized he was looking for new friends to get him through the summer. He gave a friendly "Hi" to almost everyone who used the library, especially the girls. No takers there, however. It didn't matter that much to him; he had his books to keep him company. He got through the entire *Democracy in America* by DeTocqueville in less than a month. He couldn't believe a Frenchman could nail the American character right on the head.

On weekends, he explored the mountains that he wasn't that familiar with. One weekend he drove up to the San Juan Mountains in Colorado and took a day-hike. Another weekend, he drove up to the Sawatch Mountains just west of Colorado Springs and took a hike. But of all the mountains he explored, nothing came close to the Sangre de Christo Mountains, three-fourths of which were in Colorado and the remaining fourth in northern New Mexico. If ever there was geography perfected, it was here. He could spend his entire lifetime here and never see everything. From Hunt's peak in the north all the way down to Wheeler's Peak at the southern end in New Mexico, the beauty here was limitless.

By the end of June, Trick would be somewhere in the Sangre de Christo Mountains every weekend. Being a St. Johnny, he wanted to know more about their history, of course. What he read was fascinating. The Spanish missionaries had intermarried with the local Indians, and their progeny were half-white and half Native American. They believed in Christ, but a lot of them still held onto their native religion. The result was a hybrid. One of these groups was known as the Penitentes. They re-enacted the crucifixion of Christ every year at Easter, carrying huge wooden crosses on their backs into the mountains and lashing themselves to it for three days. The sect had all but disappeared by the end of the nineteenth century, but to this day there were still wooden crosses dotting the Sange de Christo where these men had mimicked the crucifixion of Christ.

The very words Sangre de Christo in Spanish mean "blood of Christ". Trick was fascinated by this and wondered if there was still a secret society of penitents still in existence somewhere.

214 | GARRET GODWIN

In late July, there was a seminar on campus entitled "Mathematical Correlatives of Newton's Calculus" that was going to be held in the Great Room. Some famous mathematician from an Ivy League school in the east was giving the seminar. Trick understood Newton's development of calculus pretty well and thought he'd go. His library shift was over at six o'clock p.m., so he had time to go to the dining hall to get something to eat, go back to his dorm to change, and be at the Great Hall by seven p.m.

Trick entered the Great Hall and walked near the back of the room and sat down. Sitting next to him was a guy with red-orange hair and glasses, about his age, who looked very serious. He was about six feet tall and very thin, and Trick had never seen him before on campus.

Since the speaker wasn't ready yet, Trick thought he'd introduce himself.

"Hi, I'm Trick Hartland," he said.

"Gil Bates, nice to meet you," the young man said.

"First time at St. John's?" Trick asked.

"Yes," Gil replied.

"Where you from?" Trick said in as friendly a tone he cold muster.

"I'm living in Albuquerque right now, but I'm originally from Washington state," Gil replied.

Trick didn't know why but he liked this guy. He seemed like a man on a mission, and he was very intensive.

"Here to bone up on your Newtonian calculus?" Trick asked sarcastically.

"No, I'm here for the mathematical correlatives," he joked.

The speaker was finally ready and took to the podium. He started off easy enough but soon was losing everyone in the audience. Mathematical equations filled the chalkboard, and Trick was probably one of the few who got what he was getting at. Gil sat there with a stone face, no expression except for that intensity.

When the seminar was over, there was applause but no questions from the audience. The speaker apologized for going over their heads.

Trick was curious about Gil, so he asked him if he wanted a tour of the campus. To his surprise, Gil said yes. Trick led him to the dining hall, the music building, showed him some dorms, and walked through one dorm's recreation center, outside to the soccer/football field, and finally to the library.

"I work here in the library," Trick casually mentioned. "If you want to borrow a book or get a copy of an article, just let me know," he added.

Gil smiled at him and said, "Actually, there are some books I need. If you could get them for me, I'd really appreciate it," he said.

"No problem," Trick said. He took out a piece of scrap paper from his wallet and wrote on it. "Here's my number," Trick said.

"It's getting late and I have to drive back to Albuquerque, so I better get going," Gil said.

"Yeah, I guess you better. It's going to get dark soon," Trick said.

The intense red-haired man started walking towards the parking lot and trick headed for his dorm room. With Mustafa, Sam, and Omar gone for the summer, Trick wanted to make new friends, and he didn't know why but he really like this guy Gil. Even though Gil was in Albuquerque and he was in Sante Fe, that was only an hour drive and that shouldn't keep them from becoming friends.

****

Trick was drawn to the Sangre de Christo Mountains like a magnet. He didn't know what it was, but his explorations there were like a need. Every Friday evening, he would pack his backpack with everything he needed so that he could take off at dawn on Saturday mornings and head north and east.

The only part of his job at the library that he enjoyed now was sending Gil the articles he requested. Most of the articles he requested were from computer magazines, but he also borrowed a few books. Trick signed the books out that Gil wanted under his own name he trusted Gil so much. And without exception, Gil always returned the books on time.

Trick was as fascinated with botany as Gil was with computers. Trick collected specimens of the wildflowers that grew in the Sangre de Christo. He pressed them into books with scotch tape and wrote copious notes about each one, where he found it, how many of the same plant were near it, altitude, and date. He had bought three oversize notebooks with blank paper from the bookstore to put them in.

Trick collected every kind of wildflower that grew at over five thousand feet altitude, including avalanche lily, alpine speedwell, scarlet gilia, purple Jacob's ladder, sickle top lousewort, tall mountain shooting star, silky phacelia, white globe flower, red Indian paintbrush, western redysarum, larkspur, American bistort, blue-leaf huckleberry, Scottish bluebells, rosy pussytoes, yellow western wallflowers, locoweed, silky phacelia, phlox, scalloped onion, purple Peavine, naked broomrape, wild ginger, shrubby penstemon, salmonberry, trumpet gentian, mountain owl clover, milkweed, deer cabbage, buckbean, mountain forget me not, common butterwort, leather leaf saxifrage, and Papaver alpinum or arctic poppy. It was this last plant that Trick was interested in the most. They were within the same family, although the arctic poppy did not produce the alkaloids that made the opium poppy famous. If arctic poppies could grow in the Rockies, why not Papaver somniferum, the opium poppy?

The summer session at St. John's was coming to an end, and Trick needed to spend more time in the library to write his finals papers. There were no "finals" per se at St. John's, only final papers, and he wanted to ace every class, so he really concentrated on his final papers. After this round of papers, only one more semester to go and he would be a college graduate.

46
CHAPTER

A WORLD OF HARD CURENCY

Trick aced all of his finals papers, and after he received his last one back and the school was in between terms, he headed back to Galileo to see his parents. He needed a break from the library and from the school. Trick knew that with his grades from St. John's he could get into any graduate program in the country in just about any subject he wanted to study. He was still leaning toward botany – plants and trees were his true love. He knew he had better start looking into graduate programs soon because he would be finished at St. Johns in four months. If he applied early enough, he may even get a fellowship. Since he had a new friend living in Albuquerque, he started thinking seriously about the University of New Mexico.

After Trick had been home a few days, Running Deer got a call from Little Dove's father. The prodigal daughter had returned! She had been incommunicado in California for over a year, and according to her father, she wasn't the same girl. Something terrible had happened to Little Dove while she was in California. Running Deer didn't get any more details, which left Trick with a lot of questions. He decided to go over to her parent's house tomorrow and find out for himself.

The next day, Trick walked over to Little Dove's house and knocked on the door. To his surprise, Little Dove herself answered the door.

"Trick! Come on in; I'm so happy to see you," she said. Trick could see right away that Little Dove was no longer the little girl he had played with as a kid. She was now five feet ten inches tall, with beautiful chocolate brown hair and brown eyes, and she had big boobs! She pointed to the white couch in the living room where she wanted Trick to sit down. Trick couldn't believe it: Little Dove had grown up to become one hell of a sexy woman. She was still very thin and it looked like she had some make-up on. Trick felt weak in the knees. Little Dove brought him a glass of iced tea.

"I see you survived Vietnam," she said.

"Just barely," Trick answered without smiling.

"I hear you're in school now – was it St. Johns College?" she asked.

"Yes, I'll be done by the end of the year," he answered without taking his eyes off her.

"It must be pretty difficult going from war back to school," she said.

"The GI bill is paying for most of my expenses," Trick said.

"I mean, it must be difficult to study after you've been shot at in war," she said trying to make the obvious clearer.

"Oh, yes," Trick said as he realized he didn't get the point.

"Trick, let's go out for dinner tonight, O.K.?" she said with a smile. "I really need to get out of this house," she added.

"O.K. Where would you like to go?" Trick asked.

"There's a new Mexican restaurant down off of Route 30," she said. "I'd like to try it."

"O.K. is seven o'clock O.K.?" Trick asked.

"That's fine."

****

The restaurant Little Dove had chosen had an unimpressive exterior, but the décor inside was beautiful. There was a tree in the center that poked out through the roof, and the tree's branches were decorated with little white Christmas lights that looked like stars in the galaxy from a distance. The prices were reasonable too.

Trying to be the gentleman, Trick pulled the chair out from the side of the table that Little Dove had chosen, and then he sat across from her. He couldn't get over how she had changed, and he was grappling with his feelings towards her now. Trick ordered a burrito with refried beans and Little Dove ordered a chimichanga with jalapenos. They both ordered Dos Xs beer.

Little Dove had a brown v-neck velour top that accented her upper torso. Was she conscious of how feminine she had become, he wondered. Trick had on a pair of jeans and a cowboy shirt. She had outdone him in fashion. Finally, Trick cleared his head and asked her some questions.

"Why didn't you contact your parents for so long and let them know you were O.K.?" Trick asked.

"I fell in with the wrong crowd, Trick, and I was embarrassed to tell my parents about it," she replied.

"What kind of wrong crowd?" Trick pressed on.

"I started doing photo shoots for girlie magazines, and the next thing I knew I was making porno movies," she said as she lowered her head.

"Porno movies!" Trick said, and then realized he had better lower his voice. "Why in the world did you make porno movies?" Trick asked.

"I was desperate for money, Trick, she answered. "Southern California is very expensive and I couldn't keep up the rent on my apartment, so I did it for the money," she said in a sorrowful tone.

"How much money did you make?" Trick asked quietly.

"Several thousand dollars per film," she answered.

Trick now realized he was looking at a sex kitten with a boob job.

"I changed my name to Jeannie Littledove because my agent thought it sounded catchy," she went on.

"Jeannie Littledove," Trick repeated trying to decide if he liked it or not. As he rolled that name around on his tongue he was conflicted. He felt both sorry for her and wanted to lick her from head to toe at the same time.

"I'm out of the business now, Trick, and I'll never go back to it. It's a dirty, seedy world, and I'll never to be a part of it again," she said.

"There are definitely other ways to make a living," Trick said before he realized he was sounding condescending.

"You're right," she said. "I got caught up in the whole LA glamour scene, and I'm sorry I did," she said as if she was looking for forgiveness.

"Well, it's over now and it's time to put it behind you," Trick said trying to be compassionate and uplifting at the same time.

"All I know is that I'll never do it again. I want to live a clean life," she said.

They both finished dinner and Trick wasn't sure how to handle himself. He thought she could tell that he was very attracted to her, but after the dinner conversation, he wasn't sure how to proceed. He was practically drooling over her, but after what she had been through, he didn't know what she wanted.

Trick paid for the dinner, got up and walked behind her chair, and pulled it out for her. She said "Thank you" and they walked out to the parking lot; he opened the passenger side of his Ford Rambler for her and she got in. On the way back to Galileo, he felt the vibe was right.

47
CHAPTER

CLOSING THE BOOKS

When Trick arrived back in Sante Fe to resume his studies and his job at the library, he couldn't wait to meet up with his friends Mustafa, Omar, and Sam. They were already sitting together in the dining hall when Trick arrived there.

"Hi guys, I see you all made it back to Sante Fe safely," Trick said.

Omar spoke first. "So good to see you, Trick; we were hoping you would return today," he said. "What did you do with your summer?" he asked.

"Well, I stayed here for the summer term, and worked in the library – it was pretty lonely without you guys," Trick replied.

Mustafa said, "Well, we won't let you be lonely anymore – before you came we were discussing what we wanted to do during the fall term," he said.

"Besides study?" Trick joked.

"Of course!" Mustafa replied.

"How was your summer, Sam?" Trick asked.

"Just great," he said. "I was a substitute teacher in California," he added.

"Classes start tomorrow," Trick said. "Let's go into town and celebrate our last night of freedom together," Trick said.

"Sounds like a plan," Omar said.

"Let's do it," Mustafa said.

"O.K. by me," Sam chimed in.

"O.K. Let's meet here at six o'clock and I'll drive us into town," Trick said.

They all nodded in agreement, and after Trick finished eating, he got up and walked to the library. He started there again tomorrow, and he needed to find out from the head librarian what his hours would be. He only needed fifteen to twenty hours per week to make enough money to cover his miscellaneous expenses, because the GI bill covered the rest.

When he got there, he saw his hours posted on the head librarian's door and he was relieved that he hadn't been given any weekend hours. After that, he walked to his dorm room to unpack for his last term at St. John's. By the time he was done, it was almost time to meet up with

Omar, Mustafa, and Sam. He thought of a restaurant he had seen just off the Palace of the Governors that he had always wanted to try. He would suggest it and see if they agreed. He couldn't remember the name of the place, just its location.

He started walking back to the dining hall at quarter of six. They were all already there waiting for him. He suggested the restaurant and they all agreed. They all packed into his Ford Rambler, and off they went.

They all sat down and told each other more detail about what they had done with their summers. Omar and Mustafa didn't have to work, of course, coming from royal families, and they traveled throughout Europe all summer. Sam described in more detail his teaching experiences in California. He didn't like it as much as he thought he would and said he wanted to go to law school after his senior year. Trick told them about his excursions to the Sangre de Christo Mountains and his classes during the summer term. His work at the library was enough for his travel money because his basic expenses were covered by the GI bill. They wanted to know more about this guy Gil Bates that Trick had met and was helping by sending him stuff from the library. Trick told them everything he knew, and when they realized he didn't know anymore, they changed the subject.

Mustafa asked Trick if he would take them to the Sangre de Christo Mountains during the term and Trick agreed he would. Trick told them there was so much to see that they should spend one-weekend camping overnight there. They were excited by this and said they couldn't wait. Trick also told them he wouldn't be able to spend as much time with them this term as last term because he was dating somebody. They all smiled and said "Good for you!"

Trick didn't go into much detail but said that she was his childhood sweetheart. After dinner, Sam wanted to go to a bar, but the other three wanted to be fresh for classes tomorrow, so he was overruled. They all got into Trick's Ford Rambler, and Trick headed back up the San Dea to St. Johns.

****

Trick's last term at St. Johns was devoted to literature. He hadn't completed his literature segment yet, and after the first few weeks, he loved every class. Learning how to read and write critically was one of the most important missions at St. John's, and his professors made that very clear. There were so many facets to literature that Trick had never been aware of until now.

Trick became one of the most vocal students in his classes. He made significant contributions to each class, and he knew he would be rewarded at the end of the term via grades.

Trick also continued to receive requests from Gil. Trick would go to the computer science magazines and make copies of the articles that Gil wanted. He knew that Gil was a very serious person and that helping him now may pay off someday.

Trick would alternate weekends between taking Omar, Mustafa, and Sam into the mountains and going home to Galileo to see Jeannie. It finally dawned on Trick that no matter what she had done in California, he had the hots for her, and he was getting signals that she might be hot for him too. With all these hormones stirring in the pot, it was getting difficult for Trick to study. Nevertheless, he persevered and was somehow acing every class.

Sometimes Trick would think about applying to graduate schools, but then he thought he could use a nine-month break before going on. The seed of an idea for a business was already starting to sprout from his brain, and it had something to do with poppies.

His outings with Omar, Mustafa, and Sam weren't as much fun as they used to be because Trick was becoming more serious about life, love, and business. He couldn't help it; maybe his father's head for business had been passed on to him. He also realized that he may have inherited another set of genes from his father – physical attraction to female Native Americans. When he left Jeannie to go back to St. Johns, he realized he would rather be with her. He wondered if he was falling in love with her, but he was so busy at school, he really didn't have time to think about it.

On his return home for his twenty-third birthday, Trick had received a beautiful birthday gift from Jeannie – an expensive pair of cowboy boots. She had gotten his size from his mother, and told her that she really wanted to get Trick a nice present because he had been so nice to her. Trick was absolutely delighted – they were black cowboy boots with silver on the pointed toes. Now he could really kick some ass! His heart was becoming softer and softer towards Jeannie, and he was really looking forward to finishing up school in three weeks to be with her more.

On the first week back at St. John's after the birthday break, he went to an Indian jewelry store and bought a beautiful squash-blossom necklace for Jeannie to give to her at Christmas. He afforded it by saving the money he made at the library.

Once again, Trick aced all his classes. The only damper on his mood was the fact that St. Johns did not have a graduation ceremony at the end of the fall term; he would have to come back to campus next May to graduate with his fellow seniors. But Trick didn't care that much that he was "ahead of the curve"; he had an idea for a business that he was young and idealistic enough to believe in.

48
CHAPTER

SCOUTING OUT OPPORTUNITIES

Trick went home for the Christmas holidays having completed the requirements for a B.A. from St. Johns College. He was unofficially a college graduate; all he needed was the sheepskin to make it official. That would be coming in the mail sometime in January.

Trick knew he would have to make the transformation from school to real life, but he knew that he had several advantages over his competitors a couple of years younger. One: he knew reality all right from Vietnam, and Two: he already had a plan.

The plan was this: why not grow *Papiver somniferum* on the slopes of the Rockies and have migrant farm workers harvest the crop? The opium could be made into morphine and be sold to legitimate pharmaceutical companies who could then sell it to treat wounded soldiers all over the world. He thought that if he got a Ph.D. in botany and did legitimate medical research he could get around the law about growing the opium poppy. He would apply to the University of New Mexico's doctoral program and start next fall.

Trick had been scouting out isolated areas where he could grow the poppies without detection. All he needed were the seeds to get the operation started. He found out that the McCormick Company, the largest spice company in the world, sold the poppy seeds right out of grocery stores. Trick thought surely if you can get the seeds at a grocery store, growing opium poppies couldn't be that illegal.

He wanted to start small; there was no need to rush. He would be in school at least another four years to earn his Ph.D., and after that he should be able to establish himself as a legitimate scientist.

He bought enough poppy seeds to grow one acre of opium poppies. In his explorations of the Sangre de Christo he had come across a very isolated area just south of Mariquita Peak where he was pretty sure his poppies would go undetected. He drove up there with a sack of black poppy seeds and found the piece of land that he was looking for and planted his seeds.

It was March, and he knew that he was probably planting his seeds too early for a fall harvest. This was his experiment to understand the growing cycle of the opium poppy in North America.

After his seeds were planted, he drew a small square on his map of the area where he thought his acre was. He didn't think he would have any trouble finding it again, but why take a chance?

When he got home, he realized he shouldn't put all his eggs in one basket and apply only to the University of New Mexico. In addition to New Mexico, he decided to apply to the University of Colorado and the University of Arizona. Boulder was practically the same distance from his home as Albuquerque, but Arizona would be a haul. He didn't want to be that far away from Jeannie, who he was starting to fall in love with. He knew the attraction was mutual too.

He knew he had better tell Jeannie what he was up to if he ever wanted to have any kind of a future with her. The question in his mind was would she put up with someone who may be breaking the law. He called her and asked her out to dinner for Thursday night.

****

Trick picked Jeannie up and drove to a Tex-Mex barbeque restaurant. He hadn't had barbeque spare ribs for quite some time, and he was really hungry for them. Jeannie ordered the spare ribs too.

"Jeannie, I have something to tell you," Trick started. "I have an idea for a new business, and I'm not sure you're going to like it. I want to grow opium poppies in the Rockies for medicinal purposes, and I've already planted my first acre," he stopped there to gauge how this was going over. No clues yet, so he continued, "I want to get my Ph.D. in botany so that people will know I'm a serious scientist who is doing this in the name of science, not some drug peddler only out for the money. I would collect the opium and eventually set up a factory to make morphine sulfate, which pharmaceutical companies could then use to make their own brand of morphine with." That was it in a nutshell.

"Isn't growing opium poppies illegal?" Jeannie asked.

"I'm not sure about the law if it's grown for medicinal purposes," Trick replied.

"I think you had better find out before you do it," she said.

"You're right. I better look into it before I go any further," Trick said.

After that, the conversation turned to how beautiful New Mexico was in the springtime. This year the cactus of the century was in bloom. This plant only blooms once every seventeen years.

"Did you notice the one at the end of your street?" Jeannie asked, happy that Trick's "confession" was over.

Trick had in fact noticed it. Not only that, he had taken a picture of it. Its bright red flower was the size of a baseball, and it was one of the most mystical plants in the Southwest – why did it bloom only once every seventeen years? Trick told Jeannie that he had taken a photograph of it.

"Oh, can I see it when it's developed?" she asked.

"Of course," Trick replied. He was happy he had gotten his plan for a business enterprise off his chest. Now he could enjoy the evening. The band was playing rock and roll music with a good beat, and he felt like dancing.

"Will you dance with me?" Trick asked.

She practically catapulted out of her chair as she said, "Yes!"

Trick let his legs go wherever they wanted as long as they stayed in sync with the beat of the music. He felt the tightness in his chest lessen as he abandoned his body to the pulse of the music. The silver tips of his cowboy boots reflected colored light, and he became mesmerized by all the different angles of light they reflected. Jeannie saw him staring down at his boots and just thought he must really like them.

Finally, Trick lifted his gaze to Jeannie. Her brown hair was pulsing to the beat of the music and her boobs were swaying to the tempo of the rhythm. Trick couldn't take his eyes off of her chest now. He stared and stared at it. He started wondering how wonderful they must be, and he realized that maybe she would let him see them, but he didn't know how to ask.

49

CHAPTER

GETTING INTO GRADUATE SCHOOL

I t was April 1977, and if Trick wanted to get into graduate school for the fall term, he realized he had better get his applications in. He was still leaning toward the University of New Mexico, but the University of Colorado was a good back-up.

He had checked his acre near Mariquita Mountain, and his opium poppies were growing like weeds. At least he knew his business venture was viable. He was also thinking how beautiful Jeannie had turned out. So what if she got into the wrong business; she was out of it now and was as sweet as honey. He knew he couldn't hold off much longer from making a move on her.

He still had to take the GREs in biology if he wanted to get into graduate school for biology, and at least he had signed up to take them in May. Right now, he wanted to think hard about how to pursue Jeannie. Even though she had experienced the underbelly of LA, she still came back home with a more cosmopolitan and sophisticated outlook on life. She learned that it was money that made the world go round, and Trick was glad for his experiences on the far side of the globe because he saw what life was really about too, and he was also just glad to be alive.

Trick didn't worry about the GREs. He knew he either knew it or he didn't and there was no sense preparing for it. For the time being, he just wanted to plan out his business and make Jeannie fall in love with him. Those two tall orders alone were plenty big enough for his plate.

Trick and Jeannie were falling in love with each other. Trick began to realize that he really didn't have to work too hard. When he told Jeannie about his plans for graduate school and his business, she became genuinely excited.

He took her with him on one of his excursions to the Sangre de Christo. He showed her his acre of opium poppies so that she wouldn't think there was something evil about them. Then they drove down to Red Mountain and Purgatoire Peak. Just south of Purgatoire Peak was a little town nestled in between two ranges where the Sangre de Christo split off. The name of the town was Angel Fire. Trick thought this a fitting name because as they arrived at sunset, the sky was filled with pink and red, and purple clouds that seemed to go on forever.

They pulled up the main street and saw a sign for a restaurant. They walked in and saw a long bar with animal heads mounted on the wall behind it. Rustic was an understatement.

The barkeep looked at them and said, "The special today is Buffalo burger."

That sounded good so they ordered two and a couple of beers.

"What did you think of my acre?" Trick asked Jeannie.

"It's a beautiful flower – I just hope you don't get in trouble growing it," she added.

"Like I said before – if they find them and want to know why I'm growing them, I will tell them it is for legitimate scientific research, and then they won't do a thing," Trick said.

"I hope you're right," Jeannie said. "Studying all that biology would be a big waste of time if you go to prison," she said with a smile.

"Not to change the subject, but I think this town has the best view of the Sangre de Christo than anywhere else," Trick said.

"Let's drive around a little bit, and see what else is around here," Jeannie said.

"Sounds good to me," Trick nodded in the affirmative.

They got back in Trick's car and started driving up the main street. About a block down the road they saw a white adobe church with an adobe bell tower. It looked beautiful and they decided to explore it. Inside were hundreds of red candles, all lit and close to the altar. It was fairly dark inside, but the candlelight cast an eerie glow all around. On the walls was Christ on the cross. The pews were made of very old dark wood that Trick couldn't identify. Finally, a priest walked out to greet them.

"How old is this church, father?" Jeannie asked.

"It was built in the late 1600s," the father replied. "It is a fairly well-kept secret," he added.

"Does it have any parishioners?" Trick asked.

"Oh yes," the father replied. "There are still about a hundred parishioners."

"Are there any Penitentes in your congregation, father?" Trick asked with curiosity.

"Yes, there are a few," the father answered.

Trick looked very pleased because deep in his heart this was the answer that he wanted to hear.

Trick and Jeannie couldn't think of anything more to ask so they just started walking around looking at the relics. Somehow, they wound up at the entrance at just about the same time and Trick just blurted out "Jeannie, will you marry me here, in this church?"

CHAPTER 50

FOR I AM EVERY DEAD THING IN WHOM LOVE WROUGHT NEW ALCHEMY

(John Donne)

"Oh Trick, I was hoping you would ask, I am in love with you. The answer is yes," Jeannie said as she threw her arms around him.

Trick stood there squeezing her back wondering how he had gotten so lucky. They looked over at the priest they had been talking to, and he already knew the question they were going to ask him, and he was nodding his head in the affirmative. He walked behind the altar and came back with his calendar book. They agreed upon Saturday, June 21, the summer solstice.

As they drove back to Galileo, Jeannie no longer held back her affection toward Trick, and she put her hand on his leg almost the whole way home. Trick's juices were flowing, but he wanted to wait until their wedding night to consummate their marriage. Jeannie said she could wait.

In the weeks leading up to the wedding, Trick took the GREs in biology and several weeks later he heard back from both the University of New Mexico and the University of Colorado – he was accepted at both. Now all he had to do was make a decision which one to accept.

He decided to go with New Mexico because in-state tuition was a lot cheaper than out-of-state tuition. That's what it came down to – the bottom line.

Trick now had to start thinking in terms of what would be best for both Jeannie and him. When Trick told his parents that he had asked Jeannie to marry him, they were both delighted and said what a wonderful girl Jeannie was. Trick had already given Jeannie a squash-blossom necklace for Christmas, but that wasn't an engagement ring. He would have to save up his money and buy her a diamond ring. He knew it wouldn't matter to Jeannie how big it was, only that she liked it.

Jeannie's parents were happy too, and when she told them that they wanted to get married in the small adobe church in Angel Fire, she sensed their relief that she didn't want a huge wedding with all the trimmings. She said she only wanted family and a few good friends there.

Fortunately for Jeannie, he mother had kept her wedding dress, and when Jeannie tried it on, it fit – close enough. It would need a few minor alterations.

Trick's job was to pick out a best man and some ushers. Unfortunately, he couldn't ask Omar or Mustafa because they had already gone back home. However, Sam was staying New Mexico until the end of June, and Trick asked him to be his best man.

By the end of May, most of the arrangements had been made, and Trick was looking for apartments in Albuquerque. He wanted a nice size apartment, two bedrooms at least, and near campus. When he found one he liked, he put an advance deposit on it for September, and the landlord agreed to hold it for him.

The days of June rolled by, and Trick could tell that Jeannie was very excited. He gave her the diamond engagement ring that he had bought in Albuquerque. She liked it and told him that she had bought him a gold wedding band.

****

On June 21, a caravan of friends and neighbors drove up to Angel Fire from Galileo. They all parked in front of the church and walked inside. The chapel was small – it could only hold up to fifty people, but it was beautifully decorated with lit red candles.

Trick took his position up by the altar, facing the priest. Sam was standing next to him and he looked so happy for Trick. Finally, the music started and he turned around to see Jeannie walking up the aisle. She looked stunning. Trick felt like he was the luckiest man in the world as he developed a knot in his throat to stop the flow of tears.

She joined him at the altar, and in that instant, time stood still, if ever so barely perceptibly. It wasn't just a marriage of flesh to flesh and blood to blood and bone to bone, it was also a marriage of guardian angel Carlos to guardian angel Quetzalcoatl. Trick tried to make this moment last forever because he knew, at this moment, he was invincible. The Carlos-Quetzalcoatl team was ordained by the stars and stood inviolable before this adobe altar in Angel Fire. It was as though Heaven itself opened up and let them see a piece of the glory that was to be theirs. The guests felt the holy presence too, all heads lowered as though their bodies could accept only so much of the beauty before them.

After the groom kissed the bride, time started again, but with a new clock.

51
CHAPTER
MESCALERO

In Mescalero, New Mexico there is a resort built by the Apache Indians. It is called the Inn of Mountain Gods. It is one of the nicest resorts on Earth. Mescalero is smack dab in the middle of the state of New Mexico by the east-west axis. But once you get there, there's no need to leave. Everything that you could possibly want is right at your doorstep – golf, tennis, swimming, and hiking.

Trick and Jeannie thought that a honeymoon at the Inn of the Mountain Gods would bring them in touch with their Native American heritage and show them how they could share that heritage in their marriage. They had both been living in the White Man's World for so long now that they were both afraid that they were neglecting an important part of themselves. Even though Mescalero wasn't Navajo but Apache, their bloodlines were related.

As soon as they got there, Trick and Jeannie never felt so at home.

They explored everything that Mescalero had to offer. But what they enjoyed the most was the hiking. For four consecutive days, after breakfast, they would devote a full day to each of the four directions.

On the first day, they hiked west to Tularosa. This was a short hike of only five miles, but they weren't out to break any mileage records, so they didn't care. The second day they headed south to Alamogorda. This was a twenty-five hike round trip, and it was the most difficult because they had to cross a ridge of the Sacramento Mountains. From the top of a hill, they could see the vast expanse of White Sands National Monument. They were tempted but decided against it.

The third day, they walked north toward Capitan. On their way there, they got to explore the Petrified National Forest. They picked up a few pieces of petrified wood for souvenirs and put them in their backpacks. The fourth day, they headed west to Hondo.

The fifth day of their honeymoon was rainy, so they decided to do something indoors. A new science fiction was playing in Alamogorda called "Star Wars". Trick really liked the sound of that so he convinced Jeannie to go with him to see it.

She wasn't all that excited about going to see a science fiction film, but once she was in the theater watching in rapt attention all those special effects, she changed her mind and thought it was wonderful. Trick was transported to a different world. As he was learning all about Jedi

Knights and The Force, he never felt so happy in his life. There he was on his honeymoon with the sexiest woman on the planet, and she actually liked science fiction. Trick knew after he walked out of the theater that this film was the beginning of a new era in filmmaking. He knew he would be high for several days.

Trick was slowly putting his past behind him. Occasionally he stumbled, like when he wondered how it would have been if soldiers carried light sabers with them into battle instead of just plain old knives and bayonets.

Jeannie could tell that Trick was in seventh heaven after seeing "Star Wars". For a guy who had just spent two years in Vietnam and two years in a tough college, Jeannie couldn't believe how giddy Trick was.

"I can just see you with a light saber Trick," Jeannie laughed as she swooshed her hand around.

"Don't laugh," Trick said. "Someday those things will probably replace knives," he added.

"Who was your favorite character?" she asked.

Trick had pondered this one before the question was ever asked. "Obi Wan Kenobi, of course," Trick said with a smile.

"He gets beaten by Darth Vader," Jeannie pointed out.

"Yes, but it was obvious from the film that he had accomplished everything he wanted to while still mortal, and he would be more useful to the Good Side of The Force as a spirit," Trick explained.

Jeannie didn't care to follow Trick's logic any further. "Well, I liked Princess Liea, of course," Jeannie retorted. "That girl had spunk!"

Trick couldn't disagree with that one. If Princess Liea was anything it was spunky. At least she didn't say she had a thing for Hans Solo, played by Harrison Ford. At least she didn't make him jealous. For the time being, he knew that his lovemaking satisfied her. They had made love at least once every night of the week, and there were no signs that she wanted it less.

The sixth and last day of their honeymoon, Trick and Jeannie finally had a hard time deciding what to do. They finally decided to drive out to Roswell, New Mexico, and check out the site of the supposed UFO crash landing site. It was only an hour drive, and they had seen just about everything in the immediate area to see so that was their decision.

Neither Trick nor Jeannie cared much about UFOs, but the incident in 1947 did put Roswell on the map as it were. After seeing "Star Wars," Trick really thought anything regarding UFOs could be possible. Maybe a renegade ship from a far distant galaxy did crash in Roswell in 1947. if it did, too bad there were no survivors or there would be a <u>real</u> story.

52
CHAPTER

JACKSON'S LIFE COMES TO AN END

By September 1977, Trick and Jeannie were set up in their apartment in Albuquerque and Jeannie worked in a flower shop while Trick went to school. He was taking a three-course load, and he had to spend many late nights in the library studying. Jeannie usually had a meal ready for him when he got home, and he was very appreciative of that.

On some weekends, he would drive up to Mariquita Mountain to see how his plants were doing. One weekend, he found the plants had flowered, which meant that they would be ready for harvest in a couple of weeks. He didn't have the manpower to harvest them, so he knew his first year's crop would go to waste. But at least he knew he could grow the opium poppies here, and that their growing season here was roughly the opposite of what their growing season was in Southeast Asia. After the seedpods died, there wouldn't be a trace of the plants because they were annuals and had to be replanted every year.

Near the end of his first term in graduate school, Trick received a call from Running Deer. The news was bad. Jackson had lung cancer and was given less than a year to live. Trick and Jeannie said they were coming home the next weekend to visit.

When Friday evening came, Trick and Jeannie jumped in the car and drove the hundred miles to Galileo. When they got there, Running Deer had a meal waiting for them. Trick and Jeannie sat across from Jackson and Running Deer.

"Why can't they do anything?" Trick asked his father.

"Because they say it's too far spread and that it's inoperable now," Jackson replied.

Trick wished cigarettes had never been invented. They had killed so many people. He himself was even prone to smoking them occasionally.

"I'm sorry, Dad," Trick said.

"I started smoking when I was a fighter pilot in World War Two," Jackson said. "They would give out cartons free at the PX because they wanted the servicemen to have everything they wanted without costing them an arm and a leg," he went on. "Back then, smoking was the height of coolness – movie stars smoked, presidents smoked, everybody. Unfortunately, I didn't quit like most people of my generation, and now I'm paying the price for it," he said.

"I never thought it would happen to you, Dad," Trick said.

"I didn't either, son," Jackson said. "That's why your mother and me are going to spend the last few months of my life traveling and having fun," Jackson said. "I've put the Wild West Show in a caretaker's hands until we get back – if we get back," he said.

Running Deer was very quiet and Trick could tell that she was feeling really sad. She had built her life around Jackson and now she would only have him for a few more months. Running Deer wasn't all that big on travel anyway, and Trick thought to himself that she probably wasn't even looking forward to it.

They stayed up late and Trick told them about his studies and how much he liked "Star Wars", and Jeannie told them about some of the quirky people she had met while working in the flower shop, and before they knew it it was after eleven o'clock and time for bed. This was the first night that Trick got to sleep with Jeannie in his childhood bedroom, but he was tired from school and the drive and didn't want to fool around.

In the morning, Trick and Jeannie drove over to her parent's house and told them the news. They told Trick that they were sorry and that they would send a fruit basket with a get-well card attached to it.

Sometime in the late afternoon, Trick told Jeannie that he wanted to get back to Albuquerque, that he had some research that he needed to write up. She said O.K. and when they got back to their apartment Trick said he needed to go to the library.

When he got to the library, Trick found a nice little cubbyhole and sat down. He knew he didn't really have to go to the library this night, but he wanted to be alone to think about his father, and how his mother's life would change once he was gone.

Trick would spend most of his weekend hours in the library studying, and he left most of the domestic chores to Jeannie. He felt a little guilty about it, but Trick never did enjoy cleaning house, and, after all, he was furthering his education so that both he and Jeannie would have a better life together. In addition, Jeannie didn't protest too much, so Trick figured she didn't mind.

After his first semester in graduate school, it was apparent to the faculty that Trick was a gifted student, and he was given a research assistantship for his second term. The research assistantship was perfect for him because not only did he not have to pay tuition, they were paying him to teach labs and to spend twenty hours a week working in the botanical garden. Trick loved this work and both he and Jeannie benefited from the extra money.

The bad news came near the end of March. Jackson had died in his hotel room in Zurich, Switzerland. He died on March 22, 1978. Running Deer said that he never lost his sense of humor right up to the end – she said he said he always wanted to die in a neutral country, and he got his wish.

53
CHAPTER

THE SHAMAN OF SAN JUAN COUNTY

It was the first week in April before Jackson's body was back in New Mexico. Poor Running Deer had to make all the arrangements. The memorial service was held the day after Jackson's body was back. Some old veterans from World War II must have seen the obituary and showed up to pay their respects. Jackson's brother from Colorado brought his family down, and Jeannie's parents came too.

The minister made a nice eulogy, talking about Jackson's heroism in World War II, and his grit and determination in starting the Wild West Show in Galileo. The setbacks he encountered trying to get his business off the ground, the trouble he had had with some banks, and finally his disposition. He was a quiet, serious man, and if he had ever made an enemy, no one in New Mexico had ever heard about it. He was a loyal husband and a good father, and all in all, he was pretty much the salt of the Earth and he would be sorely missed by everyone who knew him.

Running Deer was somehow able to keep her eyes dry, which was something of a mystery to Trick. Jeannie was a little surprised by this too. Maybe it was because Jackson had been cremated and his ashes put in a coffin. Jackson had always wanted to be cremated, and he was sorry but he didn't want his body cut up and used for medical research.

The day came and went, and Trick was now without one of his parents, and the thought occurred to him that now he was the male head of the family. He realized that from now on, he would be thinking and acting with a new sense of responsibility. In death begins responsibility. Trick thought that he was up to the task.

Trick got through his spring semester even easier than his first semester. Because of his extra duties teaching and working in the botanical garden, he was better able to manage his time. He learned how to schedule himself and he became more organized. Jeannie really liked this aspect of his discipline. The few hours he was home he took his cleaning duties seriously and didn't waste a minute. He could vacuum the whole apartment if five minutes and wash the dishes in the sink in ten minutes. He didn't dawdle and he didn't complain.

His faculty advisor had found a job for him over the summer. He could continue his research assistantship at the branch campus at Farmington, near the four corners.

They had a botanical garden there too, which was actually larger than the one on the main campus. He could work there part-time while teaching and taking his own courses. Jeannie was delighted because Farmington was much closer to home than Albuquerque, and she really didn't like the big city that much.

On their scouting mission to find a new apartment near Farmington, they had a little luck. A faculty member at the branch campus was going on sabbatical for a year and was looking to rent his home for the year. It was an old adobe house with a courtyard full of flowers in the center; it had two bedrooms, and a beautiful living room with a vaulted ceiling with exposed beams. Trick loved it, even though it was in Aztec, about ten miles northeast of Farmington. When the faculty member gave him a reduced price because he was an R.A. at the school, which made Trick even happier. Trick and Jeannie made plans to move in the first weekend in June.

Trick and Jeannie liked northwest New Mexico so much more than Albuquerque. They were back in the Rockies again. Jeannie started looking for a new job the week after they moved in, and Trick was establishing his new routine day by day.

Jeannie found a job in a bakery during their second week in Aztec, and Trick had established his class and teaching schedule fairly well by week two. The only difference between Aztec and Albuquerque as far as their routine was concerned was that now the mountains were much more accessible to them. The other nice thing for them was that almost half of San Juan County was Navajo

Reservation land, at least ten times the size of the Santo Domingo Pueblo.

Every day while Trick was working on cataloguing some plants at the botanical garden, he noticed an ancient man, obviously of some Native American tribe, watering the plants. Trick was busy, and he never got up the impetus to say hi to him, until finally one day in July when he wasn't that busy he decided to make the effort to say hello.

"Hi, I'm Trick Hartland and I'm a botany doctoral candidate at the university. What's your name?" Trick asked.

At first, the old man just stood there spraying some flowers, and then he finally said, "Zeeleaf Tso".

"Pleased to make your acquaintance, Mr. Tso," Trick said. The old man's skin looked as tough as beef jerky and was about that same color too. "Do you mind if I ask how old you are?" Trick asked.

"One hundred and one," the old man replied.

"Geeze, that means you were born in 1877?" Trick asked in awe.

"That's correct," the old man said.

"Well, nice meeting you – I don't want to keep you from your job," Trick offered as he retreated.

When Trick got home, he told Jeannie about his encounter in the botanical garden. When he told her his name, Trick could tell that something was registering with her.

"I remember my father telling me that the chief of the Navajo in the northwest reservation was a man whose name was z something," she said. "I'll bet that's him," she added.

Trick's curiosity was aroused now. He would have to ask Zeeleaf tomorrow if he was chief of that tribe.

"God, that man was born in 1877; the things he must have witnessed," Trick gushed.

"I remember my father telling me that the chief of that tribe was a very wise man," Jeannie said.

"I can't wait to talk to him some more," Trick said.

"Don't chase him away," Jeannie warned. "I'm sure he's a very private person. Make sure you tell him that you're part Navajo and maybe he'll open up to you a little more," Jeannie added.

****

The next day during his shift in the botanical garden, Trick couldn't wait to see Zeeleaf. He had so many things he wanted to ask him. The things a Navajo born in 1877 must-have experienced and seen! Trick had called his mother last night to see if she had heard of him. She hadn't – she only heard a few stories about her own tribal leader of the Santo Domingo Reservation.

Finally, an hour into his shift, Zeeleaf appeared from behind a greenhouse. Trick walked up to him and said, "Hi Zeeleaf, I forgot to tell you yesterday that I am half Navajo. My mother is Running Deer of the Santo Domingo Reservation."

"I know a few people from that reservation," Zeeleaf replied.

"Tell me, are you the chief of your tribe?" Trick had to ask.

"They call me the elder now, but once, yes, I was the leader of my tribe," Zeeleaf answered.

"Where do you live?" Trick asked.

"I live on the reservation," Zeeleaf replied.

"Do you have a family?" Trick asked.

"My wife is gone now, but I do have three grown children and many grandchildren," he replied.

"I am married to a full-blooded Navajo," Trick said. "We got married about a year ago," Trick added.

"Congratulations," Zeeleaf said. "I wish you many happy years together," he said.

"My father just passed away a few months ago," Trick said. "He died of lung cancer," Trick added.

"I'm sorry to hear that," Zeeleaf said.

"I'm working on my doctorate in botany at the university," Trick told Zeeleaf again. "I should be done in a few more years."

"Good for you," Zeeleaf said.

"Then I want to grow plants for medicinal purposes," Trick said.

"That's a very noble calling," Zeeleaf said.

"Well, I have to get back to work now," Trick said. "But I'd love to talk with you some more tomorrow," he added.

"I'm here almost every day," Zeeleaf said.

Trick was so happy when Zeeleaf basically gave him the go-ahead to ask any questions that he wanted to. What a treasure trove of wisdom he must be, Trick thought. He focused hard on his work so that it would free up more time to talk to Zeeleaf. Trick started thinking about all the questions he wanted to ask Zeeleaf. Where was he born? Did he ever serve in the military? In what year, if any, did he vote? Why was he working in a university botanical garden?

Trick brought these questions home with him that night, and when he told them to Jeannie, she said, "You know, Trick, you ought to ask him what he knows about plants. After all, he does work in the botanical garden with you."

"You're right. I'll ask him tomorrow," Trick said.

The next day, Trick saw Zeeleaf about the same time as he did yesterday. He approached him and asked him, "Do you know a lot about plants native to the Southwest?"

"I am known now as a medicine man for my tribe," Zeeleaf said. "I work here in this garden because there is always something new to learn," he said. "I know enough about the plants and herbs to cure most minor afflictions. There are several secrets, though, that must stay within the Navajo tribe, as they are part of our culture and heritage. Since your mother is Navajo, I will teach them to you, if you wish," he said.

"Yes! Please yes!" Trick said with excitement. "I want to follow the Red Path," he added.

Zeeleaf nodded in approval and said, "O.K. We start tomorrow."

54
CHAPTER

LESSON ONE

T hat night, Trick told Jeannie that Zeeleaf was going to teach him everything he knew about herbal medicine. She was excited for him because she knew that this would give Trick more exposure and status within the Navajo nation. Jeannie asked Trick if he had mentioned anything about his poppy venture to Zeeleaf. Trick said no.

Trick felt that Jeannie was starting to look at him through fresh eyes because a medicine man in the Navajo tribe was second in importance to the chief. In other words, it was a power calling.

That night, as Trick was making love to Jeannie, she called him her "big shaman". Trick loved that. He didn't know why, but he loved being called that. He felt imbued with a new sense of mystery and power, and, for some reason, it brought out more of his masculinity.

When he awoke the next morning, he couldn't wait until it was time to go to the botanical garden. He couldn't wait to tell Zeeleaf about his plans for an opium poppy business. He wondered how Zeeleaf would react to that. He gobbled down his breakfast, then hopped on his bicycle to ride the ten miles to the university.

After he was finished with his lab work at the university, Trick got his bike and headed for the botanical garden. He was at his station by noon, and he couldn't wait for Zeeleaf to show up.

At around two p.m., Zeeleaf finally did show up. Trick saw him standing over by the cacti greenhouse. As Trick approached him, he noticed that he was wearing different clothing today. Instead of his usual jeans and flannel shirt, he was wearing a black denim shirt with a bolo and suede or deerskin pants.

"Hi Zeeleaf!" Trick said when he was within speaking distance.

"Hello there, Trick," Zeeleaf replied.

"What are you going to teach me today?" Trick asked.

"Lesson one," Zeeleaf replied.

"O.K.," Trick said. "What plant are we going to start with?" Trick asked.

"None of them," Zeeleaf said. "Lesson one is about the nature of reality," he said. "God put plants on the Earth for food and for healing, but what I want to talk about is much more important," Zeeleaf said.

"I thought you were going to teach me about medicinal plants," Trick said.

"All in good time," Zeeleaf said. "But first you must be able to distinguish between what is real and what is unreal," he added.

"O.K. Tell me what is real, Zeeleaf," Trick said.

"The white poet William Blake was actually pretty close to the truth," Zeeleaf said. "He sought a triumph of the imagination over the senses and the alienation that comes with materialism. We live in the material of a fallen world. To be a healer, one must see the world correctly; plants are just the tool to affect one aspect of life – healing, and the real skill of the healer is in the diagnosis," Zeeleaf said as he grabbed the water hose and started to spray some yucca plants.

"Is that it?" Trick asked as Zeeleaf started to move away.

"That's it for today," Zeeleaf replied. "Let lesson one sink in for a while; when you're ready for lesson two, I'll give it to you," Zeeleaf said as he moved off down the row of plants.

Trick walked back to his station a little disappointed. He was hoping to have at least one medicinal plant thoroughly covered, and they hadn't even covered plant one yet.

When Trick got home that evening, and Jeannie asked him how his session with Zeeleaf went, she could sense Trick's letdown.

"Well what did you expect?" she asked.

"I thought we were going to discuss botany, not philosophy," Trick answered.

"Maybe he was discussing botany and you just weren't able to hear him," Jeannie offered as she set the table.

"What does the "imagination" have to do with botany?" Trick retorted a little irritated.

"All I know is that Zeeleaf is considered the greatest medicine man of the western Navajo tribe," Jeannie said a little hurt.

Trick didn't want to start an argument with his wife. He still revered Zeeleaf, and he knew he had to become more flexible to go with the flow of Zeeleaf's sense of priority. On the other hand, he didn't want to be a pushover either. He was a little confused, his hormones were acting up, and he wanted to make love to his wife tonight so he knew he had better shut up.

55
CHAPTER

A SENSE OF HISTORY

Ever since the dawn of man, scribes have tried to record the major events of their times, and the best of them did so in an objective way and didn't let personal feelings dictate their narratives. Even the Gospels are sort of objective, telling the story of Jesus from the third person point of view.

Having graduated from St. John's College, Trick knew what constituted good history, and he knew deep in his heart that Zeeleaf was living history and that from now on he wouldn't question him but respect him as much as any of his professors at St. John's if not more. He knew that in Zeeleaf's scheme of things, he was an absolute beginner, and he should be humble and be grateful for anything that Zeeleaf taught him.

It was with this new attitude that Trick met with Zeeleaf that day. Trick would no longer question Zeeleaf's teachings; he would simply be his humble apprentice. Zeeleaf noticed the difference in Trick immediately, which caused him to smile.

"Are you ready for lesson two?" Zeeleaf asked with a mischievous grin.

All Trick could say was "Yes, I am."

"Have you ever heard of Wovoca?" Zeeleaf asked.

"No, I haven't," Trick replied.

"He was a Paiute Indian who lived at the end of the last century and into the beginning of this century. He was a medicine man who had the gift of visions, and one of the visions he had was of the Ghost Dance. Tribal leaders from all over the West came to meet with him for him to explain his vision."

"What year are we talking about here, Zeeleaf?" Trick asked.

"This happened in the late 1880s," Zeeleaf replied. "In any event, most of the tribal leaders recognized it for what it was – a ceremonial dance, but the Dakota Sioux saw it as a restoration of the old ways before white man ruined the land. Sitting Bull and Big Foot were the Dakota Sioux chiefs who brought this vision of the Ghost Dance back to their tribes, and when they performed it, the white soldiers thought it was a war dance."

"Why did they think it was a war dance, Zeeleaf?" Trick asked.

"Because they did it with such fervor and because Little Big Horn happened only a dozen or so years before this, and it was still fresh in the minds of many white people," Zeeleaf replied.

"So what happened?" Trick asked.

"There was a massacre, which happened at a place called Wounded Knee in the Dakota Territory," Zeeleaf replied.

"How many were killed?" Trick asked.

"About two hundred, including many women and children, and Sitting Bull and Bigfoot," Zeeleaf replied. "You see, some things plants can't cure. I wrote a poem about Wounded Knee; I'd like you to read it and then think about what I taught you in lesson one," Zeeleaf said as he handed him a folded piece of paper. Trick opened the paper and started to read:

Wounded Knee

O Brave soldiers of the white race
You chose your battles well
When the Sioux wanted one last show of dignity
You sent them to their graves to dwell.

You thought one hundred braves and two hundred and
        fifty women and children
Were too big a threat, so you ordered their relocation and
        arrest
You were five hundred strong and willing
So you sent most of them to their deaths

In the process, you killed Sitting Bull
A noble warrior of his race
And sent Big Foot to his grave
To me, it was nothing but a disgrace.

The innocent children, you slaughtered with your guns
Who would have started a new nation
But instead, oh brave soldiers,
You gave them annihilation.

Was it so evil the Ghost Dancer's dance?
To wish a return to greatness
It was not a war dance
It was their version of salvation.

To give back some dignity to their tribes
After the white conquerors had taken from them everything
        of worth
Instead of giving aid and mercy
You drove them from this Earth.

"That's enough for today," Zeeleaf said, and as he started to walk away he added, "Why don't you start a journal?"

"I will," Trick replied as he walked away towards his station, and as he did so he realized he was caring less and less about plants. The poem that Zeeleaf had given him had affected him in a profound way, more than any botany textbook could. The poem told the story of an event that was a part of his history as a Native American. He didn't care anymore if Zeeleaf never taught him another thing about botany.

56

CHAPTER

OF POETS AND PROPHETS

Trick was beginning to see that his dream of a botany business was just that – a pipe dream. Zeeleaf hadn't taught him anything about plants yet, and he didn't even care. There were more important things in this world than plants.

Jeannie noticed the difference in Trick too. Gone was his quest to conquer the sciences; in its place, a new vision was starting to take shape. She didn't know what it was, and she wasn't sure whether she liked it or not, but Trick was changing.

In his spare time, Trick started to read the works of William Blake. Trick became fascinated with Blake's cosmology, and he couldn't believe a one hundred and one-year-old Navajo Indian would be the one to turn him on to him.

Reading about the four Zoas in "Jerusalem", Trick really took a liking to Los, the demi-god represents the imagination. He admired Los' attempt to build Golganooza, the City of Arts. The closest thing to a city of art that Trick had ever experienced was Sante Fe, with its new opera house and chamber music hall and St. John's College, of course. But he knew that even Sante Fe was a dim representation of what Los had in mind. Nevertheless, he admired Los for what he attempted, and he wanted to emulate Los and attempt to create a new world based on this image.

His excursions into the Sangre de Christo became solitary searches for identity. He no longer wanted to plant opium poppies up and down the Sangre de Christo; he realized he'd probably wind up in jail. He figured that if these plants weren't indigenous to this land, God probably didn't want them there. So he realized he needed a new dream – or business plan, for what he wanted to do with the rest of his life.

Trick also realized that he wasn't making any headway with Zeeleaf, at least not in the realm of medicinal botany. Maybe he had made some headway in philosophy, history, and poetry, but not botany. He decided to confront Zeeleaf directly and ask him why he wasn't teaching him the art of being a medicine man.

After the mid-summer break, Trick returned to his part-time job at the botanical garden and he saw Zeeleaf pull into the parking lot in his Ford pick-up truck. Trick couldn't wait any longer and he walked up to Zeeleaf and asked him point blank – "Why aren't you teaching me about plants?"

"You're not ready," Zeeleaf replied.

"Why am I not ready?" Trick asked.

"You were a soldier?" Zeeleaf asked.

"Yes," Trick answered.

"You've killed?" Zeeleaf asked.

"Yes, I have," Trick had to answer.

"It's not easy to teach the art of the healer to a man of war," Zeeleaf said.

"I'm not a man of war anymore," Trick replied.

"But I can see that it is a part of you," Zeeleaf said.

"You have grand designs of using what you know to further your own ends," Zeeleaf said.

"That's what America is all about," Trick said.

"I won't teach you until you become a different person," Zeeleaf said flatly. "I suggest you take a hike in the mountains and find out what you really want from me," he added.

Trick was speechless. He realized that Zeeleaf didn't even like him, let alone want to teach him everything he knew about plants. Trick decided to take Zeeleaf's words to heart. Maybe he did need to change his attitude; maybe he did need God's forgiveness. Maybe it was time he searched his soul. Maybe he needed a whole new identity.

57

CHAPTER

FROM ATOP MUSIC MOUNTAIN

Trick had no idea that getting in good with Zeeleaf would prove to be so difficult. What did Zeeleaf have against soldiers? Trick knew that he couldn't change his past even if he wanted to. He thought that his being half Navajo would make Zeeleaf treat him like kin. In reality, it wasn't doing a thing for him.

He decided to avoid Zeeleaf for a few days. There was no sense beating a dead horse. It was obvious that Zeeleaf wasn't going to budge until Trick "changed" himself, whether that meant asking forgiveness from God or just becoming a more spiritual person, he didn't know.

He took off for the Sangre de Christo Mountains every weekend. One weekend near the end of the summer, he ended up climbing Music Mountain. He found the trail getting more and more difficult, and the final mile was extremely difficult. He sat down on a rock, and he could hear someone calling his name, only it wasn't his name. He listened again. There it was again – his name but not his name. He set up his camp. He cooked himself dinner and then jumped into his sleeping bag in the tent.

It was dawn, and just as he regained consciousness, even before he could open his eyes, he heard the name again. Pulling his journal out of his backpack, he wrote this poem:

On Hearing Music Mountain

The mountain spirit here gently whispers names
If you hear him, do not be afraid
He lets you walk on the wind over snowy glaciers
To leave your old self behind
Then, before he tells you your new name
He'll tell you some secrets about this place, like

Over the timber line the world stands still – nothing ever
    changes here
The wind forms invisible bubbles around you giving you
    air to breath
Otherwise, so high above life, you would die
You are so light up here, you must ride the stern currents
    like a bird

And learn like a fledgling to glide.
(At night, the spirit rests, you are left alone
to stare at the stars above and below
and wonder if you are one
In dreams you fall, but never hit bottom)

Awaking, the spirit beckons you to a ledge and look down
Below, the clouds' mystery-play enshrouds your soul
As the newly-risen sun melts away your past
The mountain spirit whispers your new name (Zecharia)
Tears of cognition stream from the face of your past.
Thanking God for his patience, your soul soars in silence
And listens again for the whispered name – (Zecharia,
    Zecharia, Itiso).

He was given his new identity. Maybe now Zeeleaf would teach him what he wanted to know. Coming down the mountain, Zeke noticed the purple Jacob's ladder extending for miles over the fields, mixed in with white shooting stars. There were more beautiful plants in the world than opium poppies.

Perhaps that is what Zeeleaf had seen in him and didn't like – taking nature's bounty and trying to make a business out of it was hypocrisy of sorts – especially for an Indian. Zeke was not as sure of himself as Trick was, but that was who he was now.

58

CHAPTER

A DIFFERENT PARADIGM

Upon seeing Zeeleaf again, it was as though the world was operating with a new paradigm. Zeeleaf was open and friendly, and it was apparent to Trick (Zeke) that he was willing to teach him anything.

There were no barriers between them now, and Zeeleaf treated him like a son. Zeke realized it was the attitude of contrition that made the difference. He wasn't the upstart, cocky St. Johnnie with a superior attitude anymore. He was humble now; his bold plan for an opium empire was gone. The new Trick – Zeke – was sorry that he had ever served in the military. He knew that killing wasn't his thing. He realized that he was so lucky that he got his childhood sweetheart to marry him, that he should never take her for granted.

He realized that the guy who was really on the ball was Gil Bates. He had a vision for a tool that would probably change the world. He was happy that he had helped him in his small way. Maybe someday he could do a favor for him.

Things were now on track with his marriage too. When he told Jeannie about his experience on Music Mountain, she was happy for him. She liked the fact that Zeeleaf was opening up to him. She also liked his new name – Zeke, she never did like the name Trick.

So Zeke entered his second year of graduate school humbled, less sure of himself, looking for a new plan. He wasn't capable of envisioning the future anymore, and he realized that in part his future would be governed by what Zeeleaf taught him. He saw that he would have to turn the tables on Zeeleaf if he wanted to understand him. He would have to ask the questions; he would have to probe into Zeeleaf's past, plumb his depth of experiences and find out what made him tick.

One day soon after his return to school, he asked him, "What do you believe, Zeeleaf?"

"I believe that every man must follow the path that is right for him," he said.

"Have you ever taken any wrong turns?" Zeke asked.

"Of course I have," he replied. "I was a Penitente when I was young," he added.

"You were a Penitente?" Zeke asked with surprise.

"Around the turn of the century, there were only a few of us left, because the church officially discouraged our activities," he replied.

"You mean you actually carried a cross into the mountains and mock-crucified yourself?" Zeke asked.

"Yes, I did," he replied. "I am the last surviving Penitente that I am aware of," he added.

This statement sent Zeke's mind in motion. Standing in front of him was the last surviving member of a cult that had been famous in the Southwest. The sense of history pervaded his thinking. He was now beginning to be in awe of this man.

"I also knew Wovoca," Zeeleaf added.

"You knew Wovoca?" Zeke exclaimed.

"Yes, my father and his father were friends," Zeeleaf said.

At this point, Zeke knew he was speaking to a living legend, and he understood now why Zeeleaf didn't like him at first. His haughty attitude was a joke to Zeeleaf. Trick's transformation into Zecharia was necessary before Zeeleaf would impart his world of knowledge to him.

59
CHAPTER

CARLOS SAYS GOODBYE

One night in his dreams, Carlos appeared to Zeke. In his semiconscious state, Zeke recognized Carlos as his imaginary friend from childhood. In this dream, Carlos told Zeke that he was leaving and that a new "friend" was coming to take his place. Carlos told him that he had served his purpose and that a more powerful "protector" was needed for him to assume his new identity as Zecharia Itiso. When Zeke asked Carlos who it was, he said that he could not tell him his name, because God did not want him to know it yet.

When he awoke in the morning, he told Jeannie about the dream. She said she could remember Trick's imaginary friend from childhood and said that she would miss him, that she always liked Carlos.

Zeke could never quite get a handle on Quetzalcoatl, Jeannie's guardian angel. All he knew is that he was very powerful, and although he couldn't protect her when she ran away to Los Angeles, he helped her come back to her senses and return home.

There were going to be some extreme changes in Zeke's life. He was losing his guardian angel, and for the first time in his life, he was afraid. The changes that he was going through were more scary than Vietnam.

Jeannie told him to be sure and pray and ask God for the right direction. He could no longer ask his father on Earth for advice, but he could ask his Father in Heaven. He should also pray for his mother, who had retreated into a life of solitude with other Navajo widows.

In the back of his mind, he "felt" that Zeeleaf would help him find a new guardian angel. He didn't know how long it would take, but he was sure that this was his destiny. In the meantime, Jeannie was his rock. She reassured him that everything that was happening to him was good and that in the end, they would be happier together. That's really all that mattered to him.

****

When he got together with Zeeleaf, Zeeleaf "felt" the absence of Carlos. He asked Zeke if anything significant had happened to him recently.

"Yes," Zeke said. "I had a dream and my imaginary friend from childhood, who was really my guardian angel, told me that I would be getting a new guardian angel."

"It's good that he told you," Zeeleaf said.

"Who am I becoming?" Zeke asked.

"I really don't know yet," Zeeleaf replied. "It's possible you are becoming a prophet," he added.

"A prophet!" Zeke repeated.

"You heard your new name – Zechariah – from the spirits of the mountain, didn't you?" Zeeleaf asked. "That sounds like a prophet to me," he added.

"Maybe you're right," Zeke said.

60

CHAPTER

QUETZALCOATL WANTS THE AMERICAN DREAM

It was time for Jeannie to meet Zeeleaf. Jeannie had heard all of Zeke's stories second-hand, and she was tired of it. She wanted to meet the legend face-to-face.

One day at the botanical garden, Zeke asked Zeeleaf if he could come over for dinner that night. When he accepted, Zeke was delighted. He thanked Zeeleaf, and, after giving him directions, thanked him for being willing to be his guest.

That evening, at seven o'clock, Zeeleaf arrived at their door. Zeke was closest to the door so he answered it.

"Hi Zeeleaf, welcome, please come on in," Zeke said. Zeke led Zeeleaf to the kitchen where Jeannie was still preparing the meal. "Zeeleaf, I'd like you to meet my wife Jeannie," Zeke said.

The wizened old man extended his hand and said, "How do you do."

"It's so nice to finally meet you," Jeannie said. "I've heard so much about you, I had to meet you for myself," Jeannie said.

They all sat down at the dining room table and Zeke asked Zeeleaf if he'd like anything to drink.

"Water would be fine," Zeeleaf replied.

Jeannie was acting like a schoolgirl in front of Zeeleaf. She had heard stories about this man since early childhood, and now she sat across from him face-to-face. She had so many questions she didn't know where to begin.

"Zeeleaf, I understand you were once a Penitente," she said.

"Yes, I was," Zeeleaf admitted calmly. "Back before the turn of the century."

"I also understand you knew Wovoca," Jeannie kept prying.

"Yes, my father knew his father and we had a special bond," Zeeleaf replied.

"You are living history!" Jeannie exclaimed.

"Any man who has lived as long as I have is living history," Zeeleaf replied.

"Tell me about Wovoca," Jeannie implored.

"Well, first of all, he was nicest man you'd ever want to meet," Zeeleaf replied. "He came from a long line of medicine men whose lineage goes back to the dawn of the Paiute tribe," he added. "Of course, he considered his most important mission was to help his own people," Zeeleaf went on. "He advocated turning back to the old ways, not war."

"So he was misunderstood," Zeke asked.

"Most definitely," Zeeleaf replied. "His vision of the Ghost Dance was not an advocation to go to war with the white man, it was a cleansing ceremony to return to the old ways before white man ever arrived," Zeeleaf said.

"Why did the white man interpret it as a war dance?" Jeannie asked.

"Because that's how the white man wanted to interpret it," Zeeleaf replied. "They just needed an excuse to try and annihilate them," he added.

"It's sickening," Zeke noted.

"I agree," Jeannie added.

"After that, every Indian nation in the West just wanted to keep a low profile," Zeeleaf said.

The dinner was finished and Zeke suggested that they have dessert in the courtyard. Jeannie put some ice cream in three dishes and took them out to the courtyard. The sun was a red fireball sitting halfway over the mountains, and the sky was a perfect pink and blue.

Finally, Zeeleaf turned the tables on Zeke and Jeannie. After taking his first bite of ice cream, he looked at Jeannie and asked, "What do you want out of life?"

"I want a nice adobe house somewhere in the mountains and two or three kids," she replied without hesitation. "I want Trick, I mean Zeke, to get his Ph.D. in botany and start his own botanical garden," she added.

"That's what I want, too,' Zeke confirmed. "But I'd like to get that adobe house first before having kids," he joked.

"You want the American dream, then," Zeeleaf laughed. "Good for you – it's a noble dream," he said. "I will teach you anything you want to know about plants," Zeeleaf said. "But as you probably realize by now, growing illegal plants will not get you the American dream – it will get you the American nightmare," he said.

"I know, I know," Zeke said. "I've given up on that idea," he added. "I think that my experiences in Vietnam twisted my thinking," he added.

"Good – we will start on a fresh course tomorrow, but I really need to be going now – I'm tired," Zeeleaf said. "Thank you so much for the wonderful dinner," he said as he got up and walked slowly toward the door.

"Let me walk you to your truck," Zeke offered. What Jeannie had said about wanting a house in the mountains and two or three kids was still reverberating in his head. He felt stupid that he had never asked that question – what do you want? He was so busy studying and planning their future for them that he forgot to do to the source – his wife – to see if their dreams were the same. Dumb. Dumb. Dumb.

61
CHAPTER

IT TAKES TWO TO TANGO

One day, after their shifts at the botanical gardens, was over, Zeeleaf told Zeke that he wanted to show him something. Zeke called Jeannie to let her know that he would be home late. Then they jumped into Zeeleaf's truck and took off for southwestern Colorado.

Zeeleaf drove them to where the Anasazi cliff-dwellers used to live. Zeeleaf told Zeke that Anasazi in Navajo means, "alien ancient ones". He told Zeke that the Anisazi Indians were the ancestors of the Pueblo, Navajo, and Apache Indian tribes.

"The Anasazi told of the great White-Robed Master who once walked amongst them," Zeeleaf said. "His eyes were grey-green like the ocean and he performed many miracles among the people," Zeeleaf added.

"Are you trying to tell me that Christ was here in the Americas?" Zeke asked.

"The story has been handed down through the generations by more than twenty tribes," Zeeleaf replied. "There were once great civilizations in this part of the world, and most of them knew of the Holy Master," he added.

"Why haven't I heard of this before?" Zeke asked.

"I guess your father wasn't a Mormon and your mother wanted off the reservation," Zeeleaf answered.

"I'm walking on holy ground then, aren't I, Zeeleaf?" Zeke asked.

"If you believe the legends, the answer is yes," Zeeleaf replied.

It was getting late, and Zeke and Zeeleaf headed back to the truck. They were only an hour away from Aztec, but they had been exploring a totally different world. The only evidence of this civilization was what was left in the rocks and cliff-dwellings.

As Zeke sat passively in the passenger seat, he made up his mind that he was going to read the Book of Mormon. He wasn't interested in mainstream Christianity; all he cared about was the truth. If Christ did have a ministry in Western America, he wanted to know about it and possibly join the Mormon Church.

****

When Zeke got home, he tried to explain everything Zeeleaf had told him to Jeannie.

"Do you know anything about the Anasazi?" Zeke asked her.

"Only that they lived a long time ago and are a dead civilization now," Jeannie replied.

"They aren't dead," Zeke countered. "Their blood is running through your veins and mine," he retorted. "The Apache, Navajo, and Pueblo are all descended from the Anasazi," Zeke said.

"I don't care about dead people, Zeke, only the living," Jeannie said with her temper getting the best of her.

"Well, that's not all. The Anasazi knew Jesus," Zeke said with passion. "I need to study the Book of Mormon," Zeke declared as though something divine had been revealed to him.

"You can study any book you want to Zeke," Jeannie said, her temper subsiding. "But please don't give up on your Ph.D. in botany. I want to be married to a plant doctor, not a latter-day saint," she said with a hint of sarcasm.

Zeke didn't know what to say. He knew he would follow his heart no matter where it led him, and if who he was becoming didn't jive with Quetzalcoatl's dream, perhaps the marriage wouldn't last.

He didn't care. He was entering into a new world of discovery with Zeeleaf as his guide. If there was one thing that St. John's had taught him, it was to always search for the truth. He had to know more about Jesus in America.

He realized that every mountain he had ever climbed, every path that he had ever walked on, and every pristine Aspen forest that he had ever hiked through could also have been explored by Jesus Christ the Savior. He wouldn't let go until he knew the truth.

62
CHAPTER

FLASHBACK

Zeke was having difficulty focusing on his studies. The world that Zeeleaf was opening up to him made botany seem unimportant. He finally started questioning his ability to persevere through to his Ph.D. His passion for plants was being superseded by his passion for history and the spiritual forces at work in the world. He had learned that being a medicine man was much more than just knowing how to use plants to heal people; rather, it was a whole cosmology that Zeke was just beginning to crack the surface of. He shifted from being a seeker of knowledge to a seeker of truth, and he knew deep down that Jeannie was none the happier for it.

The more he wanted to investigate this new world, the more he could feel his past weighing him down. It was like trying to fly with dumbbells attached to his feet. Even with a new name, and the possibility for a completely new identity, his past was there, each image of it engraved somewhere in the cells of his brain. He thought about Bernfeld. Was it his destiny not to come home from Vietnam? He wondered if Agent Red would ever find out where he was and slit his throat in the middle of the night. He never told Jeannie about Agent Red. Was that a mistake?

He heard on the news how Pol Pot had made Cambodia one big killing field. He wished now that the Special Forces had wiped him from the face of the Earth when they had the chance. How could he ever forget these things? He wondered if he should become a junkie and destroy his mind; at least the past would be gone with it. Each day it became harder to persevere with his studies. Each day he felt heavier and more burdened, almost like a Penitente carrying a thousand-pound cross on his back.

He got through his third semester of graduate school with the minimum required G.P.A. to stay in the program – a 3.0, all Bs. Fortunately, he had done much better his first year, so these grades wouldn't pull him down that much. Jeannie was starting to get on his case about his grades, and told him not to let Zeeleaf destroy his future. She pointed out that Zeeleaf was pure Navajo, and he couldn't care less what it took to make it in the white man's world.

At least Jeannie knew that Zeke's future science career was in trouble. There were countless students across the country who didn't bother to mention to their spouse that they were having academic difficulties. At least Zeke owned up to the fact to his wife that his motivation was wavering.

For her part, Jeannie tried to be more supportive, loosening the tether around Zeke's neck a bit to let him stay late at the library without coming down on him. Zeke appreciated that.

Secretly, of course, he wasn't staying late at the library, he was becoming Zeeleaf's apprentice. One day after their shifts at the botanical garden, Zeeleaf invited Zeke home with him. Zeeleaf lived in the southwestern corner of San Juan County in an abandoned mining shack. There were dream catchers hanging from the beams of his front porch and Navajo pottery containing various plants all around the house.

Inside, the wood floors were covered with Navajo throw rugs, and there was an old rocking chair in one corner of the living room. An old radio sat on the mantle where an old iron wood-burning stove was placed in the chimney.

"As you can see, I live a simple life," Zeeleaf said.

Zeke wasn't surprised. He half expected that Zeeleaf lived like this, and hadn't bought into the capitalistic notion that more is better. What he didn't expect was that his children and grandchildren would let him live like this. Why hadn't any of the children or grandchildren taken him in? Zeke decided to ask him the question.

"Zeeleaf, why don't you live with one of your children or grandchildren?"

"I didn't want to impose myself on anybody, not even my own children," Zeeleaf replied. "I like living out here in the desert by myself. If I lived with any of my children, they would expect me to constantly be entertaining my grandchildren. I'm not like that," he added. Then he turned the tables on Zeke. "Are you planning to start a family with your wife?" he asked.

"It's something we haven't discussed much," Zeke replied. "If it happens it happens, if it doesn't it doesn't," he added.

"Having children in these days is difficult," Zeeleaf said. "I can tell you are like me – a seeker of the truth," he added.

"Yes I am, more than you know, Zeeleaf," Zeke replied. In the back of his mind, Zeke wondered if he should tell Zeeleaf about the life he had given up in Southeast Asia, that he could have been a wealthy drug runner in the backwoods of Burma. He decided against it. That had nothing to do with his life now.

"I like seekers of the truth," Zeeleaf declared. "Zeke and ye shall find. I would never have invited you to my home if you weren't one," he added as he put a teapot on the stove.

"Tell me more about Wovoca," Zeke asked.

"O.K., but with him, it's difficult to know where to start," Zeeleaf replied as he took two teabags out of a cupboard. "He claims he actually met Jesus in 1896," Zeeleaf said with a wry smile. I never knew quite what to make of that."

"Are you serious? Where did he meet Jesus?" Zeke asked.

"On a Paiute reservation in Nevada," Zeeleaf replied.

"Did you believe him?" Zeke asked.

"I had no reason to disbelieve him," Zeeleaf replied. "If Jesus appeared to Joseph Smith in 1820, I see no reason why he couldn't appear to Wovoca in 1896," he added.

Zeke heard the sincerity in Zeeleaf's voice and knew that he was telling the truth. If he had been raised Mormon he knew all this wouldn't seem so amazing to him. As it was, he had a lot of studying to do – and not about plants. He was starting to come to terms with the fact that he would never be a doctor of botany. What he was learning was far more fascinating, and he knew he had to pursue it no matter where it led him. He thanked Zeeleaf for the tea and for showing him his home, such as it was, hopped in his car, and started driving back to Aztec. He resolved to go back to Mariquito Mountain to say goodbye to his dream of starting an opium business, and as he did so, he realized he needed a completely new business plan.

CHAPTER 63

POPPY REDUX

The plants had already flowered and the wind had scattered a few seeds, but on the whole, the field looked like a withered dream. It was like one of those historical sites that nobody had given a damn about, and as the decades rolled on, there was nothing worth rehabilitating to a pristine condition.

Hell, Zeke wasn't even the same person who had planted these seeds, and like Trick, the vestige of what once was was all but dead. Trick lived on a little bit in Zeke, but the opium poppies did not live on in anything. Nature had taken its course, and the Scottish bluebells and purple Jacob's ladder and white shooting stars had taken over the field, and Zeke saw that the field was still beautiful, but it was no longer his field of dreams. Perhaps it was just as well that the opium poppies died off, just as Trick had.

Zeke decided to give up his dream of being an opium poppy grower. Now he was focused on how to grow Monstera fruit and plantains in the soil of the Southwest. These two fruits were tropical, but Zeke was devising a way whereby they could be grown in subterranean greenhouses. Monstera and plantains were a favorite fruit among Mexicans, Central Americans, and South Americans; why not try to get North Americans to acquire a taste for them.

There was a better kingdom, a kingdom without flaw if he believed. It was difficult for Zeke to put his faith in God because the Hartlands were a determined lot who had always tried to do their best for themselves. They always believed in God, but they relied on themselves to make a living and create something out of nothing.

Zeke felt relief in the fact that God wasn't calling him to be a prophet, only a student of Zeeleaf. He knew he didn't have the commitment it takes to be a prophet. He wanted success for himself and Jeannie in this corporeal world, which meant playing the capitalist game of work hard and prosper.

Monstera fruit and plantains. Monstera fruit and plantains. That was his new mantra.

All this time, for the past two years, he had kept up a correspondence with Gil Bates. Gil had written to him about his vision of a world connected by computers. Zeke admired Gil for his passion and really wished that computers were his bag, but they just weren't. What he and Gil had in common, though, was a passion for business, making money the old-fashioned way, one mistake at a time. Zeke wrote Gil and told him about the subterranean greenhouses to grow exotic fruit, and Gil actually liked the idea. It was Gil who suggested to Zeke that if he was getting tired of studying plants, he should study business administration. That degree would be useful in any field, Gil said. After thinking about that for several days, Zeke saw the logic in that recommendation and had to agree with it. He planned to change his major to business administration for the spring term. What better major in a capitalistic world than business administration? Gil Bates hadn't even finished Dartmouth, but Zeke just had a feeling that he was going to change the world. He had also planted the seed in Zeke that would change him, too. He liked the idea of being a prophet with an MBA.

64
CHAPTER

BUSINESS 5.0

It was spring, 1979, and Zeke had told his science advisor that he wanted to switch majors to business administration. Professor Plank was disappointed, but he certainly understood. Zeke had lost his passion for science and wanted to get into the world of business. Jeannie thought it was a good move too; there were more choices of careers with an MBA than with a Ph.D. in science.

With his mathematical mind, the accounting courses were a breeze for Zeke. He was acing everything. Even Zeeleaf noticed the difference; to him, Zeke seemed happier and less stressed out. The school even let him keep his part-time job in the botanical garden.

In the courtyard of his rented adobe home, Zeke would stay up late at night studying business cases. He had a knack for understanding how businesses thought. He could diagnose a business' problems in a matter of hours and then come up with real-world solutions. He learned to think like an entrepreneur. The school converted his research fellowship into a full scholarship. Dr. Plank had helped with this, and Zeke wrote him a thank you letter.

Zeke and Zeeleaf took hikes together throughout the southwestern corner of San Juan County. They talked about the history of the Navajo nation, and how many Navajo had overcome poverty by becoming businessmen. The curse of the Navajo of course was alcohol – firewater as it was called a century ago. So many Navajo couldn't handle it and drank themselves to death.

The Apaches and Navajo built casinos on their reservations. It turned out to be quite a profitable business, and many of the initial investors were now millionaires. Zeeleaf didn't like their spirit, however. He called them apples – red on the outside, white on the inside.

Zeeleaf himself was living on social security plus the meager amount he received working at the botanical garden. Occasionally, one of his children would send him some money, and he would mail it back to them. He was too proud to accept any charity.

It turned out that Zeeleaf had been a Navajo code talker during World War II. He had been recruited in the first wave of Navajo recruits when a very bright young lieutenant realized that the Japanese would probably never be able to crack the Navajo language – and they never did.

He had also earned a Silver Star when he single-handedly wiped out a Japanese machine-gun nest at close range. This humble man was integrity personified, Zeke thought to himself. He also realized that Zeeleaf was pretty happy with Zeke's decision to give up on botany and study business administration instead. Zeke no longer pressured Zeeleaf to teach him about plants so their friendship became easier.

Zeke now was more interested in Zeeleaf's history and poetry than anything else. Zeke thought Zeeleaf's poetry was pretty good, and he asked him if he could see more of his poetry. Zeeleaf went into his bedroom and came back with a sheet of paper. He gave it to Zeke; it read:

Hailstorm

It happened one summer's eve
While camping in the Pecos
A giant hailstorm rolled in
And then the hailstones started to pelt us.

Golfball-sized chunks of ice
Rained down on our encampment
Never before in our lives had our eyes
Seen a storm pour down with such abandonment.

We ran for cover under the trees
But that only somewhat relieved the agony
Of getting stoned by golfball-size hailstones
We needed a better sanctuary.

And I thought to myself how dumb I was
For not wearing a hat at least
To lessen the force of impact on my head
Of those golfball-size hailstones which beat me.

Each hailstone was a reminder
Not to go camping unprepared
Our camping party was now covered with welts
And we realized that next time we'd better take more care.

The storm was done and we looked around
The mountain was covered with a foot of ice
And we dug out our summer camping gear
And prepared for a cold night.

Snuggled in our sleeping bags in tents
We tried to go to sleep
But the tents were only summer weight
And didn't prevent us from freezing.

So I write this poem from heaven
As a warning to campers below
Not to take Mother Nature for granted
It's something each human should know.

"Gee, that's a great poem, Zeeleaf," Zeke said. "When did that happen?" he asked.

"Nineteen thirty-six," Zeeleaf replied.

"No kidding," Zeke said.

"Yep, down in the San Deas," Zeeleaf added.

"Well, I'm glad you survived," Zeke joked.

"Me too," Zeeleaf replied.

65

CHAPTER

IT TAKES MONEY TO STUDY MONEY

Despite his scholarship, money was tight in the Hartland household. His job at the botanical garden only paid what a research assistantship paid, which was less than minimum wage. Jeannie made just above minimum wage at the bakery, so their combined income was somewhere in the neighborhood of twenty thousand a year. They were barely able to make their rent payment on their house and still eat.

There's an old Navajo saying that if you have too much money you're not living your life right. Zeke wished he could believe that. The more he learned about money, the less satisfied he was with his current state of financial affairs. By the time he finished his first semester of business school, he realized that the next year and a half was going to be very rough.

He needed a full-time job during the summer so that they would have a little cushion when the fall term began. He drove to Bandolier National Monument and applied for a job as a forest ranger. He wrote on his application that he currently worked at UNM-Farmington botanical garden and was very good with plants and that it should only be a small step from plants to trees. The head forest ranger liked that and he liked Zeke so he gave him the job. He was issued a uniform and told he could start the first workday after Memorial Day.

Jeannie was delighted. She always did love a man in uniform. Zeke's main duties were to keep the trails clean, help lost people, and help prevent forest fires. Sometimes Jeannie would drive down to Bandolier and follow Zeke around for hours at a time. They would drive around in the U.S. Park Service jeep and admire the sunsets together.

It was only a half-hour drive from Bandolier to Aztec. Zeke liked his job so much, he thought about being a forest ranger for the rest of his life. Jeannie made it clear she wouldn't be disappointed if that were his choice. Between not having to study all the time and wearing his macho forest ranger uniform, Zeke was feeling more horny than he had ever felt in his life. Zeke realized that his forest ranger uniform made him feel hard, and the harder he became the softer Jeannie felt to him. So he decided to write a poem about this phenomenon, and he titled it *The Softer You Feel, The Harder I Get*.

The Softer You Feel, The Harder I Get

You are soft, my love, and feeling
Your softness makes me get harder
Your tenderness is only exceeded,
By the softness of your skin.

The tender folds of flesh around your breasts
Make my mouth water
There is deep affection as well as tenderness
In the way you make love to me.

Let us go together into the unknown,
Let us explore new worlds together
Don't become hard my love
Let me be hard for the both of us.

Zeke always kept this poem hidden because he never wanted Jeannie to find out how much pleasure she gave him. He also thought it was pretty bad poetry and she would be more than disgusted with it. Zeeleaf was the true poet; Zeke knew he was just a hack.

66
CHAPTER

GIL AND ME

Those summer days in 1979 were halcyon days. Jeannie got excited every time she watched Zeke put on his forest ranger uniform. Zeke got excited because he knew he was getting Jeannie excited. All in all, this was the summer of sheer joy.

Zeke was spending more time with Jeannie and less time with Zeeleaf. His wife had grown into such a beauty that Zeke was proud to be seen with her wherever they went. For his part, Zeke played his role as the macho forest ranger to the fullest hilt.

All through the summer, he kept getting letters from Gil Bates. In one of his letters, Zeke told Gil that he had switched his major to business administration and he wanted to know what Gil thought about that. To his surprise, in his next letter back, Gil said that he thought that it was a good idea. Gil went as far as to say that maybe someday he could use Zeke in his company. Zeke replied back that he would consider that.

After that, Zeke started thinking a lot about Gil, and he decided to write a poem and send it to him to see what he thought. Here was the poem:

Better To Be Lucky Than Smart

Some people bump into big money by happenstance
Some invest heavily in their education
Some pamper their children with precious gifts
And why some lose everything is a conundrum.

Better to be lucky than smart they say
And that is really an understatement
Why do some fools wind up on top
And some geniuses in the basement?

Perhaps life on planet Earth is charted by serendipity
Where everything is already secretly planned
By a hoaxer God who confuses us -
After all, to Him, we are all but a grain of sand.

In the end, it doesn't matter if you're lucky or smart
The ultimate goal is the same – to be happy
Some need wealth and status in order to attain that goal
For others it's just a decent meal and enough energy to
make it to the crappy.

Zeke did show the poem to Jeannie before he sent it, and she didn't like it. Zeke sent it anyway because he thought maybe Gil would like it. In his next letter back to Zeke, Gil never mentioned the poem, so maybe Jeannie was right.

As the summer came closer and closer to an end, Zeke started thinking again about which business courses to take. Jeannie thought that he should focus more on marketing, but Zeke really liked project management. They had some courses in common, but project management was more mathematically focused than marketing. Jeannie finally agreed that it was his life and that he should study whatever he wanted to. A week before classes started, Zeke made up his mind – Project Management it was.

67
CHAPTER

OUT ON A LEDGE

The transformation of Zeke from soldier/poet to forest ranger/businessman was nearly complete by the fall of 1979. Another year and a half of education and the transformation would be complete.

Jeannie liked what she saw too. She saw a good-looking, serious-minded man who could provide for her, give her a home and children. That's all she ever wanted in a man, besides a man who loved her. And Zeke did remember to tell her that he loved her on just about every special occasion, such as birthdays, anniversaries, and Valentine's Day.

For her part, Jeannie tried to show her love for him by cooking dinner for him every night when he got home from campus, by making love with him whenever he felt like it, and by offering advice whenever he asked for it.

They settled into a routine where Zeke would get home from campus at about eight o'clock, they would have dinner, and then watch TV for a couple of hours. Sometimes they would make love after the lights went out, but most nights they didn't. It wasn't that Zeke was becoming less sexually attracted to his wife, it was just that the life of the mind was so much more important to him.

There were now two things that Zeke did in his spare time, which wasn't much. First, when he got tired of his business studies he would pull out his Book of Mormon and start reading. Second, he took up rock climbing. It started out slow, on the weekends, and then he couldn't stop thinking about which rock face he was going to climb next. He didn't use ropes and pylons, just his feet and bare hands.

What he discovered while rock climbing was quite astonishing. The rock climbs were therapeutic for him because rock climbing required such intense concentration that he couldn't think about the past. He could just feel that with each rock climb, he became more Zechariah Itiso and less Trick Hartland.

The rock climbing also almost made him as strong as Superman. Every sinew and joint in his body was taut with strength. There were so many mesas in the area that he knew he would never cease to find new challenges.

Just as his body could not do without rock climbing, his mind could now no longer do without the Book of Mormon. He was fascinated by the Mormon's belief that after Christ established his church in the Middle East, he also established one right here in the American West. He chose twelve North American apostles just as he had chosen twelve in Palestine. He was even more convinced when Zeeleaf told him the Mormons had it right, and they were the only Christians who did. Zeeleaf told Zeke that Christ had visited not only the Navajo, Apache, and Hunkpapa Sioux, but also the Choctaw, Cherokee, Chippewa, Chicksaw, Creek, Algonquin, Seneca, and Shawnee. They all had different names for him, but the Algonquin name Eeseecoatl was closest to Quetzalcoatl, which was what the ancients called him.

The Book of Mormon even gave the names of Christ's twelve apostles in North America. They were: Nephi, Jeremiah, Jonas, Timothy, Mathori, Jonas, Kumen, Shemnon, Zedekiah, Kumenonhi, Isaiah, and Mathonihah. Only the Book of Mormon explains why these names were so similar to Palestinian names.

One day, Zeke decided to go rock climbing near Mount Adams in Colorado. It was a beautiful day, and Zeke was looking forward to the climb. The first seven thousand feet were a piece of cake; the gradient of the trail wasn't very steep. Things started to get a little difficult above eight thousand feet, as the terrain became more and more rocky and the trail became only a foot wide. By nine thousand feet, only an experienced rock climber could succeed in getting to the top. The mountain trail now was almost worthless, so Zeke decided to just rock climb up the remaining two thousand feet.

He was slow but sure, making sure that each outcropping that he put his feet on could support his weight. He liked to lead with his left hand and then follow with his right. At ten thousand feet, the rock that had been supporting his right foot broke off and his left foot slipped off the rock it was on. He was dangling from his hands, and he couldn't swing his body far over enough to the left to regain a foothold. He didn't know what to do so he started to pray, and as he hung there at ten thousand feet, he felt a presence near him, and it told him to look down. He saw a five-foot wide ledge about twenty feet below him; if he swung himself just a little to the left he would reach it. Before letting go, he asked God who this presence was, and the name John just popped into his mind. Zeke asked – John the Apostle? And he heard the words "John the Revelator".

Zeke swung himself as far to the left as he could and let go, and somehow, he didn't feel that he was falling as fast as he should have. He landed on the ledge and somehow his knees absorbed the impact. He was unhurt, and he knew that he had just met his new guardian angel.

68

CHAPTER

THE APOSTOLIC TRIO

When Zeke got home, he told Jeannie that his new guardian angel John had saved his life. Jeannie looked at him like he was crazy.

"How did your new guardian angel save you?" she asked.

"I fell slower than I should have and a ledge broke my fall," Zeke answered.

"How do you know his name is John?" she pressed him.

"Because he told me so," Zeke said. "And when I asked him if he meant John the Apostle, he said yes – I'm John the Revelator," Zeke said looking his wife straight in the eyes so he could see her reaction.

314 | GARRET GODWIN

"You mean to tell me that John the Beloved is your new guardian angel," she said in disbelief.

"That's right," Zeke said. "Believe me, Jeannie – I shouldn't have survived that fall," he added.

"Well, maybe God does have a special plan for you," Jeannie said.

"Maybe so," Zeke reiterated. "I just hope it has nothing to do with the military," he added.

"I'm sure it doesn't," Jeannie said. "You've already paid your dues," she added.

Zeke retreated to the courtyard to read the Book of Mormon. In its Doctrines and Covenants section, Zeke came across a passage that talks about how the three apostles Peter, James, and John bestowed the higher priesthood (the Melchizedek priesthood) on Joseph Smith and Oliver Cowdery, and in so doing reestablished God's covenant with man on earth. John the Baptist had already baptized Joseph Smith and Oliver Cowdery into the Aaronic priesthood in Harmony, Pennsylvania in the Susquehanna River, but it was the higher priesthood that brought God's covenant back to the Earth.

By having one of the Apostolic Trio as his guardian angel, Zeke wondered what his spiritual destiny would be. He was worried that Jeannie wasn't interested in Mormonism at all. Zeke could tell that she felt uneasy about the guardian angel business; she only wanted Zeke to succeed in school and then in a good job.

Zeke was still interested in business administration, but what he was learning from Zeeleaf and what was happening to his soul was far more important to him. He did some research and found out that the closest Mormon Church was about an hour north in Colorado. He would have to invent a clever way to get Jeannie to go with him some Sunday.

Zeke was fascinated by the fact that all of Jesus' North American apostles lived long lives, unlike the fate of the apostles in Palestine, except John. They were not persecuted like their poor brethren in the Middle East, almost all of whom were martyred.

He thought there must be some significance to the fact that Jesus' last living apostle from Palestine was now his guardian angel. He prayed for an answer, but none came.

The Sunday came when Zeke convinced Jeannie to go to the Mormon Church in Colorado with him. She was reluctant at first but said she would keep an open mind. After the service, Zeke walked up to the bishop and asked him if he could speak with him. His name was Bishop Emerson.

"Is there a Mormon Bible study group within the church, bishop?" Zeke asked.

"Yes, it meets every Wednesday night at seven o'clock," Bishop Emerson said.

"May a non-church member attend?" Zeke asked.

"Certainly, our church welcomes everyone who wishes to study the gospels," the bishop said.

"I'll be here on Wednesday," Zeke said. "And thank you for the information," he added.

On their way home in the car, Jeannie asked Zeke if he could afford to take one night off from his studies to study the Book of Mormon. Zeke said he could, but that he would have to work later on the other nights of the week. This did not please Jeannie, and she remained quiet the rest of the way home.

69
CHAPTER

THE GREAT DIVIDE

The silence continued on the home front. Zeke couldn't tell if Jeannie was angry or just felt that it was all a big waste of time. Perhaps she didn't like the fact that only men were allowed to be priests in the Mormon Church, and the women had to settle for lesser offices.

Zeke could tell that within the silence trouble was brewing. There was an ocean of discontent beneath the still waters. Unfortunately, Zeke couldn't control the spiritual journey he was on any more than a cat can control its taste for milk. He would have thought that Jeannie would understand that.

That night, Jeannie lay on the extreme edge of her side of the bed and faced away from Zeke. He was getting the cold shoulder. He touched her exposed shoulder, and she said, "Not tonight."

Zeke put his head back on the pillow and stared straight up at the ceiling. All he could think about was John the Beloved, his new guardian angel. He thought back to the incident at Mount Adams. Had he seen John? No – only "felt" him and heard him. What really happened during that fall? Why was all of this driving Jeannie crazy? Those were the questions running through his mind as his eyelids started to get heavy and he could feel that he was nearing sleep. He wondered if John the Revelator would appear in his dreams.

****

Two seconds after he opened his eyes, he knew something was terribly wrong. He looked to his right and Jeannie wasn't there. He looked at the clock and it was only seven a.m. Jeannie usually slept at least until seven-thirty. Then he saw the note Jeannie had left on her pillow, right next to Zeke's head. It read:

"Dear Trick a.k.a. Zeke:

I do not know who I am living with anymore. All I know is that you are not the same person I married. I do not want to live the rest of my life married to a latter-day saint. Please forgive me. I am going back to L.A. to try to become a legitimate actress. I know now that pornography is morally wrong, and I'll never do that again. I wish you luck in your search for truth. May the Force be with you.

Jeannie"

Zeke felt waves of nausea running through his abdomen. He bolted out of bed and started throwing clothes on. He checked every room in the house before looking out at the driveway and noticing that the Rambler was gone. Damnit, he thought, he'd have to rent a car to go after her. Her parents liked him. Perhaps they would help him find her. He called her parent's house. No answer. Maybe she told them not to let him know where she was. First things first. He'd have to go to the bank and take out enough money to rent a car for a few days if she hadn't depleted the account.

After throwing up in the bathroom, Zeke collected his wits and started walking towards the bank. He was sick with the idea that Jeannie may have wiped out both their savings and checking accounts. He would know the truth in less than five minutes because the bank was only a block from their house.

Then the thought occurred to him that she couldn't have wiped out their accounts because they came home after bank hours last night, and the bank had not opened yet because it was only a little after eight a.m. and the bank didn't open until nine a.m. A wave of relief came over him, and then he felt sick forever thinking that his wife could be that greedy. He felt ashamed of himself. He didn't need to go to the bank, so he turned on his heels and started walking back home. He would try her parents again.

He dialed the number. No one was home. She must have driven back to her parent's house, told them the situation, received some assets, and taken off somewhere.

Zeke thought about how dumb he had been. Then he cut himself some slack. He couldn't help the changes he was going through, and all he did was tell Jeannie the truth instead of trying to hide it from her. He was wrong. She must have gotten fed up with his getting home late every night and then still needling time for himself to go rock climbing. He should have seen it coming, but he didn't.

He had to wait until nine o'clock to take money out of the bank. He figured he'd need three hundred dollars to rent a car for the week and stay in L.A.

70

CHAPTER

THE CHASE

Zeke had to walk to Avis rent-a-car in Farmington to rent a car. After renting a Corvair, he drove back to his house to pack. After packing his clothes, he went to the kitchen and put some fruit and cheese into a knapsack – he figured he could save some money on food. He put two suitcases in the trunk of his car and the knapsack full of fruit and cheese on the back seat. He almost forgot his sunglasses. He had heard that almost everyone in L.A. wears shades.

He was on the road by ten a.m. He figured he should reach L.A. by four or five o'clock. He had to compete for the road with the truckers who used Route 666. He was doing seventy in his little tin can, and if a trucker wanted to smash him there would be nothing left of him.

He got to Route 40 near the Arizona border. Route 40 would take him straight through Flagstaff and then on through all the way to L.A. Zeke couldn't even enjoy the scenery. His mind was so preoccupied with ideas of how to get Jeannie back that he didn't even look to the left or the right; he just kept his eyes on the road straight ahead of him.

He was starting to realize what a fool he had been. He was going to be a botanist – no, a businessman – no, a prophet/businessman. No wonder she got fed up – her husband didn't have a clue what he wanted to do with his life.

By noon, Zeke was just outside of Flagstaff and he needed to get gas. He pulled off Route 40 at a gas station and filled the tank. Zeke wished he was familiar with L.A., but he wasn't. He would have to find a cheap motel somewhere on the outskirts to hunker down in for a few days.

After getting back on Route 40, he thought he had better develop a strategy. There were more than seven million people living in and around L.A., and he didn't know who her friends were here, where she had lived, or even what company she had worked for. He knew that she wanted to bury that part of her life, so he never asked. Now it was working against him.

What about the police? No, wives left their husbands every day and the police are usually on the wife's side. What about hiring a private investigator who knows how to find missing people? No, he didn't have the money. What else could he do? There had to be a way, he thought.

He entered California and figured he had three or four hours to go. Maybe he would think of a strategy by then. He was tired of thinking for now and just focused on his driving and let his mind go blank. He would figure out what to do when he got there.

At sixty miles from Barstow Zeke let his mind start churning again. Maybe he could track her down if she used one of their credit cards. She couldn't have very much cash on her unless her parents gave her some. Zeke knew Jeannie liked to charge things without even thinking about it. Maybe she would make the same mistake now.

Zeke passed through Barstow and then got on Route 15 southwest to L.A. It was already five o'clock and Zeke was finally starting to get hungry. He decided he would wait until he found a motel and get settled in before eating. Zeke decided to get off route 15 and head straight for Pasadena, on the northern border of L.A. He had always heard that Pasadena was nice – it had to be or they wouldn't hold the Rose Bowl Parade there.

He finally arrived in Pasadena and he felt relieved when he saw a vacancy sign on a Motel 66. He pulled in, got out of the car, and walked into the office. The motel manager said the rate was thirty-eight dollars a night – just what Zeke had in mind. He gave the man a hundred-dollar deposit, walked back to the car to get his suitcases and knapsack, threw everything into the room, and then started looking for a restaurant.

He walked into what looked like a cheap restaurant, sat at the counter, and ordered a cheeseburger, fries, and a coke. When it came, he downed it all in about two minutes he was so hungry. Satiated, he started thinking about tomorrow's plan of attack. Sadly, he realized that he was clueless. He was clueless in L.A.

****

When Zeke opened his eyes the next morning, he didn't like what he was feeling. He didn't like waking up in a strange bed in a strange city with no one beside him. This wasn't what he had worked so hard for. How could Jeannie do this to him? Didn't she know that he loved her and that despite all the distractions, she was the most important thing in his life? He showered, got dressed, and started walking to the cheap restaurant for breakfast. A small window sign advertised two eggs and bacon for two bucks. That fit his budget and he walked in and ordered it.

He started observing the people in the restaurant. He could tell that Californians were much flashier than New Mexicans. He saw lots of gold chains, and gold bracelets and almost everybody did have a pair of sunglasses. Some he could tell had designer clothes, and some of the women were gorgeous, models perhaps. All in all, he hated it and thought most of them were phonies living out the capitalistic American dream. There were a lot of sports cars, as well as Mercedes and BMWs, and there were a lot of convertibles. Zeke thought about his rented Corsair and laughed.

He decided to try her parents again when he got back to the motel. Maybe they or Jeannie had had a change of heart. Jeannie's mother answered the phone.

"Is Jeannie there?" Zeke asked.

"No she isn't Zeke," her mother said.

"Will you tell me how I can get in touch with her?" Zeke asked.

"She asked us not to do that, Zeke," her mother answered. "She'll call you, but she doesn't want you to call her. Give me your number and she'll call you," her mother said.

Zeke gave Jeannie's mother his number at the motel, and then he said, "I love Jeannie very much; I always wanted the best for her."

"I know, Zeke, but Jeannie always had her own dreams, and she knew she couldn't live her dreams with you," her mother said.

"I don't see why not," Zeke said with a little anger in his voice.

"Goodbye, Zeke," her mother said, and she hung up.

Zeke thought about the conversation and realized things didn't look good. At least he didn't have to blindly search L.A. for her; he knew she would at least call him. On the other hand, Zeke didn't want to sit in his motel all day waiting for her call. He figured as long as he was here he might as well take in the city. Surely she would call and leave a message if he wasn't there.

With the ball in her court, Zeke set out to see downtown L.A. he got on Route 110 South and figured he'd park at Dodger Stadium and walk to the Hollywood Walk of Fame. Route 110 was congested with traffic and Zeke couldn't wait until he could park the car and walk. He had never seen so many people in his life. There were people in cars, people walking, people in buses, people on motorcycles; the streets were just chock-full of people, and Zeke didn't like it. There were far too many people. The only thing he liked was the Santa Monica Mountains to the west.

He got to Dodger Stadium and parked his car. He started walking south toward the Hollywood Walk of Fame. There was nothing serene about L.A., and he wondered how a Navajo girl from New Mexico could stand it here. To Zeke, it was a phantasmagoria of sights and sounds, and being in it made him feel small and insignificant. When he got to Santa Monica Boulevard, neon signs blared from the stores, and every type of product produced by capitalism could be found there. He guessed that movie stars must roam the streets with sunglasses and hats to remain incognito, unless, of course, they were promoting themselves at a premiere or looking for a new lover.

He finally reached the Hollywood Walk of Fame and gazed down at the stars on the sidewalk. This is what Jeannie longed for? Big deal. How many of these names had ever written a novel? How many had invented something? How many really improved humanity? Most of them were just photogenic and lucky.

He was already tired of the whole scene after fifteen minutes. He started back north, keeping his eyes open for a cheap restaurant. He found one halfway back to Dodger Stadium. He ordered a cheeseburger, fries, and coke. The people in this restaurant looked a little seedy, so Zeke figured it must be cheap, and it was. He got his cheeseburger, fries, and coke for four bucks. Not bad.

When he got to his motel, the blinking light on his phone told him he had a message. He dialed the manager who told him the message – "Meet me at the north entrance to Dodger Stadium at seven o'clock." It was only two o'clock now, and it would only take ten minutes to get to Dodger Stadium, so he had some time to kill. Zeke thought that expression was stupid. How can you kill time? You can waste time, but you can't kill time. Time is not a living organism that can be killed. Time is just a concept, and different peoples have different concepts about time. His time with Jeannie may be over permanently, but that was time well spent. Zeke tried to make the best of their time together, but she wasn't satisfied with it. Zeke was so busy, maybe Jeannie didn't feel that Zeke was trying to make the best of his time with her. He wanted to spend the rest of his life with her, but he couldn't do it here, in this monstrosity of a city. He wanted a peaceful life in the mountains of New Mexico, not a stress-filled life in a big city.

71
CHAPTER

A PARTING IN ELYSIAN PARK

Zeke looked at the clock on his nightstand. It was four fifteen. He planned to leave at six to allow plenty of time to get there, park, and find the north entrance to Dodger Stadium. In the meantime, Zeke was preparing his mind for the showdown. He thought about buying her flowers, but then he decided against it, as she may interpret it as a cheap bribe.

Somewhere in the back of his mind, an incoherent strategy was formulating. It wasn't based on logic but on pure emotion. He would tell her that he would stop the religious crap if only she would come home with him. He would treat her like a queen for the rest of his life. He would buy the groceries, cook the meals, and wash the dishes if she came back. He would even bring her breakfast in bed every morning.

The clock was ticking even as Zeke's mind was churning. It was now dinnertime, but he wasn't hungry. He was nauseous with anticipation. He put on the best shirt that he had brought and the best pair of pants. He looked in the mirror over the dresser – not bad, but he needed a haircut. It was time to go, and the pit in his stomach was growing. He walked out to the car and drove onto Route 110.

He took the Dodger Stadium exit and pulled into the north parking lot. It was only six thirty. Elysian Park was to the north, and Dodger Stadium was to the south. He got out of the car and walked south to the northernmost entrance to Dodger Stadium and sat down on a concrete wall.

At quarter of, he started to get fidgety. His knees started shaking and he kept twisting his body to the east and west to look for Jeannie. He didn't want to stay here the whole time, so he decided to would ask her to walk in Elysian Park with him as they talked. At least he would be on the move. He saw a woman approaching from the far end of the parking lot, but he wasn't sure yet if it was Jeannie or not. At fifty yards, he recognized that it was Jeannie. He raised his right arm and waved. She saw him and waved back.

The first thing he said to her when she finally reached his was "Why don't we go for a walk in the park?"

"Good idea," she said nervously but with a smile.

As they reached the entrance to Elysian Park, Jeannie said, "I'm sorry Zeke, but I just don't love you anymore."

"I know. I should have seen it coming. I was taking you for granted," Zeke replied.

"I don't want to spend my life in New Mexico," Jeannie said. "I want to become an actress," she added. "And to do that, I need to live here."

"I hope you make it, Jeannie, I really do," Zeke said. "I hope to see you on the big silver screen someday," Zeke said.

"I think you need to find your mission in life, Zeke. I don't think you've found it yet," Jeannie said. "And I got impatient waiting for that to happen," she added.

"I know, I know, I'm really a slow learner," Zeke said.

"You're not a slow learner, Zeke; you just don't know what you want to do with your life, but I do," Jeannie said.

Zeke realized the war was already lost and there was no point in putting up more of a fight. She had made up her mind and wasn't coming back. The clock on his marriage had stopped, and there was no way to get it started again. He had survived Vietnam, come back home and had found heaven for a few years, only to have it all taken away from him. How appropriate that his final goodbye to Jeannie would be in Elysian park, just like the Elysian fields where Greek heroes were transported without dying to a life without sorrow. Rather, how ironic, that for one hero, he would lose his happiness in Elysian Park. He knew this walk would be etched in his memory for the rest of his life, and he didn't want it to end on a sour note.

"Goodbye, Jeannie, I love you," Zeke said as he started walking toward his car. She turned and started walking to her car.

As he started driving back to the motel, he realized that Jeannie's love for him was just gone. It had run its course, and now it was over. There was no point thinking about all the what-ifs; perhaps this was his destiny.

72
CHAPTER

EVEN SUPERMAN GETS THE BLUES

The drive back to Aztec was a long drive along memory lane. The joy he had experienced with Jeannie would always be a part of him, no matter how miserable his life became. On the other hand, he was still young; he could still achieve great things without her. He thought he was married to his soulmate for a lifetime, but he was wrong. So what. Better to have loved and lost than never to have loved at all, so the saying goes. How many other women would love to be married to a Vietnam vet nearly done with an MBA? Surely they were out there.

Zeke thought that on the phoniness scale, L.A. rates a ten. He'd take Aztec over L.A. any day of the week. He thought about how to break the news to his mother. She really liked Jeannie. The other issues were mundane ones. How was he going to afford the rent on his house without

Jeannie's extra income? He would probably have to move and find a small apartment. He hated the thought of that because he really liked his house. Then another thought flashed across his mind. Would Zeeleaf think he was a loser because Jeannie left him? He hoped not. He would have to rely on his friends now more than ever. He couldn't imagine Zeeleaf turning a cold shoulder towards him just because his marriage to Jeannie didn't work out. He had only met Jeannie once, so it wasn't like they had a great friendship.

He pulled into the driveway at dusk, took the suitcases out of the trunk, and carried them into the bedroom. He decided to call his mother.

"Hi Mom, I have some bad news," Zeke started. "Jeannie and I are getting divorced," he said.

"I know, I heard it from her parents," Running Deer said.

"Oh, word travels fast," Zeke said.

"I'm sorry, son, but maybe you'll learn from your mistakes," his mother said.

"I didn't know that I made any," Zeke replied.

"We all make mistakes, Zeke," his mother said.

"Well, I'm still going to finish school and do something with my life," Zeke tried to sound upbeat.

"I know you will, son, and I'm still proud of you," Running Deer said.

"Thanks, Mom, I love you," Zeke said.

"I love you too son," Running Deer said.

The conversation was over and they both hung up. Zeke was glad he still had his mother who he could lean on for support. Then a crazy thought occurred to him. He wondered if Superman would get the blues if Lois Lane dumped him. Superman had human emotions even though he was a Kryptonian, and Zeke figured that he probably would. But, being Superman, he could probably get just about any woman on Earth he wanted. That was the bright side.

Zeke realized that he shouldn't whine and pout, but instead pour himself into his studies and make something of himself. He was a warrior, after all, and most warriors don't win every battle.

****

The day after he told Zeeleaf the news, it sank in hard. Zeke knew he was going to be alone for a long time. His good study habits at least provided the discipline for him to finish out his semester. During the winter break, he knew had had some real soul searching to do. He went back to studying the Book of Mormon and he resolved not to let depression get the better part of him.

73

CHAPTER

THE GREAT ONES KEEP MY COMPANY

Zeke persevered and finished his MBA, and it slowly dawned on him why he wanted to study at St. John's College. The answer was that even if friends and lovers abandon you, you always have the great ones to keep you company. There were times when he missed Jeannie so much that he thought of giving up, but something inside him said no – persevere. It was as though the great ones were talking to him, giving him strength.

Zeeleaf didn't abandon him, of course. Zeke actually got to know him better because now it didn't matter if he came home late. Zeeleaf and Zeke became the best of friends, and they traveled throughout the Southwest together, and in so doing, Zeeleaf taught Zeke an appreciation of history that never left him.

In 1981, Zeke joined the Mormon Church and became a Mormon. Then he got a job as a marketing manager for a pharmaceutical company in Boulder, Colorado. This job gave him the opportunity to use both his science skills and his marketing acumen, and he was only an hour and a half drive away from home. Living and working alone, Zeke matured and was finally able to see why he lost Jeannie. Simply put, he put his needs before hers, and that was his big mistake. Maybe someday he would be able to forgive himself.

How ironic it seemed to Zeke that the pharmaceutical company that he worked for did manufacture morphine sulfate. Not only that, but Zeke became the product manager for this product. Zeke goes to travel to different countries to try and help market his product in foreign countries. He liked this international perspective that his job gave him. His salary wasn't bad either.

Living alone did have its drawbacks. Sometimes he had nightmares about Vietnam. Sometimes he felt guilty that he couldn't save Bernfeld's life. Other times, he wished he had never enlisted.

As the years rolled by, Zeke liked to keep abreast of what was happening in Southeast Asia. He read in Southeast Asia magazine that Khun Sa finally surrendered to Burmese authorities in 1986. Instead of putting him in prison, they only put him under house arrest and treated him like a king because the Shan people still loved him so much. In reality, all he did was turn the keys of his business over to his son Chaouhang, who still runs the day-to-day operations of the business. After Khun Sa's surrender, the price of heroin doubled.

It should have come to no surprise to the U.S. government that the new junta in Rangoon refused an offer of two million dollars to extradite Khun Sa to the U.S. to stand trial. The rulers in Rangoon said he was a leader of one of their nation's races and they protected him from U.S. prosecution. He virtually got off scot-free.

Lo Hsin Han became the chairman of Asia World Company Limited, where his son runs the day-to-day operations. With the Burmese government's blessing, this company has invested more than two hundred million dollars in construction projects in and around Rangoon. It seems that both of the world's biggest drug warlords ended up very well.

Zeke kept his mind on his work. His company formed a joint venture with Ecto Pharmaceuticals in Manhattan to co-promote a new morphine sulfate product around the world. That really kept him busy.

Zeke met several women he was attracted to, and, although he went out on several dates with all of them, nothing serious ever developed. When it came to romance, Zeke felt like he was in some kind of purgatory for screwing up his marriage to Jeannie. They didn't even stay in touch.

Zeke continued to go rock climbing on most weekends. He kept hoping that he would meet a female rock climber who would understand him. Unfortunately, most of the ones he did meet were already married. He didn't know if he would ever meet another woman he was attracted to as much as he was attracted to Jeannie. He never gave up hope though.

By the end of the 1980s, Zeke was poised to become the Assistant Vice-President of Marketing. All those long hours had paid off. His salary would jump thirty to forty percent, and he would be given a portfolio of products to manage. It came through for him in December 1989. He was to start the new decade as the number two man in marketing.

He kept in touch with Zeeleaf, and brought him presents every time he visited him. Zeeleaf retired from the botanical garden at 110. His responsibilities as tribal chief of the Four Corners Navajo tribe required more attention than he had been able to give it, so he graciously resigned as chief horticulturist at UNM-Farmington.

In 1991, Zeke read that Cambodia had restored Prince Norodom Sihanouk to the throne. The country had finally come full circle after all that killing. It turned out that prince Sihanouk wasn't such a bad guy after all. He became a film director and a music composer. The people of Cambodia came to love him, and he became very forward-thinking. After watching gay couples in San Francisco obtain marriage licenses, he proclaimed that God loves "a wide range of tastes," and his people loved him even more. He was one of the first Cambodians to develop his own website, and it developed a cult following around the world. All in all, maybe the U.S. screwed up in picking General Non Lol to run the country. Now Cambodia has the once and future king on the throne.

74

CHAPTER

A NAVAJO IN NEW YORK

Zeke had to visit Ecto Pharmaceutical's main office in Manhattan to hammer out the fine points of a co-marketing agreement with them. After the work was over, he planned to spend an extra week of vacation time exploring different places in New York. He particularly wanted to see Palmyra, New York where Joseph Smith was guided to the Book of Mormon, and Harmony, Pennsylvania, just below the New York border, where he was baptized. He figured that after three days in Manhattan, he would be ready for the countryside of New York.

His secretary made the travel arrangements and found him cheap places to stay in Palmyra and Harmony. It was spring, 1996, and the flowers were in bloom all over New York. Zeke had some distant relatives from his father's side in the area, but he decided he wouldn't look them up. He had his own agenda, and he really didn't have the time to be flexible.

Having been a Mormon for fifteen years, Zeke was really looking forward to visiting his spiritual homeland. He figured there must be a reason why the prophet Moroni decided to bury the gold tablets on which the Book of Mormon was written in western New York state. He prayed to God that the reason for this would be made clear to him.

As the trip approached, he thought again about calling his father's brother's son, his cousin, but this deal would require some wining and dining after work hours and he just didn't know if he could fit a family visit in. So he decided against it. The trip was tomorrow and he should've made plans earlier if he really wanted to do it.

****

Zeke arrived at JFK airport in the middle of the afternoon and was glad that all he had to do today was get checked into his hotel – The Park Plaza Hotel on west 57th Street. He was hoping that there was a restaurant in the hotel so that he didn't have to leave the hotel once he was checked in.

He hailed a taxicab in front of the airport and hoped he got an honest taxicab driver because he was totally unfamiliar with New York. He looked honest enough, even though he said he was from Lithuania. As they surged through the traffic on the Long Island Expressway, Manhattan finally came into view. Zeke had never seen anything like it. There were skyscrapers everywhere and the noise was astounding. The streets were so large you could corral a herd of buffalo through them.

They finally reached the hotel, and after paying the taxicab driver, Zeke grabbed his garment bag and headed for the reception desk.

"Reservation for Zeke Itiso," Zeke said.

"Yes, Mr. Itiso, a third party has upgraded you to a penthouse suite," the clerk said. "You will be in Suite 1640," he said.

"Fine. I can carry my own luggage," Zeke said.

"Just call down to the desk if you need anything Mr. Itiso," the clerk said.

"Thank you," Zeke said as he turned around and headed for the elevators.

Zeke planned to just throw his baggage in the suite and then head downstairs to have an early dinner. He wanted to retire early so that he would have his best game on the following day.

In the restaurant, he noticed that several women were staring at him. His reddish-brown complexion must have informed them that he was from somewhere else and perhaps they were curious. He never dreamed that he would draw so much attention. He decided he liked it and gave a few flirtful smiles back. He was wearing some Indian jewelry, which should have given them some clue where he was from.

After finishing his dinner, he went straight back to his suite, took off his clothes, and went to bed. His meetings started at nine a.m., so he set his alarm clock for seven to give himself plenty of time to get ready and walk the five blocks to Ecto Pharmaceutical's main office.

****

There were ten people at the first meeting. There was the Director of Sales, the Director of Marketing, the Product Manager, the Director of Marketing Communications, the Director of Pricing, the Director of operations, the Director of Contracts, the Chief Financial officer, and Zeke. The only important negotiating point was which company would market the product where. In other words, their mission was to divide up the world. Zeke had instructions from his boss to negotiate only for U.S. states west of the Mississippi. Ecto could have the rest of the world.

Zeke set the ball in motion by telling them what his company wanted. That set off a frenzy of activity amongst the Ecto people. It was difficult to tell who the biggest fish were. In the end, the Director of Marketing spoke up.

"We agree to your terms," he said.

"Great, let's draw up the contract and sign it," Zeke said.

The Director of Contracts left the conference room to prepare the document. The Director of marketing invited Zeke to lunch at Morton's Steakhouse to celebrate completion of the deal in less than a day. Zeke was secretly glad that he only had to spend one night in Manhattan. He was already ready for the countryside.

After lunch, he checked out of his hotel and rented a car. He was on his way to Palmyra by two p.m. The four-hour ride west went quickly and Zeke pulled up to the Best Western where he would be staying the next few days. He told them that his reservation was for two days later, but fortunately, they had a room.

He changed his clothes again and headed out for Joseph Smith, Sr.'s farm. When he got there, he was disappointed. Modern progress had taken its course, and there was a slew of fast-food restaurants and chain stores that had been built in the area. The area was kept anything but pristine. Perhaps it shouldn't have come as such a surprise to Zeke because the same thing was happening all over the country.

Things got better once he got off the main roads. He pulled up to the Smith estate and started walking towards the Sacred Grove where the angel Moroni first appeared to Joseph Smith. There was an aura about the place that Zeke couldn't quite put his finger on. He could tell that what happened here was real, and he felt it from the heart.

He walked back to his car because he wanted to see the Hill Cumorah, where Moroni's gold plates were buried. The hill was only maybe fifty feet high, and only one end of it was covered by woods. Zeke had always thought that Hill Cumorah was north of the Smith homestead, but in actuality, it was south. Zeke wondered why he had always thought that it was north, but he didn't know why he thought that.

From Hill Cumorah, he walked north until he came to Hathaway Brook. It was here in this brook where some of the first baptisms in the Mormon Church were performed. The small brook flowed northward all the way to the Erie Canal. Zeke got here two days early, so he decided to walk along the brook all the way to the Erie Canal, a ten-mile hike.

From Hill Cumorah, Hathaway Brook headed almost due west for two miles, and then almost due north for eight miles. Zeke figured the walk should take him between three and four hours. He started at Canandaigua Road and headed west. He wanted to get a sense of the geography of the area, and walking was the only way to accomplish that. He crossed Stafford Road after nearly an hour of hiking, and he looked at the map again. Hathaway Brook ran right through the Sacred Grove, but he hadn't noticed it when he was there before. He wondered how close to Hathaway Brook Joseph Smith was when the angel Moroni first appeared to him in the Sacred Grove. Geographical trivia had always fascinated Zeke.

He was glad he had packed a lunch and put it in his knapsack before he left because he knew he would be hungry by the time he reached the Sacred Grove. He was hoping he would find a peaceful spot near the brook to eat his lunch. He waited patiently until he came to a place where he cross the stream without getting his feet too wet. He wanted to be on the east side of the stream when he came to the Sacred Grove.

Under the canopy of trees in the Sacred Grove, Zeke stopped for lunch at a little clearing. From where he was, he could see through the trees to the Smith's homestead. Through the trees, he could see a group of tourists walking throughout the Smith homestead. He wondered where they were from.

After he finished his lunch, he got back on the path and headed north. He still had about five miles until he reached the Erie Canal. He felt like he was missing something. He let his mind circulate in the stratosphere for a few minutes, and then it came to him. If in fact, John the Beloved was Zeke's new guardian angel, he wanted to know how and when he died. When he got to Palmyra, on the banks of the old Erie Canal, he would go to the library and find out everything there was to know about the death of John the Revelator.

When he got to the library, he went straight to the section on religion. He found that John had lived to be well over one hundred years old. Some accounts say that he did not die but was assumed into heaven like Elijah and Enoch. Most accounts, however, place his death at around 104 A.D. in Ephesus. According to some witnesses, God loved John so much that He gave John a forewarning of his death. He was one of the few figures in history who received this gift. Other accounts say that a miracle attended his death. A powder, called manna, exuded from his tomb for years after his death, and this substance could cure every kind of disease.

He had been in the library for four hours and during that time he had been unaware of time. He realized that he had to get a taxi to drive him all the way back to Hill Cumorah to retrieve his car. He walked outside the library and started walking up the main street of Palmyra. He couldn't believe his eyes when around a corner came a bright yellow taxicab. He hailed it and jumped in.

"Hill Cumorah," Zeke said.

"O.K. Kemosabe," the driver said. Evidently, the driver could tell that Zeke had some Indian blood. "You from the West?" the driver asked.

"New Mexico," Zeke replied.

"A lot of Western Mormons come to visit these parts," the driver said. "How long you stayin?" the driver asked.

"Just three days," Zeke said, realizing that he actually meant to say five days. Then he thought maybe he had seen enough of Palmyra. Maybe he should leave tomorrow and spend the rest of his vacation in Harmony, Pennsylvania.

The taxicab driver let him out back at Hill Cumorah, Zeke paid him, and he headed for his car. He drove back to Palmyra's Best Western. He wondered what people did here for a living. He decided he had seen enough here. Tomorrow it was on to Harmony.

75
CHAPTER

HARMONY

After checking out of the Best Western, Zeke headed east towards Harmony, Pennsylvania. According to the Book of Mormon, it was here that the resurrected John the Baptist baptized Joseph Smith and Oliver Cowdery. It was also here that the resurrected Peter, James, and John the Beloved restored the priesthood to Joseph Smith. Zeke wanted to see what the geography of this area looked like and try to understand why God chose this place for these events.

The Susquehanna starts in the Catskills of New York and then does a little loop in northeastern Pennsylvania for only ten miles or so before turning back north and flowing through Binghamton, New York. Then it turns south through Pennsylvania and roughly divides Pennsylvania in half.

Zeke was four days early for his reservation at the Comfort Inn in harmony, so he hoped that getting a room wouldn't be a problem. This wasn't the height of the tourist season, so he thought this shouldn't be a problem.

After a three-hour drive, he finally was driving down Main Street in Harmony. The Comfort Inn was at the south end of the street. He told the clerk his reservation wasn't for four more days, but fortunately, they had a room. There were a few restaurants along Main Street, so he decided to eat before setting about to see the town.

Harmony was the birthplace of Joseph Smith's wife, Emma Hale. It was here that Joseph Smith translated most of the Book of Mormon. Was it a coincidence that Emma Hale was born in this little piece of bucolic heaven? Zeke put his spiritual antennae on high beam as he set out to explore this village. Since he was here early, he decided he would just visit the village today, and save the river for tomorrow.

He visited the first house where Joseph and Emma lived. He didn't "feel" anything special there. He came upon a local bar and realized there were sinners even in this holy place. There were sinners everywhere, Zeke had learned by now. A little disappointed that Harmony now looked like just another small Pennsylvania town, Zeke started walking back to the Comfort Inn. He was hoping that he would feel differently about the river tomorrow. There he had a breakthrough thought. Why not see the river <u>from</u> the river? Kayaking had become such a common sport in America that maybe there was a kayak rental company in town. When he got back to the Comfort Inn, he asked the clerk. There was an outfit that rented kayaks in town just off Front Street. He was in luck. He went to bed early that night because he wanted to be at his full physical strength tomorrow.

****

He got up at seven a.m. and headed for the free continental breakfast in the lobby. He could walk from there to the outfitters off Front Street. He rented a touring kayak, pushed off from the bank, and headed upstream. He'd rather do the hard work earlier rather than later.

Willow trees lined the banks of the Susquehanna River on both sides. The current was strong and Zeke found himself using muscles that he hadn't used in a long time. A late spring breeze behind him made his paddling upstream a little easier. He wasn't paddling very fast, but his strokes were efficient. The rolling hills of the Pocono Mountains were to the south, while the Catskills were to the north. The river was only three or four feet deep and Zeke could see clear down to the riverbed. Occasionally, a brook trout swam by. There were a few boaters in the water, but as far as he could see he was the only kayaker.

He rounded a curve to a beautiful vista. Yes, what the Book of Mormon says happened here to Joseph Smith and Oliver Cowdery really happened here. As he paddled along, he tried to imagine how the angel John the Baptist appeared to Joseph and Oliver in 1829.

After several hours, he spotted an island in the middle of the river and he decided to stop there for lunch. He pushed up onto the shore, stepped out, and pulled his kayak safely to the beach. He pulled his knapsack out of the kayak and took out his lunch of KFC chicken. After eating, he decided to explore the island. Birds he had never seen before were flitting about the trees. He discovered that the island was only a hundred yards long and maybe fifty yards wide. From the north end of the island, he scanned the horizon. He had probably reached the New York/Pennsylvania border. He hadn't felt anything of a celestial nature on this part of his journey, so he decided it was time to turn around and head back downstream.

Although the wind was now against him, the current was so strong that all Zeke really had to do was steer, and he was still moving twice as fast as he moved going upstream. He covered the distance he had covered going upstream in an hour. As he approached the towns of Harmony on the south bank and Oakland on the north bank he tried to envision how these towns looked a hundred and sixty-seven years ago. Most of the houses would have been log cabins, and there certainly wouldn't be the railroad tracks that ran along the banks of the river. There wouldn't have been any telephone poles, no fast-food restaurants, and not even any paved roads. If he hadn't been from the Southwest, this would have been very difficult to do. He realized what he was attempting to do was "see" through history, and if ever how ephemerally, he was succeeding.

The vision was gone within a minute. The present ripped up his little reverie, and now it was gone. He paddled on for several hours until the sun was starting to get lower on the horizon. Then he remembered what one of his guidebooks said. "Susquehanna" means "sparkling waters" in the Susquehannock Indian language. And as the sun sank lower and lower on the horizon, he could see why the local Indians named it that because a line of "sparkling water" was now visible on the water in line with the sun. It was a color he had never seen before. He took out a notepad from his knapsack and wrote down this poem:

Shimmer

From gurgling springs the water spouts
And courses through meadows and glades
And sometimes when the sun hits it right, the water shimmers
But then at disk it fades.

At sunrise, when the light first shines upon the water
The sparkles are sometimes orange
Then they turn whiter throughout the day
Until at dusk, the hue turns close to watermelon.

In freezing winter, the ice can look like diamonds
It glistens, shines, and sparkles
But cold limits the time to appreciate its beauty
Because our bodies need warmth to keep a focus on the
    glimmering.

When water is in liquid form, it is most beautiful in summer
When it is near my body temperature
It beckons me; I feel its pull
The better half of water in me wants to merge with the
    shimmer.

That last line is what inspired Zeke to write the poem. In essence, baptism is like merging with the shimmer, which is caused by the sun, without which there would be no life on Earth.

He could envision how a shimmering John the Baptist could emerge from these waters. He already believed it, now he could see it. These waters were sacred. Something divine did happen in this little loop of water in northeast Pennsylvania.

Satisfied that he had seen enough for one day, he turned his kayak around and headed back to Harmony. Although he had rented the kayak for the whole day, he didn't want to get back after dark.

He pulled up to the outfitters, hopped out of the kayak, and walked up to the building. He turned in his life-vest and paddle and said he may be back again tomorrow.

He showered in his room and got dressed for dinner. All he could think about though was the sparkling water. It looked like glistening diamonds on a bed of reddish-orange rose petals. He had never seen such beautiful water. How pure that water was, emerging out of the Catskills only fifty or sixty miles to the north. How much purer it must have been more than a hundred and fifty years ago. No wonder the restoration of the priesthood happened here.

With that thought in mind, he started walking down Main Street looking for a restaurant. He was ravenous after all the exercise he had gotten all day. He spotted a restaurant that had a small outdoor café, and as it was a beautiful late spring evening, he chose it because he wanted to sit outside and watch the passers-by.

He was seated and given a menu. He ordered a steak and a glass of wine, even though Mormons aren't supposed to drink alcohol. He noticed a couple being seated outside a few tables away from him. There was something curious about the couple that Zeke couldn't put his finger on. The man was seated facing the street, like Zeke, while his wife or girlfriend sat facing the restaurant. Zeke hadn't gotten a good look at the man, but there was something. . . His curiosity got the better of him and he decided to chance a sideways glance, hopefully without being noticed. As he looked, chills went down his spine – he recognized the man – it was Doug price, Agent red. He was bulgier and had lost a lot of hair, but it was definitely him, the man who had vowed to kill him more than twenty years ago.

Zeke could barely eat his steak. He wondered if Doug Price had recognized him when he looked over. Probably not – he was having some sort of conversation with his wife/girlfriend. He had already asked the Lord for his forgiveness for what had happened in Vietnam; he never thought he would see Doug Price again, so he put him out of his mind. Twenty-one years later, here he was, less than twelve feet away from him. Zeke realized that you don't ask a man's forgiveness for killing someone, you ask for God's forgiveness. And he had, and he was no longer Trick Hartland, the killer in Vietnam. He was Zechariah Itiso now, Mormon pharmaceutical marketing manager. Without moving his head, Zeke took another sideways glance. Now Doug Price was looking straight at him. He wondered if he had been recognized. Nothing happened. He continued eating, staring straight ahead.

When he finished his meal, Zeke calmly asked for his check. Zeke was now a middle-aged man, not the puppy the U.S. government sent to Vietnam. Perhaps Zeke recognized Doug Price because he was already in his thirties during Vietnam, and other than his weight, his features had not really changed that much. Zeke, on the other hand, was a puppy back then – 19 years old.

The check came, and Zeke pulled out his wallet. He gave the waiter his money and waited for his change. When it came, he left the waiter a nice tip, stood up, and turned to walk towards the entrance to the outdoor café. At that moment, their eyes locked and Zeke knew in that instant that Doug Price had recognized him. Price, still nimble, blocked Zeke's path to the entrance. Zeke walked straight up to within a foot of him and looked him square in the eye. Neither one of them blinked. Doug Price said, "Come with me, I have something to show you."

Gathering his courage, Zeke followed Doug price out to the parking lot. He unlocked his car and pulled something out of his glove compartment. It was a picture album. He flipped through it until he came to the photograph he wanted to show Zeke. It was a picture of the Vietnam Veterans Memorial Wall in Washington, D.C. He pointed to Sergeant Allen Pope's name on the wall.

"If I had seen you again over there, I would have killed you," he said.

Zeke just nodded his head and started walking away.

"Don't you want to know why I didn't?" Price shouted to him. "Somebody high up over there liked you," he said.

Zeke didn't feel safe until he was out of earshot. He kept his head low wondering what the odds were that this had happened to him. Price knew in his heart that back then he was just a kid trying to save Bernfeld. Now he was just a forty-year-old man trying to get a new life. He had found what he was looking for in Harmony – his past. Tomorrow he would head home.

76
CHAPTER

ROCKY RIDGE

On his flight back to Boulder from Newark, New Jersey, Zeke had nothing to do but think. He sat in a window seat and looked at the puffy white clouds. He wondered if he had really repented before the Lord for his sins, or if his salvation somehow depended on the opinion of Doug Price. He felt humble and contrite.

His bullheadedness had ruined his marriage, there was at least one soldier who wanted him dead, and he hadn't proven himself a winner in life. He had one friend on this planet, and one knew how much longer he would be around. His mother still loved him, but he hardly ever visited her. So this is what being grown up is all about.

After the plane landed, he took the shuttle to his parking lot and headed back to his empty apartment. At least the business trip had been a success, even though the deal had taken less than a day. At least his boss would be happy that Zeke had gotten what he asked him to negotiate for.

He realized that he still had five days of vacation left, so he decided to drive down to the Four Corners and visit Zeeleaf. He wanted to tell him what had happened in Harmony.

When he got to Zeeleaf's house, Zeeleaf wasn't there. He decided to wait for him. About two hours later, Zeke could see Zeeleaf's truck winding its way up the dirt road towards the house. From about fifty yards away, Zeeleaf waved at him and he waved back. When he jumped out of the truck, he walked up to Zeke and said, "Something's happened. I'll tell you what I heard."

"An elderly Navajo woman and her daughter had eaten their evening meal and were preparing to go to bed when suddenly the frail, elderly mother said, 'We're going to have company'. The daughter didn't know what to make of this strange announcement, so she decided to ignore her mother. Then there was a loud boom coming from the roof of the house. After that, she heard talking outside. When she opened the front door, there were two white-haired Navajo men who told her not to be afraid. One of them told her, 'You already know what we're here for'.

"After that, they told her that the Navajo should return to their traditional ways, and continue to pray. Then the two men vanished into thin air, leaving behind only their footprints in a circle of corn pollen."

"The daughter told what had happened to her circle of friends, and word quickly spread throughout the reservation that there had been a holy visitation. Whites

and Indians alike from all over the southwest have already heard the story. It had happened in one of the most isolated corners of the Rocky Ridge Reservation.
We Navajo elders got together and prayed about it, and from the descriptions, we decided that the two angels were probably Talking God and White Body. Talking God was dressed in blue and White Body was dressed in white."

"As a tribal leader, I was summoned to counsel with all of the tribal elders. After conferring with all of the elders, it was proclaimed that this was a sacred event, but that only Navajos and their cousins the Apaches should be allowed to visit the site because the prophecy concerned only the Navajo nation."

Fortunately for Zeke, Zeeleaf felt that his Navajo blood was strong enough for him to visit the site. For his part, Zeeleaf felt that a visit from the deities was overdue. He too had seen that the Navajo were neglecting their prayers and offerings and that there was much disunity among his people.

Zeeleaf and Zeke drove the two hours to the eastern edge of the Rocky Ridge Reservation and set up camp. Zeke had bought all new camping supplies with his last Christmas bonus, and now he was glad he had. He had bought an eight-man tent, new sleeping bags and air mattresses, Coleman cooking ware, and an assortment of knives and utensils.

There was to be a major ceremony held at the site on the coming weekend. Navajos and Apaches from all over the southwest were pouring in and setting up camp just like Zeeleaf and Zeke. It was officially dubbed "Spiritual

Unity Week" by the elders, and the excitement was felt by every Native American in the area.

As Zeeleaf's guest, Zeke was allowed to attend the ceremonies. The first ceremony was held on Friday night. There were thirty to forty tribal elders from all different clans there. At this first ceremony, the elders decided that Navajo families must stress love, respect, responsibility, and peace as the four most important attributes of a Navajo family. If these four virtues don't exist in the family, the people are not living according to the Navajo way.

On the next evening, the tribal elders convened again. From this meeting, the elders said that their language and culture were being lost and that this should never happen. Also, the Navajo were taking Mother Earth for granted, which was the reason for the terrible drought. Prayers would end the draught.

Although the message was serious, Navajo families were allowed to have a lot of fun this night. There was a big cookout, and there were games for the children and entertainers. Ceremonial dances were performed, and Zeke joined in the fray with everyone else. He hadn't felt this happy in a long, long time. When he was done being a whirling dervish, he sat down to recuperate, and the thought occurred to him that Navajo angels must be as holy as white angels because they were both saying the same thing. They both reported to God and wanted the best for all men on Earth.

When Zeke and Zealeaf got back to their tent late that evening, Zeke told him about his meeting in Harmony with a figure from his past. After telling him every last detail,

Zeeleaf lifted up his head and said, "Life moves in circles. That event was the end of one of your circles in life. Learn from it. Pray to God to help you understand it. And never forget it."

"I am no longer the man that that man knew," Zeke said. "I was lucky to survive my original conflict with him. He must have seen that I had grown into another man, and still he had given me a warning."

"Yes he did," Zeeleaf replied. "You may still have some reckoning to do with the man you killed when you reach the spirit world. Try to atone for it while you are still on this Earth, and maybe things will go better for you from now on," Zeeleaf added.

"I have tried, Zeeleaf, but maybe I haven't done enough," Zeke said.

With that, they crept into their sleeping bags and fell asleep under the stars.

77
CHAPTER

THE CIRCLE OF LIFE

The sun rose over the peaks of the San Dea Mountains, and its first rays just touched the top of their tent. Zeeleaf was already outside sitting down facing the sun and offering a morning prayer. Zeke crawled out of his sleeping bag, sleepy-eyed, and out of the tent and sat down next to Zeeleaf. The sky was a reddish-orange, with a touch of pink thrown in. As the first rays of the sun moved further down the tent, Zeke realized that he only had a minute or two before the rays would directly reach his eyes. He prayed for forgiveness, and then he prayed that he might have a happy life. And then he saw something as the first rays of the sun hit his eyes. He saw fourteen cycles of the sun before the heavens opened up.

He didn't even attempt to tell Zeeleaf what he saw. He somehow knew that the message was for him and him alone. He continued to pray in silence sitting beside Zeeleaf.

Then for some reason, he started thinking about where he was from. Galileo is a ghost town now, a piece of flotsam in the jet stream of history. All the people who ever lived there or grew up there are gone now, even Zeke's mother. The streets are quiet, except for the occasional sagebrush that rolls down the streets. The town that Jackson Hartland had built is now abandoned, a footnote in the annals of history.

All of the people who lived there and are still alive are different people now, their identities affixed to a new geography or new enterprise. But then, Zeke thought, that is America at its best - people changing themselves to become better people, moving into a new life, and facing the endless possibilities that this country provides.

He had heard through his mother that Jeannie had remarried a stockbroker and had two children with him. If only he hadn't taken her for granted. She's made a few commercials, and every time Zeke sees one he winces. She hasn't made it big in Hollywood so far, but at least she's living where she wants to live and raising her family.

Running deer lives on the San Dea Reservation where she has many friends. She's taken up rug weaving, and she has made quite a reputation for herself as a Navajo rug maker.

Zeke lost track of Sam Newell, his roommate at St. John's College. The last he heard from him he was heading off for law school at Pepperdine University in California. Zeke knew he would be a successful lawyer. He also lost track of Omar and Mustafa. He hoped that they would become wise leaders in their countries in North Africa. Gil Bates went on to become a huge success. He still corresponds occasionally with Zeke.

Dr. Richard Brown, his mentor, and professor at St. John's College wrote a book on philosophy that won the Pulitzer prize. He is now teaching at Harvard in Boston.

Richard Armitage went on to become one of the top men in the CIA during the Bush administration, and he played a key role in the Gulf War.

Zeeleaf wants to leave New Mexico and move to Nevada and live on the Walker Lake Paiute Reservation. He knows his time is near and he wants to remember the way it was when Wovoca walked the Earth. Of all the people he had ever known, Zeeleaf had the kindest and most courageous heart. He witnessed more than a century of history, and he always tried to do his best to help his people.

As for himself, maybe he's grown up enough now to find a new happiness and hold onto it for dear life. You only go around once, the saying goes, so you better make the best of it. He continues his work in pharmaceuticals in Boulder, Colorado, and there is joy in his heart because he knows that it is only fourteen more years before the coming again of the Lord.

ABOUT THE AUTHOR

Garret Godwin received his BA in English from the Indiana University of Pennsylvania and his MA in English literature from Temple University in Philadelphia. He was the Robert Sterling Clark scholar in classics at St. John's College in Sante Fe, New Mexico, and he holds an MBA from the University of Pittsburgh. He is the author of True Philadelphia Stories (a collection of short stories and essays), three novels - Chasing Quetzalcoatl to The American Dream, Down and Out in Philadelphia and New York, and Through the Dark Looking Glass, and an anthology of poetry - As You Sow, and he lives in Mechanicsburg, Pennsylvania.

CPSIA information can be obtained
at www.ICGtesting.com
Printed in the USA
BVHW040043190523
664415BV00002B/45

9 781959 197300